AUTOCAD® CIVIL 3D® 2016

ESSENTIALS

Eric Chappell

AUTODESK.
Official Press

SYBEX®
A Wiley Brand

Acquisitions Editor: Stephanie McComb
Development Editor: Kathi Duggan
Technical Editor: Josh Modglin
Production Editor: Christine O'Connor
Copy Editor: Judy Flynn
Editorial Manager: Mary Beth Wakefield
Production Manager: Kathleen Wisor
Associate Publisher: Jim Minatel
Book Designer: Happenstance Type-O-Rama
Compositor: Cody Gates, Happenstance Type-O-Rama
Proofreader: Sarah Kaikini
Indexer: Ted Laux
Project Coordinator, Cover: Brent Savage
Cover Designer: Wiley
Cover Image: iStock/Dan Barnes

To Logan

Acknowledgments

What an amazing year it has been! I get to continue writing this series and updating it for yet another great release of Autodesk® AutoCAD® Civil 3D® software. And after a wonderful 16 months on the Premium Support Services team at Autodesk, I have changed roles and I'm now serving as Community Evangelist for InfraWorks® 360. This new role gives me the opportunity to focus on reaching the Autodesk infrastructure software (including InfraWorks, Civil 3D, and others) community and try to be a positive force to inform and enable this great group of people.

In addition, I will be updating the entire InfraWorks 360 series of books to address all the exciting changes there. These are certainly exciting times to be involved in the civil/infrastructure design industry and to be using Autodesk products. I'm blessed to be in such a wonderful position to observe and participate in the transformation that is taking place. For years, we have been talking about 3D and BIM in the civil/infrastructure industry and now we're finally putting our money where our mouths are. There will be big changes over the next few years, so invest in yourself through training and learning, and hold on and enjoy the ride!

I've said it before on past books and I'll say it again on this one: This book was a team effort. Kudos to Stephanie McComb for getting the book off the ground and for keeping it moving along throughout the process. Thanks to the wonderful editors, Christine O'Connor and Kathryn Duggan, for correcting all my mistakes (there were many) and making the book hold up to the high standard of quality that is characteristic of Wiley/Sybex. It was an honor to once again work with my good friend Joshua Modglin and to know that, as technical editor, he had my back on the technical aspects of the book.

And as always, thanks to my wife, Dixie, and my four children for enduring yet another "book season" and all of the not-so-fun stuff that comes with it. I love you all, and I do it all for you.

About the Author

Eric Chappell has been working, teaching, writing, and consulting in the world of civil engineering software for more than 20 years, and he is a recognized expert in the world of Autodesk® AutoCAD® Civil 3D® software. Eric joined the Autodesk family in September 2013 as a Premium Services Specialist and has recently taken on the role of Community Evangelist for InfraWorks® 360. In the 12 years prior to working for Autodesk, he wrote training materials and performed training for end users, trainers, and Autodesk employees around the globe. For several years, he has worked with Autodesk in authoring and developing two Autodesk certification exams. He also served as design systems manager for Timmons Group, a civil engineering and surveying firm based in Richmond, Virginia, where he managed software, standards, and training for more than 200 users. Eric is also a highly rated instructor at Autodesk University, where he has taught for the past 10 years.

Prior to writing and consulting, Eric spent nearly 10 years in the civil engineering and surveying fields while working for the H.F. Lenz Company in Johnstown, Pennsylvania. During his time at H.F. Lenz, he gained considerable practical experience as a survey crewman, designer, engineer, and CAD supervisor. Eric also holds a BS degree in Civil Engineering Technology from the University of Pittsburgh at Johnstown and is certified in Pennsylvania as an EIT.

Eric is originally from southwestern Pennsylvania, but he has lived in the Richmond, Virginia, area for the past 13 years with his wife and four children. He enjoys being outdoors and spending time with his family. He can sometimes be seen playing drums for the band Sons of Zebedee, which performs at a variety of events in the Central Virginia area.

Eric is also the author of a series of Wiley/Sybex titles for Autodesk InfraWorks 360 and InfraWorks 360 LT. Be sure to check out *Autodesk InfraWorks 360 Essentials* along with *Autodesk Roadway Design for InfraWorks 360 Essentials*, *Autodesk Bridge Design for InfraWorks 360 Essentials*, and *Autodesk Drainage Design for Autodesk InfraWorks 360 Essentials*. Other titles may also be available throughout the year based on the release of more InfraWorks 360 modules.

If you would like to contact the author with comments or suggestions, please email CivilEssentials@gmail.com. You're also welcome to visit Eric's blog at http://ericchappell.blogspot.com.

Contents at a Glance

CONTENTS

INTRODUCTION

When the first version of this book was born just over four years ago, my hope was for it to be one book in a long and successful series that would educate, inspire, and even excite many people about using the Autodesk® AutoCAD® Civil 3D® software. In order to make that happen, I decided that each book in the series had to meet the following criteria:

- ▶ It should be basic enough to enable *anyone* to learn Civil 3D.

- ▶ It should be in-depth enough to enable a person to be productive using Civil 3D for basic tasks.

- ▶ It should foster understanding by associating the things you do in Civil 3D with familiar things you see every day.

- ▶ The examples and exercises should be based on the real world.

- ▶ The book should not simply demonstrate random software features but should also teach the process of project completion using Civil 3D.

Since the first version of the book was released, I have received tons of great feedback about how well this book functions in many learning environments. I have also used the book myself to teach classes in a corporate environment, and I am very pleased with how it performs. I am confident that the goals I listed have been met, and for that reason I have held to the same writing style, format, and delivery that proved to be so successful in the previous versions.

As you work your way through the book as a teacher, a student, or an end user, you'll find that the first two chapters, although very important, are more general and introductory. After that, you're going to take a journey through the completion of a residential land development project—start to finish. In fact, the example project is based on a residential development that was built about 10 years ago, not far from my home. The topics are presented as though you have never touched a CAD program before, and wherever possible, there are sidebars and other forms of augmentation that relate what you're doing to the real world.

You'll also find that as I wrote this book, I tried to sympathize with future readers by thinking back to my college days when I was learning about surveying and civil engineering for the first time. There were many times when I felt frustrated and lost because I was learning new and foreign concepts and did not see how they related to the real world. I can remember being out in the field during my surveying class—looking through the survey instrument, writing down measurements, and having no idea why. That wasn't an enjoyable feeling, and it isn't one I want you to experience as you learn the new and foreign concepts in this book. Eventually I learned all about surveying, and now I have an in-depth understanding of how those measurements relate to designing and building roads, buildings, and other things—but it took many years. It's my sincerest hope that this book gives you a head start on some of those types of concepts while at the same time relating them to Civil 3D in ways that hit home for you.

What's New in This Book?

If you already own *AutoCAD Civil 3D 2015 Essentials*, you'll be happy to know that *AutoCAD Civil 3D 2016 Essentials* has been updated to address important changes in AutoCAD Civil 3D 2016. All applicable images have been updated in this version of the book to account for changes to the user interface and changes to functionality. The dataset files have also been updated to ensure compatibility with AutoCAD Civil 3D 2016.

Who Should Read This Book?

This book should be read by anyone who needs or wants to begin learning AutoCAD Civil 3D. It's appropriate for ages ranging from high school to retirement, and although it's intended for those who have no experience or skill with Civil 3D, it can also serve as a great resource for refreshing your knowledge base or filling in any gaps. In addition, this book can be used as a resource for preparing to take the AutoCAD Civil 3D 2016 Certified Professional exam. See www.autodesk.com/certification for more certification information and resources. You can also refer to this book's appendix to see which certification topics are covered and where they can be found in the book.

In addition to those pursuing a certification, here are some specific examples of individuals who would benefit from reading this book:

- ▶ High-school students following a design-related educational track

- ▶ College students learning to be designers or engineers

- ▶ Employees who have recently joined a company that utilizes Civil 3D

- ▶ Employees who work for companies that have recently implemented Civil 3D

- ▶ Experienced Civil 3D users who are self-taught and who want to fill in gaps in their knowledge base

What You Will Learn

This book covers the basic skills and concepts needed to begin using Civil 3D to design land development projects. The concepts include those related to Civil 3D as well as those related to civil engineering and surveying in general. It doesn't cover all topics or all Civil 3D features, but it provides a solid foundation you can use to perform basic tasks. This foundation can then serve as a stepping-off point as you learn more advanced skills and work toward an in-depth understanding of Civil 3D.

The first two chapters will give you a basic understanding of Civil 3D and help you to understand and appreciate how it "thinks." The remaining 16 chapters will teach you how to use the tools that Civil 3D provides to complete a typical land development design project.

What You Need

Specific hardware requirements for running AutoCAD Civil 3D 2016 had not been released as this book went to press. See the Autodesk website (www.autodesk.com) for current requirements.

To perform the exercises in this book, you must have AutoCAD Civil 3D 2016 installed on your computer. It's recommended that you use the default software setup with two exceptions: Change your drawing screen color to white, and dock the command line at the bottom of the screen. This book contains many screen captures of Civil 3D drawings, which were all produced with these distinctive changes to the user interface. Also, at times, the exercises refer to drawing entities by color, which is sometimes dependent on the background color.

To complete the exercises, you'll need to download the necessary files from www.sybex.com/go/civil3d2016essentials. Here you'll find a list of Zip files, one for each chapter. When you unzip the file for the first chapter to the local C: drive of your computer, a folder named Civil 3D 2016 Essentials will be created with the chapter folder inside it. As you unzip additional chapter files to the local simply merge the new Civil 3D 2016 Essentials folder into the old one. The resulting files and folders will appear similar to the following image:

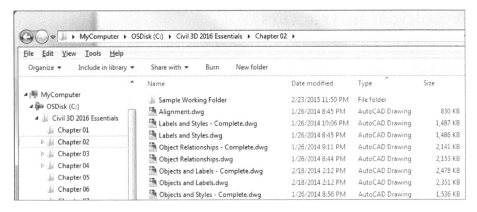

Zip files are available in imperial and metric units. As you complete the exercises, metric values will be shown in parentheses. The imperial and metric values for a given item usually are *not* equivalent, to avoid using irregular values for the design. For example, the value for the width of a sidewalk would be shown as 3' (1m) even though 3' doesn't exactly equal 1m.

Finally, be sure to check the book's website for any updates to this book should the need arise. You can also contact me directly by email at CivilEssentials@gmail.com or visit my blog at http://ericchappell .blogspot.com to read even more about the book and Civil 3D in general.

FREE AUTODESK SOFTWARE FOR STUDENTS AND EDUCATORS

The Autodesk Education Community is an online resource with more than 5 million members that enables educators and students to download—for free (see the website for terms and conditions)—the same software used by professionals worldwide. You can also access additional tools and materials to help you design, visualize, and simulate ideas. Connect with other learners to stay current with the latest industry trends and get the most out of your designs. Get started today at www.autodesk.com/joinedu.

Attention: Instructors

As you know, the best classes start with good preparation, and you can get off to a good start by downloading the instructor materials that accompany this book. Please visit www.sybex.com/go/civil3d2016essentials to access the instructor materials, which contain suggested syllabi, PowerPoint files, additional exercises, and quiz questions that you can use to assist you in making your class a success.

What Is Covered in This Book?

AutoCAD Civil 3D 2016 Essentials is organized to provide you with the knowledge needed to master the basics of AutoCAD Civil 3D 2016:

Chapter 1: Navigating the User Interface   Familiarizes you with the Civil 3D environment so that you can navigate more easily in the software.

Chapter 2: Leveraging a Dynamic Environment   Demonstrates the dynamic Civil 3D environment to establish its importance and encourage you to take full advantage of it whenever possible. This chapter focuses on important relationships between different components of a typical design model.

Chapter 3: Establishing Existing Conditions Using Survey Data
Demonstrates how to convert survey field measurements into a Civil 3D drawing while focusing on the survey functions of Civil 3D. This chapter covers creating a survey database, importing data, and processing the data to create a map of the project.

Chapter 4: Modeling the Existing Terrain Using Surfaces   Demonstrates how to create a model of the existing terrain of the project while focusing on the surface functions of Civil 3D. This chapter covers creating a new surface and adding data to it to form a 3D model of the before-construction condition of the project.

Chapter 5: Designing in 2D Using Alignments   Demonstrates how to perform basic 2D layout while focusing on the alignment functions of Civil 3D. This chapter covers creating alignments, applying design criteria, and editing alignments.

Chapter 6: Displaying and Annotating Alignments   Demonstrates how to control the appearance of alignments and provide annotation while focusing on Civil 3D alignment styles and alignment labels. This chapter covers applying alignment styles, creating alignment labels, and creating alignment tables.

Chapter 7: Designing Vertically Using Profiles   Demonstrates how to design the vertical aspect of a linear feature while focusing on the profile functions of Civil 3D. This chapter covers creating profiles, applying design criteria, editing profiles, and displaying profiles in profile views.

Chapter 8: Displaying and Annotating Profiles   Demonstrates how to control the appearance of profiles and provide annotation while focusing on Civil 3D profile styles and profile labels. This chapter covers applying profile styles, creating profile labels, and object projection.

Chapter 9: Designing in 3D Using Corridors   Demonstrates how to design a 3D model of a linear feature while focusing on the corridor functions of Civil 3D. This chapter covers creating assemblies, creating and editing corridors, and creating corridor surfaces.

Chapter 10: Creating Cross Sections of the Design   Demonstrates how to generate and display cross sections of your design while focusing on the sample line and section functions of Civil 3D. This chapter covers creating sample lines, sampling various sources, and creating section views.

Chapter 11: Displaying and Annotating Sections   Demonstrates how to control the appearance of sections and provide annotation while focusing on Civil 3D section styles and section labels. This chapter covers applying section styles, creating section labels, and object projection.

Chapter 12: Designing and Analyzing Boundaries Using Parcels Demonstrates how to design a lot layout for a residential land development project while focusing on the parcel functions of Civil 3D. This chapter covers creating and editing parcels.

Chapter 13: Displaying and Annotating Parcels   Demonstrates how to control the appearance of parcels and provide annotation while focusing on Civil 3D parcel styles and parcel labels. This chapter covers applying parcel styles, creating parcel labels, and creating parcel tables.

Chapter 14: Designing Gravity Pipe Networks   Demonstrates how to design underground gravity pipe systems for a residential land development project while focusing on the pipe network functions of Civil 3D. This chapter covers creating and editing pipe networks.

Chapter 15: Designing Pressure Pipe Networks   Demonstrates how to design underground pressure pipe systems for a residential land development project while focusing on the pressure pipe network functions of Civil 3D. This chapter covers creating and editing pressure pipe networks.

Chapter 16: Displaying and Annotating Pipe Networks   Demonstrates how to control the appearance of pipe networks (both gravity and pressure) and provide annotation while focusing on Civil 3D pipe styles, structure styles, fitting styles, appurtenance styles, and pipe network labels. This chapter covers displaying pipe networks in profile view, creating pipe network labels, and creating pipe network tables.

Chapter 17: Designing New Terrain   Demonstrates how to design a proposed ground model for a residential land development project while focusing on the feature-line and grading functions of Civil 3D. This chapter covers creating and editing feature lines and grading objects.

Chapter 18: Analyzing, Displaying, and Annotating Surfaces   Demonstrates how to perform surface analysis and display the results as well as annotate design surfaces. This chapter covers managing multiple surfaces, labeling surfaces, and analyzing surfaces.

Appendix: AutoCAD Civil 3D 2016 Certification   Provides information about AutoCAD Civil 3D certification as well as how this book will help you to prepare for the certification exams. This appendix includes specific certification objectives along with where related material appears in the book.

The Essentials Series

The Essentials series from Sybex provides outstanding instruction for readers who are just beginning to develop their professional skills. Every Essentials book includes these features:

- ▶ Skill-based instruction with chapters organized around projects rather than abstract concepts or subjects.

- ▶ Downloadable tutorial files showing the start and end state of each exercise.

- ▶ Digital extras so you can work through the project tutorials yourself. Please check the book's web page at www.sybex.com/go/civil3d2016essentials for these companion downloads.

Certification
Objective
The certification margin icon will alert you to sections that are especially relevant to AutoCAD Civil 3D 2016 certification. See the appendix for a quick snapshot of the certification objectives covered in the book.

The Autodesk certification exam objectives listed in the appendix were accurate at press time; to find the latest information about the exam and what is covered, go to www.autodesk.com/certification.

CHAPTER 1

Navigating the User Interface

If you're new to the AutoCAD® Civil 3D® software environment, then your first experience has probably been a lot like staring at the instrument panel of an airplane. Civil 3D can be quite intimidating, with lots of buttons, strange shapes, and unusual icons—all packed into a relatively small area. In addition, you may be even more intimidated by the feeling that there is a lot of power under the hood.

This leads us to our main objective for this chapter, which is to alleviate that feeling of intimidation and make you feel much more at ease within the Civil 3D environment. Let me start you down that path by saying that there's a big difference between an airplane and Civil 3D. In Civil 3D, if you really mess up, you can simply close the drawing file without saving. When piloting an airplane, it's a little more difficult to undo your mistakes.

After completing this chapter, you will have achieved a greater comfort level within the Civil 3D environment by being able to identify the main user interface components and utilize them for basic functions. You will also be able to use two specific features that will serve you well throughout the program: the Transparent Commands toolbar and the Inquiry Tool.

In this chapter, you'll learn to:

▶ **Navigate the Civil 3D user interface**

▶ **Launch general commands through the application menu**

▶ **Launch key software commands and functions using the ribbon**

▶ **Navigate the design contents using the Toolspace**

▶ **Navigate the model using the drawing area**

▶ **Communicate with Civil 3D using the command line**

▶ **Access and modify design information using Panorama**

▶ **Access specialized commands using the Transparent Commands toolbar**

▶ **Get information about your design using the Inquiry Tool**

Getting to Know the Civil 3D User Interface

Certification
Objective

To begin learning about the Civil 3D environment, let's take our airplane analogy down a notch and think about this as learning to drive an automobile. When
your parents first sat you down at the wheel and talked about the car's controls,
they probably didn't mention the air conditioning or the radio. Those, of course,
are important parts of the driving experience, but I'm betting they started with
the most important parts, such as the steering wheel, the gas pedal, and, most
important of all, the brake pedal. We're going to approach your first experience
with "driving" Civil 3D in much the same manner.

There are many, many parts to the Civil 3D user interface. For the purpose of this
book, I'll cover just the ones that will be most important in enabling you to navigate
the software effectively. Figure 1.1 shows the major components of the user interface.

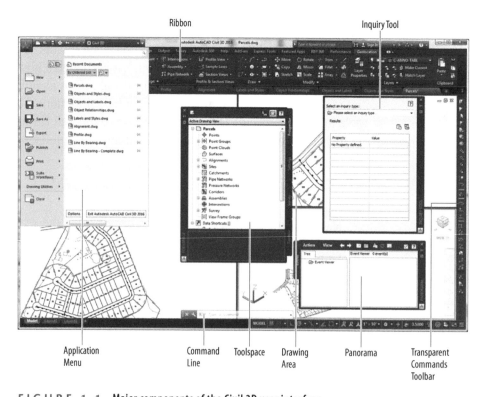

FIGURE 1.1   Major components of the Civil 3D user interface

Application Menu   The place where you can find everyday file-handling commands that enable you to do things like open, save, and print your drawings

Ribbon   The place where most Civil 3D commands are launched

Toolspace   The Civil 3D "command center" where all the data and settings are laid out in an organized fashion

Drawing Area   The place where the drawing is created

Command Line   The "chat window" where you and Civil 3D talk to one another

Panorama   A multipurpose window where you can view and/or edit drawing information and properties

Inquiry Tool   A tool with many smaller tools within it that enable you to get information about your design

Transparent Commands Toolbar   A toolbar with special commands that allow drafting and geometric construction to be done in the way that civil engineers and surveyors do it

Working with the Application Menu

The application menu (see Figure 1.2) expands out from the square AutoCAD Civil 3D icon located at the top left of your screen. Here, you'll find commands for creating, opening, saving, and printing your drawing files.

F I G U R E   1 . 2   Part of the Civil 3D application menu

The Quick Access Toolbar just to the right of the AutoCAD Civil 3D icon is a handy subset of your most commonly used general-purpose tools. It can be customized to add more tools if you like.

Exercise 1.1: Use the Application Menu to Open a File

In this exercise, you will use the application menu to open a file.

1. Launch Civil 3D by double-clicking the Civil 3D 2016 Imperial (Metric) icon on the desktop of your computer.

2. Click the application menu icon.

3. On the application menu, click Open.

4. Browse to the Chapter 01 class data folder, and open User Interface.dwg.

5. Open the application menu once more, and investigate the commands that are listed there. You'll notice that most of them have to do with creating, opening, saving, and printing drawing files.

6. Keep this drawing open for the next exercise.

Because nothing changes in this drawing file as a result of the exercise steps, no User Interface – Complete file is necessary.

> **If you haven't already done so, download and install the files for Chapter 1 according to the instructions in this book's Introduction.**

IT's ALL IN HOW YOU LOOK AT IT

This drawing, like many other drawings you'll open while working through this book, is set up with three viewports. The one on the left is top-down, or *plan view*, showing the entire project. The one at the top right is also plan view, but it is zoomed in to a different part of the drawing. The lower-right viewport is a *3D view*. These are three views of the same design, and what happens in one will happen in the other two. Think of it as three cameras showing three different viewpoints of the same subject, with each viewport being like a television monitor.

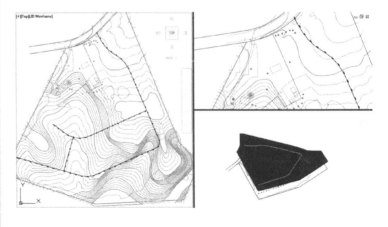

Working with the Ribbon

The *ribbon* is located at the top of your screen, and it is the launching pad for most of your Civil 3D commands. The commands that it contains are organized into groups through the use of *tabs* and *panels*. The ribbon itself is divided into a series of tabs that include Home, Insert, Annotate, and so on, as illustrated in Figure 1.3.

FIGURE 1.3   **Tabs arrange large numbers of similar Civil 3D commands into groups.**

Each tab is divided into panels. For instance, the Home tab shown in Figure 1.4 includes the Palettes, Create Ground Data, Create Design, Profile & Section Views, and Draw panels.

FIGURE 1.4   **Panels provide another level of grouping within a ribbon tab.**

Because Civil 3D groups the commands in this way, you never have to choose from more than a handful of commands once you've taken your best guess at the correct tab and panel. Also, you'll find that the more you use Civil 3D, the better you will get at knowing the location of the commands. It's not so much memorizing their positions as it is learning how Civil 3D "thinks"—that is, the way in which it relates commands to one another and categorizes them into tabs and panels.

One other thing you should know is that most panels expand downward to show you the less frequently used commands in a particular category. You'll know that a panel expands when you see a downward-pointing white triangle next to its name. For example, Figure 1.5 shows the Home tab's Create Design panel expanded with more commands. Don't forget to look on these hidden panels when searching for commands.

FIGURE 1.5   Most panels expand downward to reveal more commands, as is the case with the Create Design panel on the Home tab of the ribbon.

One of the best features of the ribbon is its ability to respond to what you select in the drawing area. For example, if you click a Civil 3D alignment, the ribbon changes and serves up alignment-related commands on a special tab. The same is true for surfaces, parcels, and so on. These special tabs are referred to as *contextual ribbon tabs*. They are a huge help when you're first learning Civil 3D and a huge time-saver even after you've become a master.

ANOTHER GREAT WAY TO FIND COMMANDS

Sometimes you really have no idea where to even begin looking for a command. The application menu has a handy tool that will help you find just about any command, regardless of where it is in the user interface. Simply click the application menu and type a keyword in the search bar. You'll be given a list of commands that match your keyword. You can launch a command right from the list by clicking it, or you can learn where the command is located by looking at the information shown to the right of it.

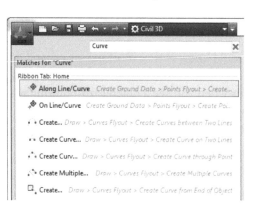

Exercise 1.2: Use the Ribbon to Launch Commands

In this exercise, you will familiarize yourself with the ribbon's tabs and panels.

1. Launch Civil 3D 2016, and open the file named User Interface.dwg.

2. Click the Home tab of the ribbon to bring it to the forefront (it may be there already).

3. Click the downward-pointing white triangle at the bottom of the Create Design panel and note how it expands down, as shown previously in Figure 1.5.

4. Click the Insert tab of the ribbon. Here, you see words like *insert*, *import*, and *attach*, which are all ways of bringing information into the drawing.

5. Click the other tabs of the ribbon, and see whether you can relate some of the words you see in the commands to the title of each ribbon tab.

6. Place your cursor in the left viewport, and roll the mouse wheel forward to zoom in to the drawing. Keep zooming in until you can clearly see the road centerlines labeled with stationing numbers (these are Civil 3D alignments). Click one of the road centerlines, and note that the ribbon displays a contextual tab to make alignment commands accessible (see Figure 1.6).

If you are continuing from the previous exercise, you can skip to step 2. If you don't have the necessary file(s), download and install the files for Chapter 1 according to the instructions in this book's Introduction.

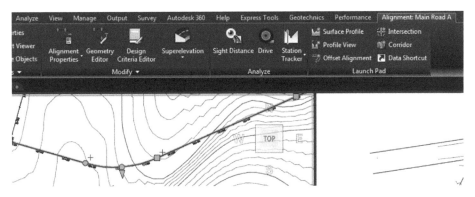

FIGURE 1.6 The ribbon displays the contextual Alignment: Main Road A tab because an alignment has been selected in the drawing (the name of the tab you see may be slightly different depending on which alignment you selected).

7. Keep this drawing open for the next exercise.

Because nothing changes in this drawing file as a result of the exercise steps, no User Interface – Complete file is necessary.

Working with the Toolspace

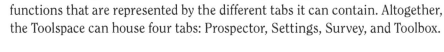

You can open the Toolspace by clicking the Toolspace icon on the Home tab of the ribbon.

Think of the Toolspace as the Civil 3D "command center" where all Civil 3D data and settings are laid out in a nice, orderly arrangement. It has several main functions that are represented by the different tabs it can contain. Altogether, the Toolspace can house four tabs: Prospector, Settings, Survey, and Toolbox.

Prospector Tab

Certification
Objective

Prospector is arguably the most important part of the Civil 3D user interface. As you build your design, *Prospector* arranges the different components of your design in a tree structure (see Figure 1.7). Why a tree structure and not just a list of items? Later in this book, you'll study how Civil 3D creates relationships between different parts of your design. In some ways, this tree structure helps represent some of those relationships as a hierarchy. Another, more practical reason for a tree structure is that it's an efficient way to show a long list of items in a relatively small area—the branches of the tree can be collapsed to make room to expand other branches.

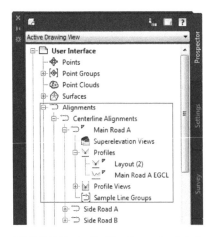

FIGURE 1.7   The Prospector tab showing a portion of the tree structure

Another way to think about Prospector is that it arranges your design categorically rather than spatially. In other words, in your drawing area, you might see road centerlines crossing through parcels, which cross through contours, which cross through survey points. Everything is in the right place spatially, but from an organizational standpoint, it's kind of a mess. Prospector sorts out this mess and puts all the points in one place, all the parcels in one place, and so on. Prospector also knows exactly where those objects are in the drawing. You can right-click an object in Prospector and use the Select command or Zoom To command to locate that object within the drawing.

If you are continuing from the previous exercise, you can skip to step 2. If you don't have the necessary file(s), download and install the files for Chapter 1 according to the instructions in this book's Introduction.

Exercise 1.3: Explore the Model with the Prospector Tab

In this exercise you will use the Prospector tab of the Toolspace to explore the model.

1. Launch Civil 3D 2016, and open the file named User Interface.dwg.

2. If the Toolspace is not already open, click Toolspace on the Home tab of the ribbon.

3. Click the Prospector tab of the Toolspace to bring it to the forefront.

4. Explore the tree structure of Prospector by clicking the plus signs to expand the different branches.

If the Prospector tab is not visible, click the Home tab of the ribbon and then click the Prospector icon on the Palettes panel.

5. Expand Alignments ➤ Centerline Alignments ➤ Main Road A ➤ Profiles. This hierarchical arrangement provides effective organization and suggests a relationship between the alignment and its profiles.

6. Click within the left viewport to activate it. Then, on the Prospector tab, right-click Side Road B, and select Zoom To. Notice how Prospector knows the location of the alignment named Side Road B, even if you don't.

7. Keep this drawing open for the next exercise.

Because nothing changes in this drawing file as a result of the exercise steps, no User Interface – Complete file is necessary.

It's important to point out that Prospector isn't just a place for viewing your design; it's also a place where you can change the appearance of your design, create new components for your design, edit your design, and so on. These types of functions are accessed through contextual menus such as the one used in step 6 of Exercise 1.3. A good rule of thumb when using Prospector is, "When in doubt, right-click it."

Certification
Objective

Settings Tab

If you are continuing from the previous exercise, you can skip to step 2. If you don't have the necessary file(s), download and install the files for Chapter 1 according to the instructions in this book's Introduction.

Civil 3D has a lot of settings that control nearly every aspect of how the software behaves. In fact, one of the things that makes Civil 3D so powerful is that you can customize its settings to accommodate nearly any type of design, any company standard, or any other factor that defines the environment within which you use it. The *Settings tab* is where these settings are managed; however, you won't be spending much time here in the early part of your Civil 3D career. This area is more often the territory of a CAD manager or Civil 3D guru.

Exercise 1.4: Explore the Drawing Settings with the Settings Tab

In this exercise, you will use the Settings tab of the Toolspace to explore the drawing settings.

1. Launch Civil 3D 2016, and open the file named User Interface.dwg.

2. If the Toolspace is not already open, click Toolspace on the Home tab of the ribbon.

If the Settings tab is not visible, click the Home tab of the ribbon and then click the Settings icon on the Palettes panel.

3. Click the Settings tab of the Toolspace.

4. Expand Surface ➤ Surface Styles, and note the list of styles shown there. These styles control the appearance of models that represent the shape of the ground.

5. Expand Surface ➤ Label Styles ➤ Contour, and note the list of styles shown there. These styles control a certain type of label that is used to annotate surface models.

6. Keep this drawing open for the next exercise.

Because nothing changes in this drawing file as a result of the exercise steps, no User Interface – Complete file is necessary.

Survey Tab

The *Survey tab* is specifically designed for working with survey data. You could call it "Prospector for surveyors" because it serves the same functions and works in much the same way as the Prospector tab. It displays survey data in a tree structure, and it allows you to launch commands through contextual menus.

Toolbox Tab

As if Civil 3D didn't have enough stuff packed into it already, the Toolbox is a place where other add-ons can be plugged in. Your company may have some custom programming that is designed to run in Civil 3D, or you may have some add-on modules provided by Autodesk. This is the place where you can load and run these additional enhancements to Civil 3D.

Using the Drawing Area

The drawing area is where you can actually see and "touch" the design model you are creating. The design model is most often viewed from above, referred to as *plan view*, but it can be viewed from any perspective. For example, because Civil 3D specializes in representing designs as 3D models, you may want to display your model using a 3D view. Figure 1.8 shows a model in both plan and 3D views.

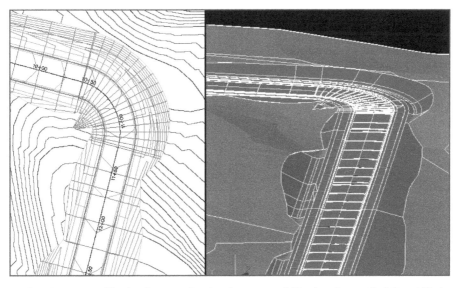

FIGURE 1.8   The drawing area showing the same model in plan view on the left and 3D view on the right

Using the Command Line

Think of the command line (see Figure 1.9) as a "chat window" where you talk with Civil 3D. Nearly everything you do is reported on the command line along with the response from Civil 3D. A response can be a request for more information, report of a result, or notification of a problem. It's good to get into the habit of always watching the command line, because it often tells you what to do next. You can also launch commands from the command line, but you will likely find it much easier to use the visual interface provided by the ribbon and other tools.

```
Command: *Cancel*
Command: LINE
Specify first point: '_NE
>_ ▾ NE >>>>Enter northing <0.0000>:
```

FIGURE 1.9 A view of the command line while a transparent command (covered later in this chapter) is used to draw a line. Notice how the command line reports that the LINE command has been started and then prompts for the first piece of information: the "first point."

Using Panorama

Panorama is a multipurpose window that is used to show and/or modify many different types of information. It works by displaying a tab for the information that you or the program has called for. For example, the Events tab (also known as the *Event Viewer*) shows up when Civil 3D needs to tell you something about the drawing. In another example, if you launch the command to edit the geometric details of an alignment, the Alignment Entities tab appears. As shown in Figure 1.10, while Panorama displays information for one task, it also displays tabs for other tasks that you can access with a single click. This enables you to multitask within the same window.

No.	Type	Tangency Constraint	Parameter Constrai...	Parameter C...	Length	Ra
1	Line	Not Constrained (Fixed)	🔒	Two points	71.890'	
2	Curve	Constrained on Both Sides (Free)	🔒	Radius	143.335'	
3	Line	Not Constrained (Fixed)	🔒	Two points	33.616'	
4	Curve	Constrained on Both Sides (Free)	🔒	Radius	181.732'	
5	Line	Not Constrained (Fixed)	🔒	Two points	613.854'	
6	Curve	Constrained on Both Sides (Free)	🔒	Radius	78.540'	
7	Line	Not Constrained (Fixed)	🔒	Two points	553.949'	
8	Curve	Constrained on Both Sides (Free)	🔒	Radius	136.280'	
9	Line	Not Constrained (Fixed)	🔒	Two points	552.610'	

FIGURE 1.10 Panorama showing the Events and Alignment Entities tabs

Exercise 1.5: Explore Panorama

In this exercise, you will open the Event Viewer and Volumes Dashboard to become familiar with the Panorama.

1. Launch Civil 3D 2016, and open the file named User Interface.dwg.

2. On the Home tab of the ribbon, expand the Palettes panel and click the icon for Event Viewer.

3. Experiment with resizing, auto-hiding, and docking the Panorama window. You'll find that it behaves much like other dockable windows in Civil 3D.

4. Press Esc to clear any selections in the drawing. Click one of the contour lines in the drawing to display the Tin Surface: Existing Ground ribbon tab, and then click Volumes Dashboard on the Analyze panel.

5. Close Panorama, and close the drawing without saving.

Because nothing changes in this drawing file as a result of the exercise steps, no User Interface – Complete file is necessary.

If you are continuing from the previous exercise, you can skip to step 2. If you don't have the necessary file(s), download and install the files for Chapter 1 according to the instructions in this book's Introduction.

Note the Volumes Dashboard tab that shows up next to the Events tab in Panorama.

Using the Transparent Commands Toolbar

As you may already know, civil engineers and surveyors draw things a little differently than architects or mechanical engineers. They use things such as bearings, curve deltas, northings, and eastings to define geometry. The Transparent Commands toolbar enables Civil 3D users to draw things based on the special geometric concepts that are unique to civil engineers and surveyors.

For example, when drawing a line, you can use the Northing Easting transparent command to specify the first point and the Bearing Distance transparent command to specify the endpoint (see Figure 1.11).

Certification Objective

Northing Easting

Bearing Distance

FIGURE 1.11   The Transparent Commands toolbar with red lines pointing to the Bearing Distance and Northing Easting transparent commands

You can dock and undock the Transparent Commands toolbar by dragging the double line at the end of the toolbar to the appropriate location.

Exercise 1.6: Use Transparent Commands to Draw Like a Civil Engineer

If you are continuing from the previous exercise, you can skip to step 2. If you don't have the necessary file(s), download and install the files for Chapter 1 according to the instructions in this book's Introduction.

In this exercise, you will use one of the Transparent Commands to draw a line by bearing and distance.

1. Launch Civil 3D 2016, and open the file named Line By Bearing.dwg.

2. Click the Type a command prompt on the command line. Type **LINE**, and press Enter.

3. When prompted to specify the first point, click a point near the center of the screen.

4. When prompted to specify the next point, click Bearing Distance on the Transparent Commands toolbar. Refer to Figure 1.11 for the location of this command.

5. When prompted for a quadrant, either type **1** and press Enter or click in the upper-right quadrant created by the crosshairs on the screen.

6. When prompted for the bearing, type **45** and press Enter.

7. When prompted for the distance, type **500** (**150**) and press Enter. Press Esc twice to exit the command. You have just drawn a line that is 500 feet (150 meters) long at a bearing of N 45° E.

8. Save and close the drawing.

To view the results of completing the exercise successfully, you can open Line By Bearing - Complete.dwg.

Using the Inquiry Tool

Most of the time, you'll be the one providing the information for a drawing. Sometimes, however, you need your drawing to tell *you* something. That's where the *Inquiry Tool* comes in. The Inquiry Tool is a separate window whose sole purpose is to give you information about things in the drawing. There is a long list of drawing items from which to choose, and beneath each item is a list of things that you can ask about (see Figure 1.12).

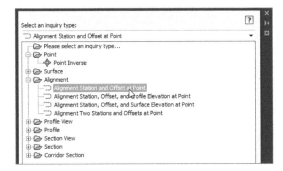

FIGURE 1.12   The Inquiry Tool showing a partial list of available inquiry types

Certification
Objective

USING SPECIALIZED LINE AND CURVE COMMANDS

Another Civil 3D feature that enables you to draw like a surveyor or civil engineer is a set of specialized line and curve commands. These commands are mixed in with the basic AutoCAD line and curve commands on the Draw panel of the ribbon. You can find specialized line commands by expanding the Line icon to reveal commands like Create Line By Bearing, Create Line By Point # Range, and so on. There is also a Curves icon that expands to reveal commands like Create Curve Through Point and Create Multiple Curves. Finally, the Best Fit icon expands to include commands for best-fit lines and curves. The following image shows the expanded form of the Line, Curve, and Best Fit icons.

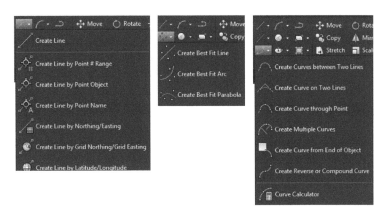

Exercise 1.7: Use the Inquiry Tool to Answer Questions

In this exercise, you will use the Inquiry Tool to analyze the line that was drawn in the previous exercise.

If you are continuing from the previous exercise, you can skip to step 2. If you don't have the necessary file(s), download and install the files for Chapter 1 according to the instructions in this book's Introduction.

1. Launch Civil 3D 2016, and open the file named Inquiry.dwg.

2. On the Analyze tab of the ribbon, click Inquiry Tool.

3. Under Select An Inquiry Type, select Point ➤ Point Inverse.

4. When prompted to specify the first point, hold down the Shift key, right-click, and select Endpoint on the contextual menu that appears.

5. Click the southwestern endpoint of the line you drew earlier.

You may need to zoom in to accurately pick the end of the line.

6. Use the Shift+right-click combination again to select Endpoint, and then click the opposite end of the line for the second point.

7. Scroll down to the Direction and Horizontal Distance values in the Inquiry Tool window. Note that they show the same bearing and distance that you entered earlier.

Because nothing has changed in this drawing file, no Inquiry – Complete file is available.

Now You Know

Now that you have completed this chapter, you are more comfortable in the Civil 3D user interface and can begin navigating it to get where you need to go. You understand how to use the application menu to access files and do other general tasks. You can use the ribbon to access Civil 3D commands and the Toolspace to explore the model contents and the drawing settings. You understand where Panorama fits in to the overall user interface makeup. You can use transparent commands to perform basic drafting using terms and geometric concepts that are unique to those working in the civil engineering and surveying fields. Finally, you can use the Inquiry Tool to answer questions about your design.

Now that you have a feel for the Civil 3D user interface, you are ready to move on in your learning experience. Next you will study the nature of the Civil 3D environment in all its dynamic 3D glory, and you will begin to build and create a design, learning new tools and concepts as you go.

CHAPTER 2

Leveraging a Dynamic Environment

Let's switch back to the airplane analogy again. So far we've sat down in the cockpit and talked about the most important gauges and controls. In several cases, we've even pushed a few buttons and looked behind a few hidden panels. You now have a greater familiarity with the user interface.

In this chapter, we're going to take the plane for a ride and observe and discuss how it works. How does it turn? How fast can it go? And, most important, how do the parts work together? You won't be able to fly solo after completing this chapter, but you will gain the experience of applying specific instructions, producing specific results, and discussing those results.

How does this translate to the AutoCAD® Civil 3D® software? Civil 3D has a unique, dynamic environment that is all about leveraging interactions and relationships. If you capitalize on this while you're working with Civil 3D, you will be much more productive and efficient. After completing this chapter, you will understand the dynamic capabilities of the Civil 3D environment and the importance of taking advantage of those capabilities.

In this chapter, you'll learn to:

▶ **Understand and leverage the connection between objects and styles**

▶ **Understand the connection between labels and label styles**

▶ **Understand the connection between objects**

▶ **Understand the connection between objects and labels**

▶ **Appreciate the richness of the 3D model**

▶ **Share data in the dynamic Civil 3D environment**

Connecting Objects and Styles

The word *object* is usually considered pretty generic, but in the world of Civil 3D it means something very specific. A Civil 3D object is an intelligent piece of your design model that stores information about itself and has the ability to interact with other objects in the drawing. Another characteristic of a Civil 3D object is that it is affected by a Civil 3D style. A Civil 3D *style* is a collection of settings that control the appearance and behavior of a Civil 3D object.

The relationship between objects and styles is one of several key relationships that you must understand and be able to take advantage of when using Civil 3D. Here are a few examples of Civil 3D objects that you'll encounter in this book as well as in a production environment:

Surface   A 3-D model typically used to represent the shape of the ground, either existing or proposed

Alignment   A series of 2-D lines, arcs, and spirals typically used to represent a linear feature such as a road centerline

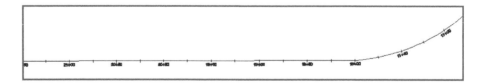

Profile   A series of lines and curves that represent changes in elevation along an alignment

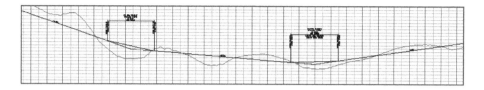

Parcel   A closed shape typically used to represent a legal property boundary

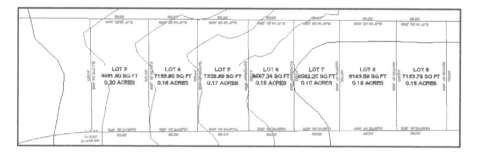

RECAP OF IMPORTANT DEFINITIONS

A Civil 3D *object* is an intelligent piece of your design model that stores information about itself and has the ability to interact with other objects in the drawing.

A Civil 3D *style* is a collection of settings that control the appearance and behavior of a Civil 3D object.

WHAT IS ELEVATION?

Depending on where you are in your civil engineering or surveying learning experience, the term *elevation* may be foreign to you. One way to visualize this concept is to think of it in terms of a piece of grid paper laid out over an area of land with the horizontal lines running west to east and the vertical lines running south to north. Elevation would be coming straight up out of the paper. So, the top of a hill would have a greater elevation than the bottom of a ravine. Another way of thinking about this is in terms of an XYZ coordinate system. X and Y would be the lines on the grid paper, and Z (elevation) would be coming out of it. Because Civil 3D combines general AutoCAD® software and civil engineering commands, elevation and the z-axis are the same.

One more thing—depending on where you live in the world, it may be appropriate to use the word *level* instead of *elevation*.

Each of the objects listed previously can be controlled by styles. For example, surface styles can be used to show a surface in many forms, including contour lines, a 3-D grid, a series of arrows pointing downhill, shading representing different elevation ranges, and more (see Figure 2.1). In addition to changing the overall appearance of an object, styles can control specific details that differ slightly between similar configurations. For example, in one case there may be surface contours that need to be shown on an existing layer, whereas in another case the same contours are shown on a proposed layer (see Figure 2.2). The configuration is the same (contours), but the way that configuration is displayed (which layer) is different between two different styles.

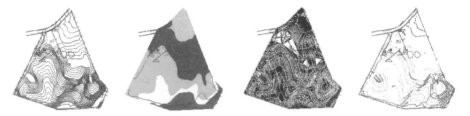

▶

The acronym TIN will be covered in Chapter 4.

FIGURE 2.1   The same surface is shown in four different configurations using four different styles (from left to right): contours, elevation banding, TIN lines and contours, and slope arrows.

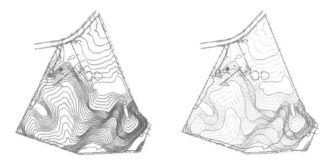

FIGURE 2.2   The contours on the left are displayed using proposed layers that are typically darker and more prominent. The contours on the right are displayed using existing layers that are typically lighter, so they appear more as background information.

Exercise 2.1: Apply Styles to Objects

In this exercise, you will use styles to change the appearance and behavior of Civil 3D objects.

If you haven't already done so, download and install the files for Chapter 2 according to the instructions in this book's Introduction.

1. Open the drawing named Objects and Styles.dwg located in the Chapter 02 class data folder.

   The plan view of the surface in the left viewport should appear similar to the first image shown in Figure 2.1.

2. Click one of the contour lines in the drawing to select the surface object.

Notice that when you click a contour, the entire surface object is selected and all the contours appear highlighted.

3. If the Properties palette is not visible, click Properties on the Home tab of the ribbon.

4. In the Properties window, change the Style property to Elevation Banding (2D).

   The surface will display as colored bands, representing different ranges of elevations, similar to the second image in Figure 2.1.

This is the style that was assigned to the surface when you first opened the drawing. Note that both of the last two styles displayed contours but on different layers. Some of the contours change to the new color as a result of this change.

5. Change the Style property to Contours & Triangles.

   The surface should now appear similar to the third image in Figure 2.1. The triangles are the fundamental framework of the surface and give it the shape that it has.

6. Change the Style property to Contours 1' and 5' (Design) (0.5 m and 2.5 m (Design)).

   The surface should now resemble the left image in Figure 2.2.

7. Change the Style property to Contours 1' and 5' (Background) (0.5 m and 2.5 m (Background)).

WHAT ARE CONTOURS?

Contours are lines that are used to represent topography or changes in elevation across the ground. Most people experience contours in things like trail maps that cover a large area (square miles or square kilometers) in comparison to what we typically see in Civil 3D. By definition, contours are lines that connect points of equal elevation. If you took a giant horizontal blade and passed it through the ground at equal elevation intervals, you would get contour lines. In flat areas, the lines would be far apart, and in steep areas, the lines would be close together. With practice, you can look at a contour map and visualize the 3D shape of the land that the map represents.

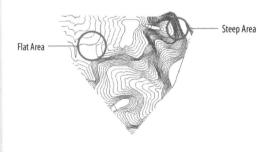

The Tin Surface: Existing Ground tab is an example of a special ribbon tab that is displayed because you selected a surface. These are often referred to as *contextual* ribbon tabs, as you may remember from the previous chapter.

8. With the surface still selected, click the Tin Surface: Existing Ground ribbon tab and then click Surface Properties ➢ Edit Surface Style.

9. Click the Display tab, and then click the color column next to Major Contour.

10. Choose a noticeable color, and click OK. Click OK again to return to the drawing.

Some of the contours change to the new color as a result of this change.

11. Save and close the drawing.

You can view the results of successfully completing this exercise by opening `Objects and Styles - Complete.dwg`.

As you worked through the previous exercise, did you notice that no extra steps were required to update or redraw the surface when a new style was assigned or the style was edited? The effect was immediate—as soon as you modified the assigned style or assigned a different style, the appearance of the surface changed. This is because of a dynamic relationship between the object and its style, a relationship that is honored throughout the software.

EDITING A STYLE VS. ASSIGNING A DIFFERENT STYLE

In steps 4 through 7 of the previous exercise, you changed the appearance of the surface by assigning a different style to it. This is the way to do it 99 percent of the time. In steps 8 through 10, you edited the style that was already assigned to the surface. Editing styles is typically the responsibility of a CAD manager. In fact, in many companies, end users are not permitted to modify or create styles. However, it is still important to understand that when a style is modified, any object using that style will change its appearance or behavior to honor the new version of the style.

Connecting Labels and Label Styles

Labels are an important part of any design because they provide specific information about the design that is often necessary for it to be properly constructed. Civil 3D enables you to create many different types of labels that associate themselves with the different types of Civil 3D objects. Labels are Civil 3D objects too, and just like the objects listed in the previous section, their appearance and behavior are controlled by styles. Also, just as with the relationship between objects and their styles, labels react when a different style is assigned or the assigned style is modified.

Certification
Objective

Here are some label types that correspond to the Civil 3D objects listed in the previous section:

Surface Spot Elevation Label   This type of label is typically used to display the elevation of a key point in the design, such as a low point that water will drain toward or a high point that water will drain away from.

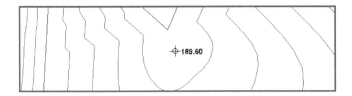

Alignment Station Offset Label   This type of label is used to express the location of a feature in reference to a linear object. For example, you can express the location of a manhole by saying that it is a certain distance along the length of the road (station) and a certain distance to the left or right of it (offset).

Profile Grade Break Label   This type of label is used to show the location and elevation of a slope change along a profile. For example, if the profile slopes upward and then changes to a downward direction, the highest point where the change occurs is considered a grade break and is a common location to place a label.

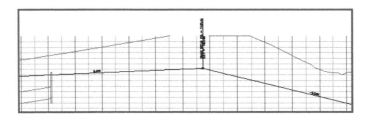

Station and Offset

Long linear designs such as roads and pipelines often use station and offset notation to express locations. Stations themselves are usually expressed in a special notation that has a plus sign in it.

For example, if you're working in imperial units, a station of 2+00 refers to a location that is 200 feet "down the road" (assuming the road begins at station 0+00). To get to station 2+00, offset 12', you would travel down the road exactly 200 feet, turn right exactly 90 degrees, and travel exactly 12 feet.

If you're working in metric units, a common format is to use three digits after the plus sign. In this case, a station of 0+200 refers to a location 200 meters down the road. To get to station 0+200, offset 4 m, you would travel 200 meters down the road, turn right exactly 90 degrees, and travel exactly 4 meters.

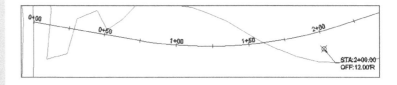

Parcel Segment Label   This type of label is typically used to express geometric information about a line or curve that forms part of a legal boundary. For example, it is common to label the bearing and distance of a straight line segment along a property boundary.

Exercise 2.2: Apply Label Styles to Labels

In this exercise, you will use label styles to change the appearance and behavior of labels.

1. Open the drawing named Labels and Styles.dwg located in the Chapter 02 class data folder.

2. In the top-right viewport, click the label. If the Properties palette is not visible, click Properties on the Home tab of the ribbon.

3. Change the value for Station Offset Label Style to Station And Offset, as shown in Figure 2.3. Notice how the content of the label changes.

If you haven't already done so, download and install the files for Chapter 2 according to the instructions in this book's Introduction.

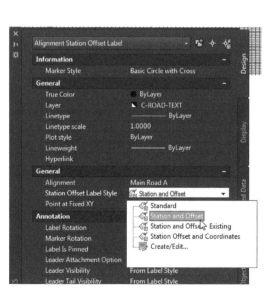

F I G U R E   2 . 3   Assigning the Station And Offset label style to the label

4. Change the value for Station Offset Label Style to Station And Offset – Existing. This time, the content stays the same but the style of the text changes.

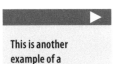

This is another example of a *contextual* ribbon tab.

5. With the label still selected, click Label Properties ➢ Edit Label Style on the Labels – Alignment Station Offset Label contextual ribbon tab.

6. In the Station Offset Label Style dialog box, click Edit Current Selection, as shown in Figure 2.4.

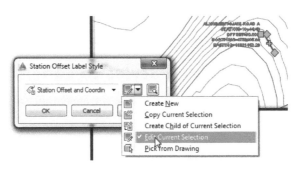

FIGURE 2.4 Clicking the Edit Current Selection command for the selected label style

7. In the Label Style Composer dialog box, click the Dragged State tab. Change the Visibility value for the leader to False, as shown in Figure 2.5.

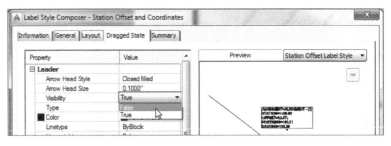

The label is updated to reflect the change to the style and no longer displays a leader.

FIGURE 2.5 Changing the visibility of the leader by modifying a label style

8. Click OK twice to dismiss all dialog boxes and return to the drawing.

9. Save and close the drawing.

You can view the results of successfully completing this exercise by opening `Labels and Styles - Complete.dwg`.

STYLES AND COMPANY STANDARDS

Civil 3D styles can make it easier for end users to meet company standards and can make graphical output more consistent. With a good set of styles that integrate company standards, all that an end user has to worry about is choosing the right style from a manageable list of choices. Conversely, if end users have to create their own styles, labels, and/or other graphical components, their drawings will most likely vary and may not comply with those standards.

Connecting Objects to Objects

The most important type of relationship that you'll see in this chapter is the one between objects. A typical land development project is a collection of dozens of mini-designs that often tie in to one another. For example, a road is designed by first drawing the 2D path of its centerline, then the proposed changes in elevation along that centerline, and finally the lanes, curbs, and sidewalks extending outward from that centerline. To provide drainage during a rainstorm, ditches must be installed along the sides of the road. The location and depth of these ditches can be traced back through the design process the entire way to the layout of the road centerline. If the layout of the centerline needs to change for some reason, that change must propagate downstream through the design process, ultimately changing the location and depth of one or more ditches.

Before Civil 3D, the many implications of such a change had to be addressed manually. An engineer or designer would have to inspect the road elevations, curbs, sidewalks, and ditches and manually address any changes required because of a change "upstream" in the design. With Civil 3D, you can build relationships between design objects and cause these changes to take place automatically, saving time and money and reducing opportunity for human error.

Exercise 2.3: Explore Object Relationships

In this exercise, you will study how object relationships are leveraged to make design changes in a drawing.

1. Open Object Relationships.dwg located in the Chapter 02 class data folder.

◄

If you haven't already done so, download and install the files for Chapter 2 according to the instructions in this book's Introduction.

2. Press the F3 key, and observe the command line. If it reports <Osnap On>, then press F3 again. If it reports <Osnap Off>, this is the correct condition for this exercise, and you can move on to the next step.

3. Click the top-right viewport, which shows a profile of the road design. The black lines represent the elevations along the centerline of the new road. The blue lines represent storm drains and pipes connecting them.

4. Click the black line representing the road profile. Zoom in until you can clearly see the triangular grip located at the intersection of two lines.

5. Click the triangular grip, and drag it upward to a location just below the top edge of the profile view grid, as shown in Figure 2.6.

    Notice that the 3-D view (bottom-right) of the road automatically updates, including the height of the Inlet 2 drain. In the profile view (top-right), the top of the drain is elevated to match the road.

▶ <Osnap Off> prevents your cursor from locking on to objects in the drawing that are near it.

▶ Be sure that your command line is docked at the bottom of your screen and that the background color is set to white before proceeding with these steps.

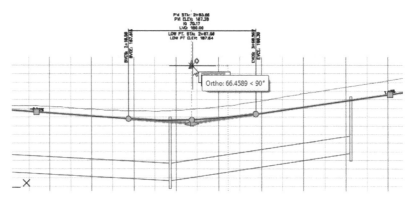

FIGURE 2.6 Grip-editing the profile

6. Save and close the drawing.

You can view the results of successfully completing this exercise by opening Object Relationships - Complete.dwg.

This simple exercise illustrates the power of relationships between objects. The ease with which you just updated the design may cause you to take the underlying processes for granted; however, there is a lot happening behind the scenes. The following is a general account of the events that took place when you changed the location of the triangular grip:

- ▶ The slopes of the lines leading into that triangular grip were changed to match the new location of the grip.

- ▶ The parabolic curve geometry at the location of the grip was updated automatically.

- ▶ The corridor object, which represents a 3-D model of the road, was automatically rebuilt and updated to match the new profile geometry.

- ▶ A surface representing the pavement, concrete, and earthen embankment elevations of the corridor was automatically rebuilt.

- ▶ The storm drain updated its top elevation to match the surface in the previous step.

- ▶ The 3-D representation of the storm drain was automatically updated (bottom-right view).

- ▶ The profile view representation of the storm drain was automatically updated (top-right view).

A simple grip edit triggered a chain of events that might have taken an hour or more to update manually. In addition to all this, other changes took place that did not affect the design of the storm drain. This is the power of the Civil 3D dynamic environment. You should know, however, that the existence of these relationships is not necessarily automatic. They have to be considered and at times consciously built in to the design by the Civil 3D user.

Connecting Objects to Labels

There is also an important relationship between objects and labels. Labeling is one of the most time-consuming aspects of preparing a set of construction documents. Although it is a very important part of the process, it really has nothing to do with the design. Usually, labels are placed when the design is already complete, as a means of communicating the necessary information for constructing the design in the field. The big advantage of the dynamic relationship between objects and labels is that it enables the user to create a single label that is valid for the life of the object. As the object changes, the label changes with it—so the label is always up to date and never has to be edited manually.

If you haven't already done so, download and install the files for Chapter 2 according to the instructions in this book's Introduction.

Exercise 2.4: Explore the Relationship Between Objects and Labels

In this exercise, you will study how dynamic labels respond when changes are made to the objects they annotate.

1. Open `Objects and Labels.dwg` located in the `Chapter 02` class data folder. Notice the elevation label, which currently reads 190.02 (57.92).

2. Click one of the dark gray contour lines. On the ribbon, click Edit Surface ➤ Paste Surface.

This step is like using a bulldozer to cut the road into the hillside, causing the elevation to drop about 3 feet (1 meter).

3. Select Main Road A FG, and click OK. Press Esc to clear the selection. In the top-right viewport, notice how the label updates and now reads 187.33 (57.07).

4. In the top-right viewport, pan southward and note the station value of 10+95.68 (0+333.96) and the offset value of 68.49L (20.88m L) in the label to the south of the spot elevation.

5. Click the road centerline to select it and display its grips. Then click the triangular grip and drag it west to a point near the west edge of the road, as shown in Figure 2.7.

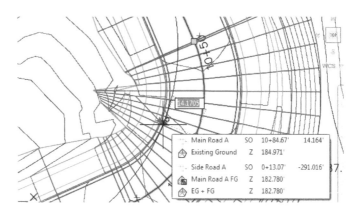

FIGURE 2.7 Grip-editing the alignment

After a pause while Civil 3D rebuilds several aspects of the design, the label updates once more. Because the road is no longer influencing the elevation of this spot, the label reverts to its original value of 190.02 (57.92). The station offset label now displays updated values for station and offset.

6. Save and close the drawing.

You can view the results of successfully completing this exercise by opening
Objects and Labels - Complete.dwg.

Appreciating the Richness of the 3-D Model

Even though what you have done to this point may seem a bit foreign at the
moment, at some point you will realize that all you're doing with Civil 3D is creating instructions for how to build something. If you've ever assembled a piece
of furniture or a bicycle that you bought at a store, you can relate to this concept. The primary purpose of Civil 3D is to help you prepare the instructions for
how to build a land development project.

Thirty years ago, the method used to prepare land development plans was
relatively the same as it had been for hundreds of years: plans were drawn on
paper, providing only a two-dimensional depiction of what was to be built. The
information that existed for the design was limited to what could be displayed
on paper. Then, with the advent of computers, something magical started to
happen. Virtual versions of design components could be modeled electronically.
They could be represented in all three dimensions and even have additional
information attached to them. Now, instead of using an ink line on paper to
represent a pipe, you could do it with a 3-D cylinder that also stored the pipe's
material, structural characteristics, and flow characteristics. This "smart"
object could be ported to hydraulic design software for further analysis in conjunction with local rainfall data to determine whether it was large enough to
handle a storm with a specific likelihood of occurring within the life span of the
pipe. And so on, and so on.

Thus, in 30 years we have progressed from ink on paper to 3-D intelligent
objects. The step from drawing with a pen to drawing with a mouse came early
in that evolution—not 3D or intelligent, but lines on a screen that could be
printed. Civil 3D contains all the basic tools to represent designs in this manner,
and unfortunately, many users create only basic 2-D drawings even though they
have access to the dynamic 3-D environment that you've seen in this chapter.
My sincere hope is that you will not be this type of end user but instead will
squeeze every dynamic relationship possible into the models you build with Civil
3D. You may not realize the full potential of the dynamic relationships you build
until you have the opportunity to use them, but you can bet that they will pay
dividends on every single project. The following are examples where it is essen-
tial to have a dynamic 3-D model.

Building Information Modeling

Building information modeling (BIM) has been a hot topic in the design, construction, and facilities management fields for quite some time now. Although some would argue that Civil 3D has little to do with the *B* (building), it definitely has the *I* (information) and the *M* (modeling) aspects. Many civil engineering projects are incidental to building construction and therefore present an opportunity for Civil 3D models to be integrated with BIM. No model, no BIM.

GPS-Guided Machine Control

Imagine being able to download the instructions to assemble your bike and then upload them to your own personal robot, which would assemble the bike for you. That might sound like science fiction, but something similar is common practice in the land development industry. Models built with Civil 3D are being uploaded to GPS-guided earthmoving machines. These giant "robots" synchronize GPS-based locations of themselves and their digging implements with the dimensions of the Civil 3D model until the real dirt and rock are a match to the model. Without a model, there is no GPS-guided machine control.

Construction Simulation

If you think about it, one thing that Civil 3D enables you to do is to simulate the project before having the contractor attempt to build it in the field. Why do this? It's a lot cheaper to undo a CAD command than to undo the placement of several truckloads of concrete. Contractors are taking this one step further by simulating the construction itself. The sequence of operations, staging of materials, arrangement of equipment, and many other aspects can all be simulated with several products available on the market. These 4-D (3-D + time) or even 5-D (3-D + time + cost) simulations are becoming commonplace in nearly all major construction projects. No model, no simulation.

Visualization

Visualization is itself a form of simulation. With design software now commonly producing 3-D models, the leap to 3-D visualization is much shorter and easier to accomplish than ever before. Clients, review agencies, and the public are beginning to expect renderings and even animations of proposed designs to be available for them to assess. No model, no visualization.

Building your designs as dynamic models does take a bit more effort and time, but as you develop more and more skills, the extra time and effort become a smaller fraction of the overall process. The resulting models are much more useful, much more information rich, and much more valuable to your clients and the other parties involved in your projects. There's no telling how this information will be used, but one thing is for sure: It won't be used at all if it's not there.

In addition, building designs as dynamic models improves the quality and efficiency of the design process. Designers who make full use of the dynamic model produce better designs by creating more design iterations and what-if scenarios than those who don't. They can respond more quickly to design changes, reducing the overall cost involved in designing the project and increasing the bottom line. Leveraging the dynamic model isn't just cool, it's also practical and very smart from a business perspective.

Sharing Data in a Dynamic Environment

So far, you have studied many ways in which relationships and interactions are used to make Civil 3D a powerful design solution, but all these relationships have been confined to a single drawing or a single user. What happens in a team environment? Are there ways in which whole drawings can interact with one another? Can multiple team members establish dynamic relationships between their designs? The answer is yes, and the feature that makes it possible is the *data shortcut*.

Certification
Objective

Earlier, in the section "Connecting Objects to Objects," you observed how a profile, a road design, and a pipe system design can be related to one another. Now, imagine a design team where Joe designs the profile in one drawing, Susan designs the road model in another drawing, and Jill designs the pipe system in yet another. Data shortcuts make it possible for these designs to be linked together just as you witnessed earlier—even across drawings.

A data shortcut is a link to a Civil 3D object that enables another drawing to get access to that object. For example, if you create a profile that represents the proposed centerline elevations of a road, you can publish a data shortcut for that profile, which makes that profile "visible" to other drawings. You or someone else can then open another drawing and use that data shortcut to access the profile. Once you have accessed the profile, you can use it as part of another design, such as the case with the road model.

When a data shortcut is created, it is displayed in Prospector beneath the Data Shortcuts heading (see Figure 2.8). Data shortcuts are stored within a *data shortcuts projects folder*. This enables related data shortcuts, such as those pertaining to a given project, to be grouped together in one location. The folder that contains data shortcuts folders is the *working folder*. It allows you to set up one location where all projects are stored.

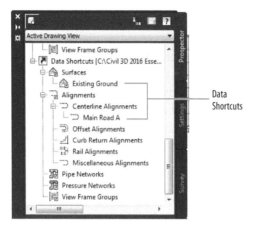

Data Shortcuts

FIGURE 2.8   Data shortcuts shown in Prospector

Once a data shortcut is made available, you can use it to create a *data reference* in another drawing. Objects that are data referenced, such as surfaces, alignments, and profiles, appear in Prospector along with other "native" objects. An icon next to them indicates that they are data references. In Figure 2.9, the Existing Ground surface and the Main Road A alignment have an icon next to them indicating that they are data references.

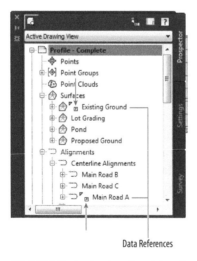

Data References

FIGURE 2.9   A surface data reference and an alignment data reference shown along with other surfaces and alignments in Prospector

Exercise 2.5: Share Data Using Data Shortcuts

In this exercise, you will use data shortcuts to share data between drawings. You will publish a surface and an alignment as data shortcuts from two separate drawings. Then you will reference the alignment and surface into a third drawing and use the information to create a profile.

If you haven't already done so, download and install the files for Chapter 2 according to the instructions in this book's Introduction.

1. Open the file named Surface.dwg located in the Chapter 02 class data folder.

2. If the Toolspace is not visible, click Toolspace on the Home tab of the ribbon.

3. On the Prospector tab of the Toolspace, right-click Data Shortcuts and select Set Working Folder. The Browse For Folder dialog box opens.

4. Browse to the Chapter 02 class data folder, and select Sample Working Folder. Click OK.

5. Right-click Data Shortcuts, and select New Data Shortcuts Project Folder. The New Data Shortcut Folder dialog box opens.

6. Type **Sample Project** in the Name field, and click OK.

7. Save the drawing. Click the Manage tab of the ribbon, and then click Create Data Shortcuts. The Create Data Shortcuts dialog box opens.

8. Check the box next to Existing Ground, and click OK.

9. Open the file named Alignment.dwg located in the Chapter 02 class data folder.

10. Repeat steps 7 and 8 for the alignment named Main Road A.

You will need to expand Alignments ➢ Centerline Alignments to find the Main Road A alignment.

11. Open the file named Profile.dwg located in the Chapter 02 class data folder.

12. In Prospector, expand Data Shortcuts ➢ Surfaces. Right-click Existing Ground, and select Create Reference.

13. Click OK to accept the default settings in the Create Surface Reference dialog box. Contours in the left viewport and a 3-D model in the lower-right viewport indicate a newly added surface.

14. Repeat steps 12 and 13 for the alignment data shortcut named Main Road A. A new alignment is created in the drawing.

When you click Add, you are in a sense *adding* the surface to the alignment to generate the profile data.

15. On the Home tab of the ribbon, click Profile ➢ Create Surface Profile. The Create Profile From Surface dialog box opens.

16. Click Add, and then click Draw In Profile View. The Create Profile View – General dialog box opens.

17. Click Create Profile View. Pick a point in the top-right viewport. A new profile is created that is the result of relating an alignment to a surface (see Figure 2.10). This profile represents the interaction among three different drawings.

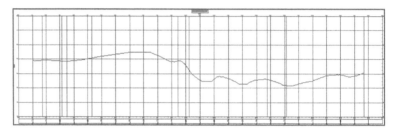

F I G U R E 2 . 1 0   **A profile created from an alignment data reference and a surface data reference**

18. Save and close all drawings.

You can view the results of successfully completing this exercise by opening `Profile - Complete.dwg`.

Now You Know

Now that you have completed this chapter, you understand the dynamic environment of Civil 3D. You comprehend how styles are applied to objects to change their appearance and behavior. This includes objects such as alignments and surfaces and also labels. You understand how objects are connected to one another and interact automatically so that you don't have to spend extra time "fixing" your design when something changes. You appreciate the richness of a 3-D model and understand how powerful it is for performing design in today's fast-paced and demanding world. And, finally, you can share data within a team by using data shortcuts to share design data between drawings.

Now that you understand and appreciate the dynamic Civil 3D environment, you will move forward into the next chapters with greater insight. As you progress through this book, be on the lookout for instances where this dynamic environment offers power and efficiency. Remember these examples and take them with you when you begin designing your own projects using Civil 3D.

CHAPTER 3

Establishing Existing Conditions Using Survey Data

With our tour of the AutoCAD® Civil 3D® software user interface and our study of its capabilities behind us, it's now time to do what we came here to do: Use Civil 3D to complete a land-development project. To begin to understand the task ahead, let's imagine land development as creating a sculpture, but on a very large scale. If sculptors were to create works of art from wood, they would probably begin by studying the original piece of wood, assessing its dimensions, shape, and surface features. These elements would all factor into how the sculptors would approach their work. A sculptor with some computer savvy might even model the original piece of wood on a computer and plan out each cut of material.

In this chapter, we are going to explore the first activities that are performed during a land-development project: the measurement, mapping, and modeling of the land in its existing form. To plan out how the land will be reshaped, you must first understand how it's shaped right now. This is analogous to the sculptor's measurement and assessment of their medium. The measurement and mapping of land is known as *surveying*, and the data that is collected during the process is known as *survey data*.

In this chapter, you'll learn to:

▶ **Understand the purpose and function of survey data**

▶ **Create a survey database**

▶ **Import survey data**

▶ **Automate field-to-finish**

▶ **Edit survey points**

▶ **Edit survey figures**

▶ **Create points**

What Is Survey Data?

Think back to the last time you played connect-the-dots to draw a picture. Ever wonder who made the dots and how they were made? I'm no expert, but I'm guessing someone took the original picture, laid a piece of tracing paper over it, and made dots along the edges of key features in the picture. Someone skilled at this would make just enough dots to define the features but not so many as to make them confusing or wasteful. The dots are a way of capturing an image and transferring it to another location.

In land development, the land is the picture and the surveyor is the one who makes the dots—referred to as *points*. Obviously, tracing paper can't be used, so the surveyor lays an imaginary grid over the land (a coordinate system) and creates the points as information by recording their coordinates on this grid paper. The tools the surveyor uses are extremely accurate and are capable of capturing the location of each point within a tolerance of about 1/8 of an inch (3 mm). Something different about the surveyor's "dots" is that their location is recorded in all three dimensions. This enables a technician to play connect-the-dots in 3-D to create a 3-D model in addition to a 2-D map of the features of the land. Another difference is that a surveyor's dots have description codes next to them instead of just numbers. A *description code* identifies the type of feature that a dot, or point, is intended to represent (see Figure 3.1).

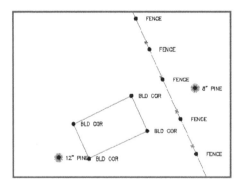

FIGURE 3.1   Survey points shown as dots, giving a sense of how they are used to create mapping

If you're thinking that it takes a lot of points to capture several acres of land, you're absolutely right. How can you keep track of all those points? How can they be easily turned into a 3-D model of the land? Is there some way of automating the connect-the-dots process? Civil 3D has the answers to these questions, and in this chapter, you'll learn how you can use Civil 3D to transform raw field points into maps and 3-D models of the land.

REALITY CAPTURE

The technology of reality capture has become more and more common in the last few years. *Reality capture* refers to the use of high-density laser scanners to collect millions or even billions of data points. The resulting data is often referred to as a *point cloud* because, due to its density, the data often looks like a cloud or fog. With this approach, there is no need to play connect-the-dots because the data points are so close together that they define the shape of the land.

Although it's not covered in this book, you should know that Civil 3D has the ability to import and use point cloud data to create a model of an existing piece of land. The image here shows an example of point cloud data that has been imported into Civil 3D.

Creating a Survey Database

In Chapter 2, "Leveraging a Dynamic Environment," you learned about the importance of relationships in Civil 3D and saw firsthand how Civil 3D makes use of interactions between different object types. When you're dealing with survey data, these relationships are managed in a *survey database*. The raw data is linked with the screen representation of the points in the survey database, which is linked with the linework generated by connecting those points, and so on. The survey database is unique in Civil 3D in that it's stored outside the drawing file.

Exercise 3.1: Create a Survey Database

In this exercise, you'll create a survey database.

1. Open Civil 3D, and click New on the application menu. When prompted for a template, browse to the Chapter 03 class data folder and open Essentials.dwt.

2. Click the Survey tab of the Toolspace.

3. Right-click Survey Databases, and select Set Working Folder.

4. Browse to and select the Chapter 03 class data folder, and click OK.

THE SURVEY WORKING FOLDER

The working folder is simply the location where survey databases are stored. In this exercise, you'll create a survey database named Essentials. This will create a folder in Chapter 03 named Essentials.

---

5. Right-click Survey Databases, and click New Local Survey Database.

6. Type **Essentials** as the new database name, and click OK.

    The Essentials database is now shown on the Survey tab. Note the components of the survey database, such as Import Events, Networks, Figures, and Survey Points (see Figure 3.2). The survey database establishes and manages relationships between these different components.

FIGURE 3.2 The Essentials survey database shown in Prospector after the completion of step 6

If you haven't already done so, download and install the files for Chapter 3 according to the instructions in this book's Introduction.

If the Toolspace is not visible, you can click Toolspace on the Home tab of the ribbon. If the Survey tab is not visible, click the Survey icon to the right of the Toolspace icon.

In Prospector, you'll see a series of Essentials survey databases that you'll use in upcoming exercises.

7. Close the drawing without saving.

There is no "Complete" drawing for this exercise because you did not modify a drawing file. You did create a new survey database, but it's currently empty. In the next exercise, you'll use the Essentials 1 survey database, which has already been created for you.

Importing Survey Data

After creating a survey database to receive the data, the next step is to transfer the raw data into Civil 3D so that the analysis and mapping can begin. There are several ways to accomplish this, but in this chapter you're going to do it the way a surveyor would do it. The process of importing data requires some important questions to be answered. For your first try, however, you're going to accept all the defaults and see what happens.

Exercise 3.2: Import Survey Data

In this exercise, you'll import survey data into a survey database and into a drawing.

1. Open the drawing named Import Survey Data.dwg located in the Chapter 03 class data folder.

2. On the Home tab of the ribbon, click Import Survey Data.

3. Select the Essentials 1 survey database, and click Next.

4. Under Data Source Type, select Point File.

5. Click the plus icon under Selected Files, and browse to the Chapter 03 class data folder.

If you haven't already done so, download and install the files for Chapter 3 according to the instructions in this book's Introduction.

If you don't see any Essentials databases listed, go back and complete steps 2–4 in Exercise 3.1. The Essentials 1 database is the result of correctly completing the previous exercise. This database is provided to ensure that you start the current exercise with the correct version.

SURVEY DATA SOURCES

Survey data can come in several forms, depending on the hardware and/or software used to create it. Here are a few of the most common forms:

Field Book File   This is considered a legacy format unique to Autodesk products such as Land Desktop and older versions of Civil 3D. Many surveyors have moved on from field book files but some have done so fairly recently. For that reason, you might still find them to be somewhat common. One difference with field book files is that they can store the measurements exactly as they were taken in the field. The other formats listed here contain points that have been reduced to coordinates.

LandXML File   Many civil engineering and surveying programs can export data in the form of LandXML, including Civil 3D. This nonproprietary format enables data to be exchanged between programs created by different software companies.

Point File   The point file is probably the most generic and universally accepted way of delivering point data. This type of file is plain text and can be opened in a program like Microsoft Notepad. Regardless of age, cost, or origin, nearly all surveying and civil engineering programs are capable of producing this type of file.

Points From Drawing   With this option, you can open a drawing that already contains points and add them to your survey database. Remember that the survey database is stored outside the drawing, so the points you see in the drawing are a representation of what is stored there.

PNEZD represents the order of the data columns in the text file: Point number, Northing, Easting, Z coordinate (elevation), and Description.

6. For Files Of Type, select the Text/Template/Extract File (*.txt) option. Then select Topo Survey.txt, and click Open.

7. Under Specify Point File Format, scroll down and select PNEZD (Comma Delimited).

8. Click Next. In the Specify Network dialog box, note that <none> is selected for the current network. Click Next.

9. In the Import Options dialog box, check the boxes next to Process Linework During Import and Insert Survey Points.

10. Verify that Current Figure Prefix Database and Current Linework Code Set are both set to Sample.

11. Click Finish.

12. Zoom in to the drawing, and examine what you see (see Figure 3.3).

Measurements can be linked so that accuracy can be adjusted across the entire project simultaneously. The survey data in this exercise does not contain any of these relationships, so no network is needed.

You may need to execute the Zoom Extents command to bring the points into view. To do this, type **ZE** at the command line and press Enter.

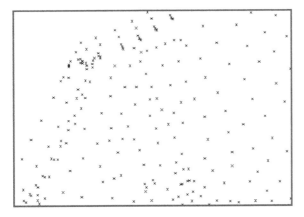

FIGURE 3.3 So far, importing data shows only a bunch of relatively meaningless *x* markers in the drawing.

13. Save and close the drawing.

You can view the results of successfully completing this exercise by opening Import Survey Data - Complete.dwg. The survey database named Essentials 2 is provided for the next exercise and matches what you should have at the end of this exercise. It contains the same points you just imported.

IMPORTING POINTS WITHOUT A SURVEY DATABASE

Sometimes you may want to import points straight into your Civil 3D drawing without the extended data-management capabilities of the survey database. You can do this using the Points From File command on the Insert tab of the ribbon, as shown in the following illustration.

The resulting dialog box (shown next) provides only one choice for file format—a text file—and no association with a survey database or linework code is set.

For that reason, some of the features you'll learn about later in this chapter will not be utilized. These include the automatic generation of linework, accuracy adjustment, and others.

(Continues)

IMPORTING POINTS WITHOUT A SURVEY DATABASE *(Continued)*

The differences continue as you work with the points you've imported. Points created without the management of the survey database are easily edited. You'll find that points created using the Points From File command can be moved as easily as moving a circle or a polyline. They can also be freely edited using the Properties window. Using the Points From File function is definitely quicker and simpler than using the Import Survey Data command; however, there are considerable differences in functionality. When you choose which method to use, be sure to consider the level of protection, ease of editing, ability to generate linework, and interrelationship between points and survey measurements. Each method serves a different purpose and should be chosen appropriately.

Automating Field-to-Finish

The term *field-to-finish* refers to the process of transforming raw survey field data into a finished drawing. Before computers, the point data collected in the field was plotted on paper by hand, and draftspeople skillfully connected the dots and employed other methods to create the desired topographic map. The process was manual in the truest sense of the word. Next came the first CAD programs, in which points could be plotted on a computer screen and the dots connected using primitive entities such as lines, arcs, and polylines. This is what many would now refer to as a "manual" process.

◄

A *topographic map* can be thought of as a 3-D map: the 2-D outlines of surface features combined with contour lines representing the third dimension.

As you might guess, the process of making a drawing out of point data is quite tedious and presents an opportunity for automation. Imagine using the result from the steps in the previous section (see Figure 3.3) to create a map of the land. With no information accompanying the points, it would be nearly impossible. In the following sections, you'll see how to use several Civil 3D features to automate this process, resulting in a drawing that is 80- to 90-percent complete immediately after you import the raw field data. However, as is usually the case, the more automation you want, the more setup you're required to perform. Automation is another way of saying that you're going to make a bunch of decisions ahead of time and ask the computer to carry out those decisions when needed.

The following Civil 3D features enable you to convert raw field data into drawing information.

Linework Code Set

To create linear features using connected points, someone has to tell those features when to start, when to end, when to draw curves, when to draw straight lines, and so on. In other words, it can be a bit more complicated than "Draw a line from point 1 to point 2." Field crews use codes to carry out these geometric instructions. For example, they might include the string BEG when locating the first point on a fence line, which means to begin a new feature at that point. The linework code set correlates these field codes with instructions that control the generation of linework in the drawing. This is the way of telling Civil 3D that BEG means "begin drawing here," BCV means "begin curve here," and so on. Another way to think of a linework code set is as a translator between field language and Civil 3D language.

Exercise 3.3: Apply a Linework Code Set

If you haven't already done so, download and install the files for Chapter 3 according to the instructions in this book's Introduction.

The Essentials 2 database is the result of correctly completing the previous exercise. This database is provided to ensure that you start the current exercise with the correct version.

In this exercise, you'll assign a linework code set to your drawing and apply it to points that have been imported.

1. Open the drawing named Linework Code Set.dwg located in the Chapter 03 class data folder.

2. Click the Survey tab of the Toolspace.

3. If the contents beneath the Essentials 2 survey database are not visible, right-click Essentials 2 and select Open For Edit.

   If you receive an error message here, you may not have installed the datasets correctly. Refer to the introduction for instructions on installing the datasets.

4. Expand Import Events. Right-click Topo Survey.txt, and select Properties.

5. Click the Browse icon next to File to open the text file. Notice the codes BEG, BCV, ECV, and END.

   These are the codes used in the field to represent Begin Feature, Begin Curve, End Curve, and End Feature. If you scroll down in the text file, you'll also see the CLS code, which represents Close Feature.

6. Close the text file, and click Cancel to dismiss the Import Event Properties dialog box.

7. Click the icon in the top-left corner of the Survey tab to edit the survey user settings.

8. Click the Browse icon next to Linework Code Sets Path, browse to the Chapter 03 class data folder, and click OK. Click OK to dismiss the Survey User Settings dialog box.

9. On the Survey tab, right-click Linework Code Sets and select Refresh. Click the plus sign next to Linework Code Sets. You should now see Essentials listed as a linework code set.

10. Under Linework Code Sets, right-click Essentials and select Make Current.

11. Under Linework Code Sets, right-click Essentials and select Edit. Notice that the codes used for Begin, End, Begin Curve, End Curve, and Close now match what you saw in the text file. The codes in the linework code set named Sample were different, and therefore no linework was drawn when you imported the survey data.

12. Click Cancel to dismiss the Edit Linework Code Set dialog box.

13. Under Import Events, right-click Topo Survey.txt and select Process Linework.

14. For Current Linework Code Set, select Essentials, and click OK.

15. Save and close the drawing.

You can view the results of successfully completing this exercise by opening Linework Code Set - Complete.dwg. The survey database named Essentials 3 is provided for the next exercise and matches what you should have at the end of this exercise.

> **◄**
>
> You should see a series of lines appear in the drawing. As you'll learn later in this chapter, these lines represent features like tree lines, fences, roads, and streams.

Point Styles

Not all points are meant to be connected with other points. Some represent stand-alone features such as power poles, manholes, or trees. These types of features are typically represented with a symbol that either resembles their true form or uniquely identifies them. With the Point Styles feature, a symbol can be used to mark a point, meaning the likeness of a power pole, manhole, or tree can be used instead of an x or a dot.

Point Label Styles

For some points, you might want labeling to be included automatically. For example, you may want trees to be labeled with their common names or manholes to be labeled with their top elevations. When the annotation is very uniform, point label styles can be employed to provide the desired labels automatically.

Description Keys

As discussed, it takes a lot of points to capture several acres of land effectively. To make things even more challenging, field crews often use abbreviated versions of descriptions to represent points, such as EP for edge of pavement, CLRD for centerline of road, and so on. The result is hundreds or even thousands of points all clumped together and labeled with cryptic abbreviated descriptions.

Description keys solve this problem by automatically sorting the points onto the appropriate layers, rewriting the abbreviated descriptions to full-length descriptions, and automatically applying point styles to control the appearance of the points. For example, a description key takes a point coded as PP, places it on the utility layer, displays it as a power pole, and rewrites the description to say POWER POLE. Imagine the time saved when this is done automatically for 10,000 points.

Exercise 3.4: Configure and Apply a Description Key

In this exercise, you'll configure a description key for the tree points in your drawing. You'll apply the description key and observe the automation that it enables.

1. Open the drawing named Description Keys.dwg located in the Chapter 03 class data folder.

2. Click the Settings tab of the Toolspace, and expand Point ➤ Description Key Sets.

3. Right-click Essentials, and select Edit Keys.

4. Click the cell in the Style column for code TR* to open the Point Style dialog box.

5. Select Tree as the point style, and click OK.

6. Click the green check mark to dismiss Panorama.

7. Click the Prospector tab, and then click Points.

8. In the listing of points at the bottom of Prospector, scroll to the right and click the Raw Description column heading to sort the points by that property.

9. Scroll to the bottom of the list where all the TR points are now located.

10. Right-click one of the points, and select Apply Description Keys. One of the points in the drawing should become a tree symbol.

11. Select all the TR points, and use the Apply Description Keys command to change them. All the trees in the drawing are now clearly visible and appropriately represented.

12. Return to the Settings tab, and edit the Essentials description key set once again. This time, assign a point label style of Description Only to the TR* code. Apply description keys to the TR points from within Prospector as you did earlier.

13. Edit the TR* description key code again, this time changing the Format value to **$1″ $2 ($1mm $2)**.

14. Apply the description keys to the TR points again. This time, the labels make more sense and read 12″ (300 mm) PINE, 15″ (375 mm) MAPLE, and so on.

15. Save and close the drawing.

The trees in the drawing are now labeled, although the label is the actual field code. A better result would be a more polished description.

You can view the results of successfully completing this exercise by opening `Description Keys - Complete.dwg`. No change was made to the survey database during this exercise.

What's Up with the Dollar Signs?

In the previous exercise, you used a code of $1″ $2 to create the full description for the trees. The $ is a special code that tells Civil 3D you want to use part of the raw description in the full description. The parts of the raw description are separated by spaces and numbered from left to right, starting at zero. Thus, in the raw description TR 12 OAK, TR is $0, 12 is $1, and OAK is $2. So $1″ $2 becomes 12″ OAK. With metric values in the raw description TR 300 OAK, TR is $0, 300 is $1, and OAK is $2. So $1mm $2 becomes 300 mm OAK. This is a great way for the person in the field to control the outcome in the drawing with as few keystrokes as possible.

Figure Prefix Database

As discussed, the linework code set handles how field codes are translated into linework commands, but what happens to those features once they are drawn? What layer are they drawn on? Do they have any special purpose such as a

Certification
Objective

property line or breakline? The figure prefix database is the means by which these decisions can be made up front for specific codes. For example, any feature drawn through points coded EP (edge of pavement) will be drawn on the pavement layer and tagged as a key component for establishing a hard edge in the 3D model of the terrain, also known as a *breakline*.

Exercise 3.5: Apply a Figure Prefix Database

If you haven't already done so, download and install the files for Chapter 3 according to the instructions in this book's Introduction.

Note that some codes are designated as breaklines: EP (edge of pavement), TOPD (top of ditch), and TOB (top of bank). These lines can be used to define hard edges in a surface model.

In this exercise, you'll assign a figure prefix database to your drawing and apply its settings to the linework in your drawing.

1. Open the drawing named Figure Prefix Database.dwg located in the Chapter 03 class data folder.

2. On the Survey tab of the Toolspace, click the Edit Survey User Settings icon in the top-left corner.

3. Click the Browse icon next to Figure Prefix Database Path. Browse to and select the Chapter 03 class data folder, and then click OK.

4. Click OK to dismiss the Survey User Settings dialog box. Right-click Figure Prefix Databases, and select Refresh. Click the plus sign next to Figure Prefix Databases to expand its contents. You should now see Essentials listed under Figure Prefix Databases.

5. Right-click Essentials, and select Make Current. Right-click Essentials again, and this time, select Manage Figure Prefix Database.

6. Scroll down, and examine the codes in the Name column. These match the codes you saw in the text file containing the survey data.

7. Click Cancel to dismiss the Figure Prefix Database Manager dialog box.

The Essentials 3 database is the result of correctly completing the previous exercise. This database is provided to ensure that you start the current exercise with the correct version.

8. If the contents of the Essentials 3 survey database are not visible, right-click Essentials 3 and select Open For Edit.

9. Expand Import Events. Right-click Topo Survey.txt, and select Process Linework.

10. In the Process Linework dialog box, select Essentials for Current Figure Prefix Database and click OK. Civil 3D redraws the linework, this time doing so on the appropriate layers. This is evident in the

linetypes that are applied to the treelines and fence lines, which are now appropriately represented on the drawing (see Figure 3.4).

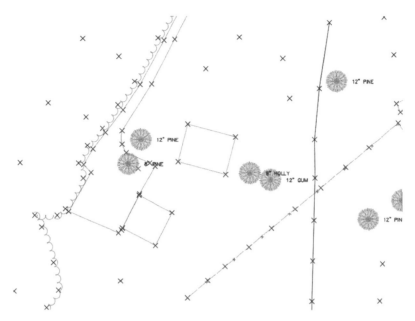

FIGURE 3.4 The appearance of the drawing makes more sense now that features such as fence lines and treelines have been drawn on the appropriate layers.

11. Save and close the drawing.

SURVEY FIGURES

At this point, you may be wondering what the word *figure* means or, specifically, what a *survey figure* is. A Civil 3D survey figure is the program's way of representing a linear feature that has been defined using survey data. A survey figure is commonly used to represent visible features such as fence lines, edges of pavement, and treelines as well as topographic features such as tops and bottoms of embankments. The topographic feature line layers are usually turned off when the drawing is plotted. Survey figures can be referenced by other Civil 3D objects such as surfaces, feature lines, and corridors, enabling design work to tie into existing features and topography, where applicable.

You can view the results of successfully completing this exercise by open-ing `Figure Prefix Database - Complete.dwg`. The survey database named `Essentials 4` is provided for the next exercise and matches what you should have at the end of this exercise.

Point Groups

Certification
Objective

Point groups are another way of managing large amounts of point data. This feature enables you to sort points based on a number of factors, such as descrip-tion, elevation, point number, and manual selection. You can set up point groups ahead of time so that points can be automatically sorted into groups as they are imported into the drawing. You can also create new point groups on the fly to sort points as you go.

Once points have been grouped, you can use them to study and manipulate multiple points at once. The groups are listed in Prospector, and you can view the points contained in each group simply by clicking the group name and viewing the contents of the point group in the item view at the bottom (see Figure 3.5). In addition, many point-editing commands allow you to select points by group, enabling you to modify large numbers of points at once.

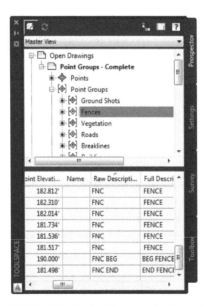

F I G U R E 3 . 5   **The contents of a specific point group shown in the item view of Prospector**

Point groups also enable you to assign default point styles and label styles to points within the group. With this capability, you can make points in a certain group take on specific graphical characteristics by controlling the point style and point label style.

Exercise 3.6: Create and Apply Point Groups

In this exercise, you'll configure several point groups and use them to organize points in your drawing as well as control their appearance.

If you haven't already done so, download and install the files for Chapter 3 according to the instructions in this book's Introduction.

1. Open the drawing named Point Groups.dwg located in the Chapter 03 class data folder.

2. In Prospector, right-click Point Groups and select New.

3. On the Information tab of the Point Group Properties dialog box, type **Buildings** in the Name field. Select Basic as the point style and <none> as the point label style.

4. Click the Raw Description Matching tab. Check the box next to BLD*, and click OK.

5. Expand Point Groups, and click the Buildings point group in Prospector. Examine the list of points shown in the Prospector item view at the bottom. Note that they all are points with a BLD description.

6. Create the following point groups with the associated raw descriptions listed. Use a default Point Style value of Basic and a default Point Label Style of <None> for each point group:

   ▶ Breaklines: BOB, BOTD, SWL, TOB, TOPD

   ▶ Roads: CLRD, DW, EP, ES

   ▶ Vegetation: ESHB, TL, TR

   ▶ Fences: FNC

   ▶ Ground Shots: GS

SECRET CODE?

You may be wondering what the raw descriptions mean in step 6 of Exercise 3.6. What you see here are abbreviations for items that are commonly located in the field by surveyors. In the interest of efficiency, abbreviated codes are typed in the field instead of the full names of the features. Here is what these particular examples stand for:

▶ Breaklines

    ▶ BOB: Bottom of bank

    ▶ BOTD: Bottom of ditch

    ▶ SWL: Swale

    ▶ TOB: Top of bank

    ▶ TOPD: Top of ditch

▶ Roads

    ▶ CLRD: Centerline of road

    ▶ DW: Driveway

    ▶ EP: Edge of pavement

    ▶ ES: Edge of shoulder

▶ Vegetation

    ▶ ESHB: Edge of shrub

    ▶ TL: Treeline

    ▶ TR: Tree

▶ Fences

    ▶ FNC: Fence

▶ Ground Shots

    ▶ GS: Ground shot

7. Click the Settings tab, and expand Point ➤ Description Key Sets.

8. Right-click Essentials, and select Edit Keys.

9. Hold down the Shift key to select all rows except the last one (TR*). Then right-click the Style column heading, and select Edit.

10. Select <default>, and click OK. Click the green check mark to close Panorama.

11. In Prospector, right-click the All Points point group and select Apply Description Keys. This applies the new style choice of <default> to all points except trees. Now the point style assigned by the point groups is able to have an effect, and most of the points change from *x* markers to circle markers.

12. In Prospector, right-click the Ground Shots point group and select Properties.

13. On the Information tab, select Ground Shot as the default point style and Elevation Only as the default point label style. Click OK, and notice what happens to all the ground shot points in the drawing.

14. Click the Output tab of the ribbon, and then click Export Points.

15. Check the box next to Limit Points To Point Group, and choose the Roads point group.

16. Click OK, and browse to your Chapter 03 class data folder. Enter **Road Points** as the name of the file, and click Open. Then click OK to dismiss the Export Points dialog box.

17. Save and close the drawing.

You can view the results of successfully completing this exercise by opening Description Keys - Complete.dwg. The survey database was not changed as a result of this exercise.

You should find <default> at the top of the list. You may need to scroll up.

All Points is a special point group that must exist in all drawings. As the name implies, it always contains all the points in the drawing.

This is an example of using a group to make a selection of points. Imagine selecting all these road points one by one.

You have just created a file that contains only points in the Roads point group. You might do this if a road designer asks for point information on a road that has been surveyed.

POINT GROUPS VS. DESCRIPTION KEYS

At this point, you may be scratching your head a bit, thinking that a few minutes ago you learned that description keys control the point style and point label style assigned to a point. Well, you're right—they do. However, you may have also noticed that when you assign these styles using description keys, the choice at the top of the list in each case is <default>. This choice could (and maybe should) be changed to say ByPointGroup, because that's what it essentially means. When you configure your description keys to use <default> as the style, you're deferring the decision about what style to use for the point groups. If you choose anything else, you're making that decision right then and there.

(Continues)

POINT GROUPS VS. DESCRIPTION KEYS *(Continued)*

Feel better about it? Well, unfortunately, there's another feature to consider that makes this a little more complicated but also gives you even more flexibility when stylizing points. One of the properties of a point group is the ability to set up an override. When you set up a point style or point label style as an *override*, it means you're going to apply that style regardless of whether it's <default> or something else. The Overrides tab in the Point Group Properties dialog box enables you to do this.

If you're wondering whether point groups or description keys are best to use, the answer is *both*. By thoroughly understanding how each method can be applied to your point data, you can use both point groups and description keys to stylize and organize your points in the best way possible. When you're starting out, however, you may want to pick one method or the other, completely develop that method, and then sprinkle in the other method little by little, observing and understanding how the two work together.

EVOLVE YOUR STANDARDS

In the previous exercises, you made some corrections and assigned a specific linework code set and figure prefix database to the data you imported. In an actual production environment, the changes you make to the description key set should be incorporated into the company template so that the tree points are handled correctly for all future jobs. The point groups you create could also be included in the company template so that they're available on all future jobs. In addition, the linework code set and figure prefix database that you use could be assigned as defaults so that they are automatically applied to future data imports. A CAD manager typically handles this type of configuration management, but end users like you usually identify the needs for the changes. When you're working with Civil 3D in a production environment, be sure to work with your CAD manager to make sure you and your coworkers are leveraging the configuration of Civil 3D as much as possible.

Editing Survey Points

As discussed, it takes many points to survey a piece of land—that's hundreds or even thousands of individual measurements and hand-typed field codes. On nearly every project, there will be items that require editing. Once the data has been imported into Civil 3D, the field crew is off to its next job, and the task of fixing things up belongs to you.

For several reasons, editing survey points is a bit different from editing "regular" points, properly referred to as *COGO points*. One reason is that survey points are considered "sacred" and are not typically moved or modified in any way without considerable thought and/or the supervision of a surveyor. The second reason, related to the first, is that Civil 3D uses a separate survey database system to store points. The points in the drawing are essentially locked and can't be changed unless the information in the survey database changes. With this system, a surveyor can send out the drawing file without sharing the survey database that goes with it. When the points in the drawing are separated from the survey database, they become locked and can't be easily modified. In this way, the survey database gives control of the points to the person who created them.

Exercise 3.7: Edit Survey Points

In this exercise, you'll edit a survey point to correct a field coding error. You'll demonstrate that access to the survey database is necessary for editing survey points.

If you haven't already done so, download and install the files for Chapter 3 according to the instructions in this book's Introduction.

1. Open the drawing named Edit Survey Points.dwg located in the Chapter 03 class data folder. If a survey database is open, right-click it and select Close Survey Database.

2. Locate and zoom in to the red point along the west treeline, as shown in Figure 3.6.

3. Open the Properties window, and then select the red point. Note that there is a typo in the raw description. It should say TR 12 PINE (TR 300 PINE) instead of TTR 12 PINE (TTR 300 PINE). You can't edit the raw description here because the data is stored in the survey database.

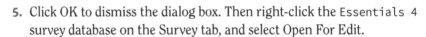

FIGURE 3.6 An error has caused this point to display incorrectly.

The survey database is needed to edit the points. This is how the points are kept safe when the drawing is shared outside the survey office.

4. With the point still selected, click Survey Point Properties on the ribbon. A dialog box opens, informing you that you must open a survey database.

5. Click OK to dismiss the dialog box. Then right-click the Essentials 4 survey database on the Survey tab, and select Open For Edit.

The Essentials 4 database is the result of correctly completing the previous exercise. This database is provided to ensure that you start the current exercise with the correct version.

6. With the red point still selected, click Survey Point Properties on the ribbon.

7. Edit the description to say **TR 12 PINE (TR 300 PINE)**, and click OK.

SURVEY POINTS VS. COGO POINTS

As previously mentioned, there are two types of points: COGO points and survey points. How can you tell the difference? Here are a few characteristics of each to help you distinguish between the two:

Survey Point Characteristics

▶ Only survey points are displayed on the Survey tab (COGO points are not).

▶ Survey points are displayed on both the Prospector and the Survey tabs.

▶ Survey points have an icon next to them that looks like a survey target (an hourglass inside a box overlaid on crosshairs).

(Continues)

SURVEY POINTS VS. COGO POINTS *(Continued)*

▶ Survey points can't be moved without accessing the survey database and using specialized commands for editing survey points.

▶ Survey points can't be edited in the Properties window.

COGO Point Characteristics

▶ COGO points are not displayed on the Survey tab.

 ▶ COGO points have an icon next to them that looks like a circle overlaid on crosshairs.

▶ COGO points can be moved, even using basic, non–Civil 3D drafting commands.

▶ COGO points can be edited in the Properties window.

---

8. Press Enter to end the command. You're prompted to update linework in the drawing.

9. Click No to dismiss the Edit Survey Point Properties—Process Linework dialog, because the change you made does not affect linework.

10. Click the red point, right-click, and select Apply Description Keys.

11. Save and close the drawing.

You can view the results of successfully completing this exercise by opening `Edit Survey Points - Complete.dwg`. The survey database named `Essentials 5` is provided for the next exercise and matches what you should have at the end of this exercise.

> ◀
>
> The effect of the description key puts the point on the correct layer, changes its marker to a tree symbol, and provides a label indicating that it's a 12″ (30-mm) PINE.

Editing Survey Figures

Mistakes in the field can lead to errors in the way linework is drawn. Once again, the changes need to be made a certain way because you're dealing with special survey objects, this time survey figures. Survey figures are linked to the survey database, but unlike survey points, they can be edited without accessing the survey database. If you edit survey figures in this way, you need to be aware that the objects you've edited are no longer in sync with the survey database. When this occurs you should take steps to keep them in sync to ensure that the correct data is used in the future.

Exercise 3.8: Edit Survey Figures

If you haven't already done so, download and install the files for Chapter 3 according to the instructions in this book's Introduction.

In this exercise, you'll edit several survey figures to correct errors that took place due to incorrect translation from the field to the drawing.

1. Open the drawing named Edit Survey Figures.dwg located in the Chapter 03 class data folder.

2. If the contents beneath the Essentials 5 survey database are not visible, right-click Essentials 5 and select Open For Edit.

The Essentials 5 database is the result of correctly completing the previous exercise. This database is provided to ensure that you start the current exercise with the correct version.

3. In the top-right viewport, locate the building that is missing its north side. Click the building figure line, and then click Survey Figure Properties on the ribbon. Notice that point 285 is missing a CLS (close) code that would provide the north side of the building by closing the rectangle.

4. Click point 285 in the point list; then set the Closed value to Yes, and click OK. The shape of the building is now closed. Because you used the Survey Figure Properties command to edit this figure, the drawing and the survey database are in sync.

At this point, you could back out and fix the point description. However, for the purposes of this exercise, you'll edit the figure instead.

5. Press Esc to clear the previous selection. Pan to the southeast until you can see the building to the west of the 6″ (150 mm) pine. This building should appear as two separate buildings.

6. Click the building figure, and then click Survey Figure Properties on the ribbon.

7. In the Figure Properties dialog box, click point 288 and then click the red X icon. Remove points 289, 290, and 291 in the same manner.

8. Click OK to close the Figure Properties dialog box. Now only the north building is shown in the drawing.

9. Right-click Figures on the Survey tab, and select Create Figure Interactively.

10. When prompted, enter **BLD2** as the figure name, and click OK.

11. Click the four points that make up the smaller building, and then press Enter.

12. In the Figure Properties dialog box, set the Closed value to Yes. If necessary, adjust the order of the points using the arrow buttons. Click Apply and then OK when the blue figure outline appears as a rectangle in the drawing. The building figure now appears as it should, and the two separate buildings are represented properly, as shown in Figure 3.7.

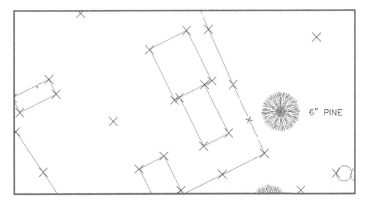

FIGURE 3.7   **The result of editing the building figures**

13. Save and close the drawing.

You can view the results of successfully completing this exercise by opening Edit Survey Figures - Complete.dwg. The survey database named Essentials 6 is provided for the next exercise and matches what you should have at the end of this exercise.

Creating Additional Points

You may occasionally need to create your own points to establish key locations in the drawing. For example, early in the design, you may want to show specific locations for proposed test borings or property corners that need to be found. Another example is that you may have a point file that you would like to import into the drawing without including it in a survey database. Civil 3D has a multitude of tools designed to create points easily and efficiently. They are found on a special toolbar that opens when you click the Point Creation Tools command on the Home tab of the ribbon.

In many ways, the points you create using these tools are treated in the same manner as those created by importing survey data. They can be placed in point

Certification
Objective

groups and can respond to description keys. They can also be affected by point styles and point label styles. There are differences, however, between these points and those created by importing survey data. For example, Civil 3D can't automatically generate linework by importing points in this manner. Also, these points don't have the protection of the survey database, allowing them to be edited by anyone who opens the drawing. Regardless of how they are created, all points can be exported to a file that can be uploaded to a portable device and taken to the field to be staked out.

Exercise 3.9: Import Points and Create Points Manually

If you haven't already done so, download and install the files for Chapter 3 according to the instructions in this book's Introduction.

In this exercise, you'll begin by importing points that represent property corners that were found on the site. Then you'll create stake-out points to assist field crews in locating several missing property corners. You'll also create points along the proposed road centerlines. These points will represent the locations of soil-test borings to be performed on the site.

Stake out is a term used by surveyors to refer to placing markers in the field at predetermined locations, often calculated in the office.

1. Open the drawing named Stake Out.dwg located in the Chapter 03 class data folder.

   This drawing contains a calculated property boundary reconstructed from a deed or other source of information. It also contains a preliminary layout of the road centerlines that will be used to determine soil-test boring locations. You'll begin by inserting points into the drawing that represent property corners located in the field.

There are points in the drawing that have the same numbers as the points that are being imported. This is resolved by using the Add An Offset option to increase the incoming point numbers by 1,000.

2. On the Insert tab of the ribbon, click Points From File.

3. In the Import Points dialog box, select PNEZD (Comma Delimited) as the format. Then click the plus sign icon and browse to the Chapter 03 class data folder.

4. For Files Of Type, select the Text/Template/Extract File (*.txt) option. Then select Found Corners.txt, and click Open.

5. Click OK to dismiss the Import Points dialog box.

6. In the Duplicate Point Number dialog box, under Resolution, select Add An Offset. Type **1000** in the box below Add An Offset From, and click OK.

7. In Prospector, expand Point Groups. Right-click Found Corners, and select Update.

   This applies the default styles from the point group to the newly imported points. Found corners appear with red markers and text. Notice that two points are missing along the south property boundary as well as one point on the east property boundary and one at the northwest corner (four points in all). Finding and locating these corners in the field will greatly improve the accuracy and validity of the property survey.

8. On the Home tab of the ribbon, click Points ➤ Point Creation Tools.

9. On the Create Points toolbar, click the button on the far left to launch the Miscellaneous Manual tool. In the left viewport, snap to the locations of the missing points.

10. In Prospector, right-click the Corners To Be Found point group and select Update.

    These points display in blue.

11. On the Create Points toolbar, click the chevron on the far right to expand the toolbar.

12. Expand Points Creation, and enter **BORE** as the default description.

13. Click the down arrow on the button farthest to the left, and then click Measure Object.

14. Click one of the magenta road centerlines. Press Enter three times to accept the default starting station, ending station, and offset.

15. Type an interval of **250 (80)**, and press Enter. The points are created at a 250′ (80-m) interval along the polyline you've selected.

16. In Prospector, update the Test Borings point group.

17. Repeat steps 13 to 16 for the remaining road centerlines.

18. On the Output tab of the ribbon, click Export Points.

19. For format, select PNEZD (Comma Delimited). Check the box next to Limit To Points In Point Group, and select Corners To Be Found.

This file could be sent to a surveyor to help locate the missing points in the field.

This file could be sent to a geotechnical company so that they can stake out the test borings in the correct location.

20. Click OK, and browse to the Chapter 03 class data folder. Specify a filename of **Corners to be Found.txt**.

21. Repeat steps 19 to 21 for the Test Boring point group to create a Test Borings.txt point file.

22. Save and close the drawing.

   You can view the results of successfully completing this exercise by opening Stake Out - Complete.dwg. There was no change to the survey database as a result of this exercise.

NOW YOU KNOW

Now that you have completed this chapter, you understand the world of survey data as it exists in the Civil 3D environment. You understand that survey data must reside in a survey database that exists separately from the drawing file. You know how to import data into the survey database and display it in your drawing as points and linework. You know how to automate the organization and graphical properties of the points and linework using linework code sets, description keys, the figure prefix database, and point groups. You can edit survey points and survey figures by accessing the survey database and making changes using the appropriate tools. Finally, you know several additional methods for importing points and creating them manually.

With the knowledge and skills you have gained in this chapter, you're ready to begin working with survey data in Civil 3D: turning it from raw field data into a drawing representing the existing conditions of a project.

CHAPTER 4

Modeling the Existing Terrain Using Surfaces

In Chapter 3, "Establishing Existing Conditions Using Survey Data," you learned how to establish the existing conditions of a project by playing a very elaborate game of connect-the-dots. So far, you've been solving the connect-the-dots puzzle in only two dimensions—creating the treelines, fence lines, buildings, trees, and so on. Now, you'll use the same data to establish the third dimension of your existing conditions model, and you'll do that using AutoCAD® Civil 3D® *surfaces*.

Many would say the goal in this process is to generate existing contours for the project. Twenty years ago, that would have been the case, but in this era of 3-D modeling, the result of your efforts will serve a much greater purpose. Although it's true that you'll be able to create contours from your surface model, you'll also create an accurate 3-D representation of the ground that can be used in many ways throughout the project.

In this chapter, you'll learn to:

▶ **Understand the purpose and function of surfaces**

▶ **Create a surface from survey data**

▶ **Use breaklines to improve surface accuracy**

▶ **Edit surfaces**

▶ **Display and analyze surfaces**

▶ **Annotate surfaces**

Understanding Surfaces

As you might guess, the 3-D game of connect-the-dots is a bit more sophisticated than the 2-D version. In addition, you need the result to be a 3D model rather than just lines. To accomplish this, Civil 3D uses a computer algorithm that connects the dots in the most efficient and accurate way possible. This algorithm is known as a *Triangular Irregular Network (TIN)* algorithm.

The TIN algorithm works by connecting one point to at least two of its neighbors using 3-D lines. Because each point connects to two or more of its neighbors, the resulting model looks something like a spider web made up of triangles (the *T* in *TIN*). Because the spacing between points is typically non-uniform, the triangles come in many shapes and sizes, which is why it's called irregular (the *I* in *TIN*). The network (the *N* in *TIN*) part comes from all the points being connected by lines and the points and lines being related to one another. Figure 4.1 shows a surface with its TIN lines visible.

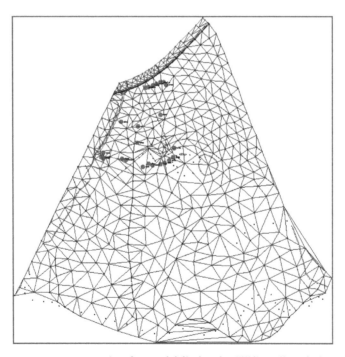

F I G U R E   4 . 1   A surface model displayed as TIN lines. Note the irregular triangular shapes that make up the surface model.

There's even more to it than the triangles, though. In fact, the triangles are just a handy visual representation of the algorithm at work, and by themselves, they aren't all that useful. What *is* useful is that the algorithm can calculate the elevation of any point within the area covered by the TIN model. So, even if you pick a point in the open space inside a triangle, the elevation will be calculated. This is what makes the TIN model a true model. It can be sliced, be turned on its side, have water poured on it, be excavated, and be filled in—all virtually, of course. The capability of using surface models for these types of calculations and simulations is what makes them so useful and puts them at the core of Civil 3D functionality.

Creating a Surface from Survey Data

You create a surface in Prospector by simply right-clicking the Surfaces node of the tree and selecting Create Surface, as shown in Figure 4.2. The newly created surface appears in Prospector immediately, but it can't be seen in the drawing until some data is added to it. The fundamental components of a surface are points and lines. It's your job to supply the source of the points, and Civil 3D takes care of drawing the lines. At this phase of the project, you'll be using survey points as the initial source of surface-point data.

Certification
Objective

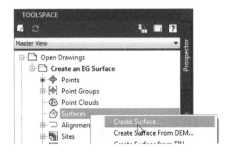

FIGURE 4.2   Creating a surface from within Prospector

If you haven't already done so, download and install the files for Chapter 4 according to the instructions in this book's Introduction.

Exercise 4.1: Create an Existing Ground Surface

In this exercise, you'll create a surface from survey data.

1. Open the drawing named Create an EG Surface.dwg located in the Chapter 04 class data folder.

2. In Prospector, right-click Surfaces and select Create Surface.

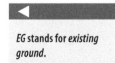

EG stands for *existing ground.*

3. In the Create Surface dialog box, enter EG in the Name field.

4. For Style, select C-Existing Contours (1') (C-Existing Contours (0.5 m)). Click OK to dismiss the Create Surface dialog box.

5. In Prospector, expand Surfaces ➤ EG ➤ Definition. Study the items listed beneath EG in the tree (see Figure 4.3).

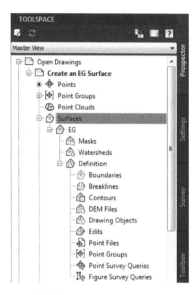

FIGURE 4.3   The contents of a surface shown in Prospector

COMPONENTS OF A SURFACE

As shown in Figure 4.3, you can use many potential types of information to create a surface and control its shape. The following list describes each one briefly:

Boundaries   Boundaries are used to control where the surface *is*. A boundary around the edge of a surface can keep it contained within a certain area. Another type of boundary can keep a surface out of an interior area, like a pond or building.

Breaklines   Breaklines force TIN lines to align with them. In this way, they help to define hard edges such as edges of embankments, curb lines, ditch lines, and so on.

(Continues)

COMPONENTS OF A SURFACE *(Continued)*

Contours   Usually, we think of contours as the end product of building a surface, but they can also be used as a source of data for a surface.

DEM Files   *DEM* stands for *digital elevation model*, and it's typically associated with large-scale mapping that has relatively low accuracy. DEMs can often be found alongside large-scale mapping data and are typically only accurate enough for rough analysis or calculations.

Drawing Objects   Drawing objects are AutoCAD® software entities such as lines, blocks, and even text. These items can be used to help define a surface as effectively as survey points, as long as they've been created at the appropriate elevations.

Edits   Edits aren't actual data, but they do contribute to the makeup of a surface. There are many ways in which a surface can be edited to improve its accuracy or usability. Some of these editing methods will be covered in this chapter.

Point Files   You've already learned that a point file is a text file containing *x*, *y*, and *z* data. So far, you've used these files to create Civil 3D points in the drawing, but the same data can also be imported directly into a surface.

Point Groups   In Chapter 3, you learned that one of the benefits of point groups is that they enable multiple points to be selected simultaneously. Using one or more point groups to define a surface is one of the most important and most common uses of point groups in Civil 3D.

Point Survey and Figure Survey Queries   These queries are created using the survey functionality and utilize a sophisticated way of selecting points and figures based on survey properties. These queries are not covered in this book, but information about them is available within the Civil 3D help content.

6. Right-click Point Groups, and select Add.

7. Select Ground Shots, and click OK.

   The surface is now visible in plan view in the form of contours and shaded 3-D faces in the bottom-right 3-D view.

8. In the lower-right viewport, click Shaded and select 2D Wireframe, as shown in Figure 4.4.

   The appearance of the surface changes to show the TIN lines.

The difference in appearance between plan view and 3-D view is a function of the surface style.

FIGURE 4.4 Changing the visual style to 2D Wireframe in the lower-right viewport

9. Click 2D Wireframe and select Conceptual. To orbit your view of the surface, click and drag the center mouse button while holding your Shift key. Observe the surface from several different viewpoints.

This way of studying the surface gives a real sense of the surface as a "solid" model in which the area inside the triangles has substance. It's also a great visual representation of the TIN algorithm and the surface model (see Figure 4.5).

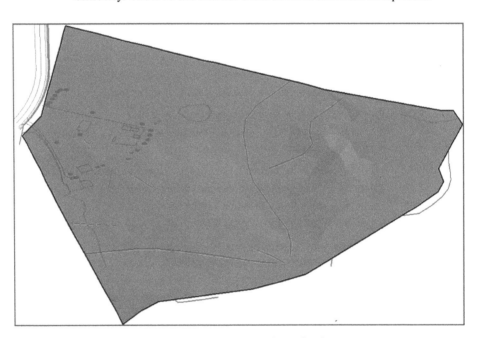

FIGURE 4.5 A surface shown using the Conceptual visual style

10. Save and close the drawing.

You can view the results of successfully completing this exercise by opening `Create an EG Surface - Complete.dwg`.

Using Breaklines to Improve Surface Accuracy

The TIN algorithm creates surfaces by drawing 3-D lines between points that are closest to each other. In certain instances, this is not the most accurate way to model the surface, and the TIN lines must be forced into a specific arrangement. This arrangement typically coincides with a linear feature such as a curb, the top of an embankment, or a wall. This forced alignment of TIN lines along a linear feature is best handled with a breakline. In Figure 4.6, the blue lines represent the edges of a channel and the TIN lines are shown in red. In the image on the top, the blue lines have not been added to the channel surface as breaklines, resulting in a rough and inaccurate representation of the channel. In the image on the bottom, the breaklines have been applied and force the TIN lines to align with the edges of the channel, producing a much smoother and more accurate model.

Certification
Objective

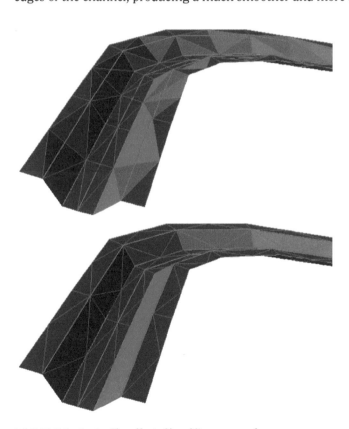

FIGURE 4.6 The effect of breaklines on a surface

From Prospector, you can add breaklines by right-clicking the Breaklines node for a given surface and selecting Add (see Figure 4.7). When it comes to survey data, there is an even easier way. From the Survey Toolspace, you can right-click Figures and select Create Breaklines. This opens a list of all your survey figures with some checked as breaklines and some not (see Figure 4.8). How does the command know which is which? This was specified in the figure prefix database you learned about in Chapter 3. As the figures were created, they were automatically tagged as breaklines or non-breaklines according to the code assigned to the points that define them.

F I G U R E   4 . 7   Adding breaklines from within Prospector

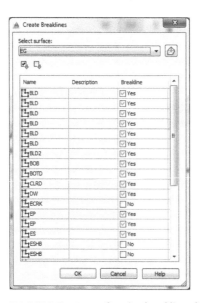

F I G U R E   4 . 8   Creating breaklines from survey figures. Note how some figures are checked as breaklines and some are not.

Exercise 4.2: Add Breaklines

In this exercise, you'll add breaklines to a surface and observe their effect on the accuracy of the surface.

If you haven't already done so, download and install the files for Chapter 4 according to the instructions in this book's Introduction.

1. Open the drawing named Add Breaklines.dwg located in the Chapter 04 class data folder.

2. On the Survey tab of the Toolspace, right-click Survey Databases and select Set Working Folder.

3. Browse to and select the Chapter 04 class data folder. Click OK.
   You should see a different survey database named Essentials.

4. Right-click the Essentials survey database, and select Open For Edit.

5. Expand the Essentials database. Right-click Figures, and select Create Breaklines.

6. Scan the list of figures, and note which ones are tagged as breaklines. Click OK.

7. In the Add Breaklines dialog box, change the Mid-Ordinate Distance value to 0.03, and click OK.

BREAKLINES IN THE FIELD

As you study the list of figures in this exercise, are you wondering why some are designated as breaklines and others are not? Breaklines are linear features that mark a change in the slope of the ground. Some of these are quite obvious, such as a set of bottom of bank (BOB) points or top of ditch (TOPD) points. Others serve double duty, such as an edge of pavement (EP). This survey figure marks the line where pavement ends and dirt begins, but typically there is also a change in slope at this line between the slope of the ground and the manmade slope of the road. For this reason, EPs are often tagged as breaklines. Other features obviously have nothing to do with the slope of the ground, such as a right of way (ROW), treeline (TL), and fence line (FENC); therefore, they aren't checked as breaklines.

You should notice a change in the contours along the red break-lines. These breaklines define the swales, edges, and ridges that were recognized in the field and explicitly located as terrain features. In addition, notice that contours now cover the road area to the north. The surface in this area is made strictly of breaklines.

8. In the top-right viewport, click one of the surface contours, and then click Surface Properties on the ribbon.

9. On the Information tab of the Surface Properties dialog box, change Surface Style to Triangles. Click OK and press Esc to clear the selection of the surface.

   Notice how TIN lines don't cross the breaklines.

10. Select the surface and open Surface Properties again. On the Definition tab, uncheck the box next to Add Breakline, as shown in Figure 4.9. Click OK, and then click Rebuild The Surface.

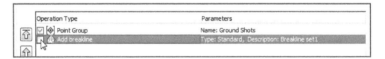

F I G U R E   4 . 9   Unchecking the Add Breakline operation for the surface

You have removed the effect of the breaklines temporarily. Notice how the TIN lines cross back and forth over the swale and ridge lines, creating a rough edge where there should be a sharp, well-defined edge.

11. Repeat step 10 but this time check the box next to Add Breakline.
    The breaklines are once again applied to the surface.

12. Save and close the drawing.

You can view the results of successfully completing this exercise by opening Add Breaklines - Complete.dwg.

This exercise shows you the importance of breaklines. Connecting a bunch of points together with 3-D triangular shapes does not necessarily generate an accurate surface. In certain areas, the shapes themselves have to be manipulated so that they align with terrain features in order to model their form accurately. Figure 4.10 compares the surface with and without breaklines in both 2-D and 3-D views.

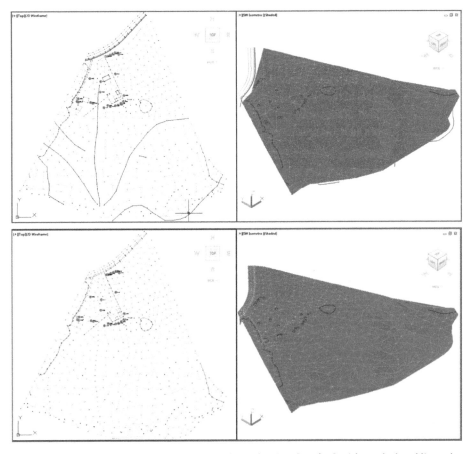

FIGURE 4.10   The two top views show the surface in 2-D and 3-D without the breaklines; the two bottom views show the surface with the breaklines included.

BREAKLINE SETTINGS AND OPTIONS

The Add Breaklines dialog box has several options and values to choose from. Here is a brief explanation of each:

Type   Of the five types listed here, only two are important to discuss at this time: proximity and standard. Standard breaklines have two jobs. First, they control the alignment of TIN lines, as discussed previously. Second, their vertices are a source of additional point information in the drawing. As you might recall, the only point group you added to the surface is Ground Shots, so you'll need the points to come along with any breaklines you add. For this to work, the vertices of the breaklines must be 3-D and must be at the correct elevations.

(Continues)

BREAKLINE SETTINGS AND OPTIONS *(Continued)*

Proximity breaklines have only one job, which is to control the alignment of TIN lines. Therefore, proximity breaklines only need to be 2-D, but they must have points in their *proximity* so that they can "steal" their elevations. If you had added all the survey points to your surface, then the survey figures could have been added as proximity breaklines.

Weeding Factors   Sometimes, the items you use for breaklines can have too many vertices on them, and you'll want to eliminate some of them so that your surface isn't overloaded with data. The selective removal of points based on distance and angle is known as *weeding*.

Supplementing By Distance   Sometimes your breaklines will have long stretches without any vertices in them. Because new TIN lines are created only where there are points, and points are created only where there are vertices, some supplemental vertices may be needed to improve the accuracy of the surface. When you check the box next to Distance, Civil 3D creates more points along the breakline that are spaced out according to the value you provide.

Supplementing By Mid-Ordinate   Curves are a bit of a challenge because TIN lines are straight and curves are, well, curved. For that reason, any curves in a breakline are approximated with a series of short TIN lines. Just how short and numerous these lines are depends on the mid-ordinate setting. *Mid-ordinate* is a geometric term that refers to the perpendicular distance between an arc and its chord. When this distance is short, the chord is also short, and multiple instances of it can fit within the length of the arc. This might seem like a strange way to define this behavior, but what's handy about it is that a single mid-ordinate value works pretty well for a fairly wide range of curve radii. The following image shows the effect of the mid-ordinate setting on a surface. The image on the left uses a value of 0.1, and the image on the right uses a value of 1.0.

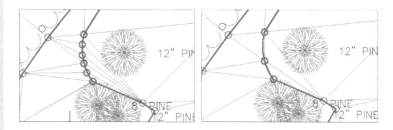

Editing Surfaces

With the inclusion of points and breaklines in the surface, you have essentially provided all the data that will be needed to create the surface model. However, you should continue manipulating this data until you achieve the most accurate representation possible of the existing ground surface. You can edit surfaces in many ways. In the following sections, you'll learn about three surface-editing methods: adding boundaries, deleting lines, and editing points.

Certification
Objective

Adding Boundaries

As discussed earlier, boundaries are a way of defining where the surface is and where it isn't. In the example project, you don't want the surface to exist outside the area that has been surveyed. Why would the surface extend beyond the survey data? If the edge of an area represented by the points happens to bend inward, the lines will extend across the "bay" (see Figure 4.11) and will create misrepresented surface data in that area. One way to avoid or correct this situation is to provide an *outer boundary* that prevents the surface from existing in these areas.

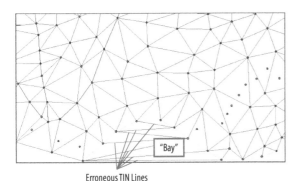

Erroneous TIN Lines

FIGURE 4.11   **Erroneous TIN lines created across a bay in the surface data**

Another common example of surfaces being where they shouldn't be is within the shape of a building. It's considered poor drafting practice to show contours passing through a building. After all, the ground surface isn't accessible in that location. Another type of boundary, called a *hide boundary*, can be used to remove surface data from within a surface, thus creating a void, or "hole," in the surface.

Types of Boundaries

The four types of boundaries you can create with Civil 3D are as follows:

Outer   An outer boundary establishes a perimeter for the surface. No surface data can exist outside an outer boundary. This type of boundary is commonly used in most surfaces.

Hide   A hide boundary creates a void, or "hole," in the surface. Hide boundaries are commonly used to remove surface data within buildings.

Show   A show boundary creates an island of data within a hide boundary. An example of a show boundary is a courtyard within the footprint of a building.

Data Clip   The first three types of boundaries hide the surface data after it has been created. A data-clip boundary is a special type of boundary that prevents data outside it from ever becoming part of the surface. Data-clip boundaries are used in cases where a small surface is made from source data that covers a large area.

Exercise 4.3: Add Boundaries

If you haven't already done so, download and install the files for Chapter 4 according to the instructions in this book's Introduction.

In this exercise, you'll add boundaries around the buildings that will remove surface data from within their footprints.

1. Open the drawing named Surface Boundaries.dwg located in the Chapter 04 class data folder.

2. Click one of the surface contours in the top-right viewport. Then, on the Tin Surface: EG tab of the ribbon, click Add Data ➢ Boundaries.

3. Enter **Bld1** as the boundary name, and select Hide as the type. Make sure the box next to Non-Destructive Breakline is checked, and click OK.

The Non-Destructive Breakline option creates a clean edge along the boundary by trimming some TIN lines and adding others.

4. Select one of the buildings in the top-right viewport, and press Enter. You should immediately see a hole appear in the surface shown in the lower-right viewport. If you've selected a building with contours running through it, you'll see the contours disappear in the upper-right viewport. It appears that they have been trimmed, but actually, the surface data has been removed from within the shape of the building.

5. Repeat steps 2 to 4 for the other buildings, even if contours don't pass through them. Use a name other than Bld1 or the software won't accept your boundaries.

6. In the lower-right viewport, zoom in to the area of the buildings, and notice that there are now voids where the buildings are located, as shown in Figure 4.12.

Remember that contours aren't the only things surfaces are used for. No matter how you look at this surface, you don't want data to appear where the buildings are.

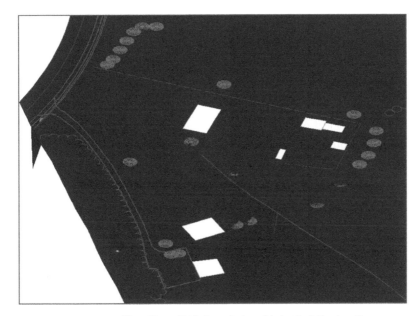

FIGURE 4.12   The effect of hide boundaries added at building locations

7. Save and close the drawing.

You can view the results of successfully completing this exercise by opening Surface Boundaries - Complete.dwg.

Deleting Lines

Another, less eloquent way of removing unwanted TIN lines is to delete them from the surface rather than use a boundary to do it for you. This method is best when you need to remove only a few TIN lines in isolated areas. There are two important things to remember when deleting TIN lines. First, in order for the lines to be deleted, they must be visible, which means you must apply a style that displays them. Second, you can't use the AutoCAD ERASE command to remove them; instead, you must use the Delete Line command created specifically for surfaces.

Exercise 4.4: Delete Lines

In this exercise, you'll delete unwanted TIN lines from the surface.

1. Open the drawing named `Delete TIN Lines.dwg` located in your `Chapter 04` class data folder.

2. Click one of the contours in the top-right viewport, and then select Surface Properties on the ribbon.

3. On the Information tab, change Surface Style to Triangles and click OK. Press Esc to clear the selection of the surface.

4. In the left viewport, zoom in to the southern edge of the surface, and note the TIN lines that extend across the bend in the stream (shown previously in Figure 4.11).

5. Select one of the TIN lines, and then click Edit Surface ➢ Delete Line on the ribbon. Select the erroneous lines as indicated previously in Figure 4.11. Press Enter after you've made your selection.

6. Pan around the edge of the surface, and delete any other TIN lines that look like they don't belong. The resulting surface should look similar to Figure 4.13.

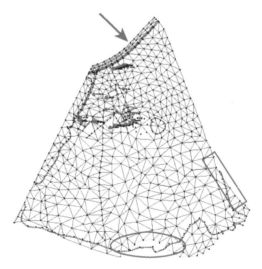

FIGURE 4.13 The extents of the surface after erroneous TIN lines have been removed. The areas of removal are highlighted.

7. Save and close the drawing.

You can view the results of successfully completing this exercise by opening Delete TIN Lines - Complete.dwg.

Editing Points

As you have learned, the fundamental building blocks of surfaces are points and lines. The points are derived from some other source of data, such as standard breaklines, contours, survey points, and so on. If there is an error in one of those source objects, there will be an error in the surface as well. When this occurs, you can either edit the source data and rebuild the surface or edit the surface itself.

Exercise 4.5: Edit Points

You have already learned about editing survey source data (survey points and survey figures). In this exercise, you'll edit the surface.

If you haven't already done so, download and install the files for Chapter 4 according to the instructions in this book's Introduction.

1. Open the drawing named Editing Points.dwg located in your Chapter 04 class data folder.

    The two right viewports are zoomed in to the location where the driveway meets the road on the north side of the property. In this area, one of the surface points is incorrect. In the plan view on the top right, the effects of the incorrect point can be seen in the densely packed contours. In the 3-D view on the bottom right, the erroneous point appears as a downward spike in the surface.

2. Click one of the contours to select the surface, and then click Surface Properties on the ribbon.

3. In the Surface Properties dialog box, click the Information tab and change Surface Style to Triangles And Points. Click OK.

    The display of the surface changes to lines and points, with the points appearing as plus-sign markers.

4. Click any TIN line to select the surface, and then click Edit Surface ➤ Modify Point on the ribbon.

5. When prompted to select a point, click the point in the 3-D view that is located well below the other points (see Figure 4.14). Press Enter.

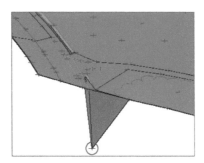

FIGURE 4.14   3-D view of incorrect surface point

6. At the command line, type **190.76** (**58.144**), and press Enter.
   Notice how the surface is modified but the survey figure is left behind. Depending on the situation, it may be prudent to go back to the source data for the survey figure and correct that as well.

7. Press Enter to exit the Modify Point command. Change the style of the surface back to C-Existing Contours (1') (C-Existing Contours (0.5 m)).
   Notice that the closely spaced contours in the top-right viewport are no longer there.

8. Save and close the drawing.
   You can view the results of successfully completing this exercise by opening Editing Points - Complete.dwg.

Displaying and Analyzing Surfaces

Certification
Objective

Because you're working with surface objects in Civil 3D, you can do much more than simply show contours. Civil 3D surfaces can help you tell many different stories about the shape of the land and how water will flow across it. They are able to do this through multiple types of analyses as well as the ability for styles to display analysis results in nearly any way you wish. With these tools at your disposal, you can study the terrain thoroughly and make smart choices about the direction of your design early in the process.

Analyzing Elevation

Elevation analysis allows you to delineate any number of elevation ranges and then graphically distinguish the different ranges by color. This is a useful tool in many instances, especially when you're working with someone who doesn't know how to read contours.

Exercise 4.6: Analyze Elevation

In this exercise, you'll perform an elevation analysis on a surface in your drawing.

If you haven't already done so, download and install the files for Chapter 4 according to the instructions in this book's Introduction.

1. Open the drawing named Elevation Analysis.dwg located in the Chapter 04 class data folder.

2. Click one of the contours to select the surface, and then click Surface Properties on the ribbon.

3. Change Surface Style to Elevation Banding (2-D).

4. Click the Analysis tab. Verify that the analysis type is Elevations and the number of ranges is 8.

5. Click the downward-pointing arrow to populate the Range Details section of the dialog box with new data.

6. Click OK to return to the drawing. Press Esc to clear the selection of the surface.

   The surface undergoes an obvious change, and it's now displayed as a series of colored bands with red signifying the lowest elevations and purple signifying the highest.

7. Change the style of the surface to Elevation Banding (3-D).

   Now the 3-D view displays the colored bands as a 3-D representation with exaggerated elevations. This tells a clear story about the existing shape of the land for this site (see Figure 4.15).

You may need to zoom out a bit in the lower-right viewport to see the 3-D color representation of the surface.

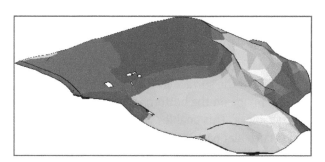

FIGURE 4.15   A 3-D view of a surface using the Elevation Banding (3-D) style

8. Save and close the drawing.

You can view the results of successfully completing this exercise by opening Elevation Analysis - Complete.dwg.

Analyzing Slope

Another important aspect of the terrain is the slope. Areas with very steep slopes are difficult to navigate either by construction vehicles or the eventual occupants of the property. Flat slopes are much more accessible, but if they are too flat, then drainage problems often occur. One of your tasks as a designer is to ensure that your project has the right slopes in the right areas. By studying the slopes of the existing topography, you can locate features where slopes are good or determine that terrain modifications will be necessary to create good slopes.

Civil 3D can display slopes in two ways. The first is to show the slopes as colored ranges like the ones you saw in the previous section. The second is to use slope arrows that can be color-coded to indicate what range they're located in, with the added benefit of always pointing downhill to show you the direction of water flow.

Exercise 4.7: Analyze Slope

If you haven't already done so, download and install the files for Chapter 4 according to the instructions in this book's Introduction.

In this exercise, you'll perform a slope analysis on a surface in your drawing.

1. Open the drawing named Slope Analysis.dwg located in the Chapter 04 class data folder.

2. Click one of the contours to select the surface, and then click Surface Properties on the ribbon.

3. On the Information tab of the Surface Properties dialog box, change Surface Style to Slope Banding (3-D).

4. Click the Analysis tab. Change Analysis Type to Slopes, and click the downward-pointing arrow.

5. Click OK. Press Esc to clear the selection of the surface and zoom in to the 3-D view of the surface in the bottom-right viewport.

   In the 3-D image on the bottom right, the darkest reds signify the steepest slopes. This enables you to see that the area north of the farm is fairly flat pasture land while the area to the south of the farm slopes dramatically toward the stream farther to the south (see Figure 4.16).

6. Access Surface Properties again, and change the style to Slope Arrows.

7. On the Analysis tab, choose Slope Arrows as the analysis type, and click the arrow again.

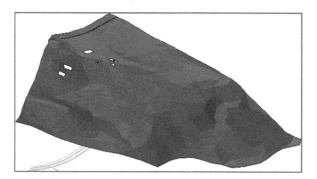

FIGURE 4.16   **Slope analysis of surface shown in 3-D**

8. Click OK to return to the drawing. Press Esc to clear the selection of the surface.

   In this view, the darker blues and blacks are the steepest slopes, and the arrows themselves always point downhill. As you study the arrows, you should notice a drainage divide that runs west to east through the farm buildings; it's delineated in red in Figure 4.17. Rain falling to the north of this area drains to the road, and rain falling south of it drains to the stream.

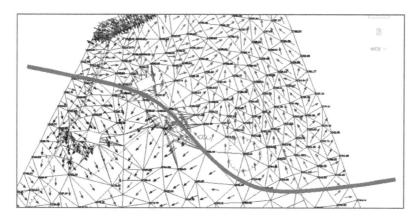

FIGURE 4.17   **Slope arrows can be used to identify a drainage divide (delineated in red) in the project.**

9. Save and close the drawing.

You can view the results of successfully completing this exercise by opening Slope Analysis - Complete.dwg.

Performing Other Types of Analysis

In addition to analyzing elevations, slopes, and slope arrows, you can perform the following types of analyses:

Contours   Contours can be used to analyze a surface. They can be color-coded, and you can create a legend table that shows the area and/or volume the contours represent.

Directions   With this type of analysis, you can see a visual representation of your surface slopes. For example, you can use the analysis to see which parts of your surface slope to the south and which slope to the north.

User-Defined Contours   Contours are usually placed at even intervals, such as the 1' (0.5-meter) contours with which you have been working so far. What if you want to show a contour that represents elevation 92.75? That's done as a user-defined contour. A user-defined contour is an individual instance of a contour, usually at an irregular interval.

Watersheds   A watershed analysis outlines areas within the surface where rainfall runoff flows to a certain point or in a certain direction. This type of analysis is yet another way of studying the drainage characteristics of the terrain.

Exploring Even More Analysis Tools

There are even more ways of analyzing your surface that aren't found in Surface Properties. For example, the following tools are especially useful on many projects:

Water Drop Tool   With the Water Drop tool, you can click any point on your surface and Civil 3D will trace the downhill path of that point until it reaches a low point or encounters the edge of the surface. This is a very detailed way to study how water will flow across the ground.

Catchment Area Tool   With this tool, you can click a point on the surface and Civil 3D will draw a closed shape that represents the area that flows to that point. This is very useful when you're analyzing the effects of rainfall on your project.

Quick Profile   With the Quick Profile tool, you can display a slice of your surface to get an edge-on view of it. This can help you understand the slope of the land and the location of high and low points.

You'll learn more about these tools and get hands-on experience with them in Chapter 18, "Analyzing, Displaying, and Annotating Surfaces."

Annotating Surfaces

Certification
Objective

As you have read, surfaces are used to tell a story about the shape of a piece of land. I have presented nearly a dozen different ways to tell that story, but I have yet to discuss the most obvious and most common way: telling the story with text. In the following exercise, you'll use three types of labels to annotate a surface: spot elevation labels, slope labels, and contour labels.

Exercise 4.8: Annotate a Surface

In this exercise, you'll annotate a surface using spot elevation labels, slope labels, and contour labels.

1. Open the drawing named Labeling Surfaces.dwg located in the Chapter 04 class data folder.

   The top-right viewport is zoomed in to the north end of the project near the location where the magenta centerline meets the centerline of the existing road. Your task is to label the elevation of the existing road where these two centerlines meet.

2. Click one of the contours to select the surface, and then click Add Labels ➢ Add Surface Labels on the ribbon.

3. In the Add Labels dialog box, select Spot Elevation as the label type.

4. Verify that the spot elevation label style is set to Elevation Only – Existing and the marker style is set to Spot Elevation.

5. Click Add. Snap to the northern endpoint of the magenta centerline. A label is placed at the location you selected (see Figure 4.18).

If you haven't already done so, download and install the files for Chapter 4 according to the instructions in this book's Introduction.

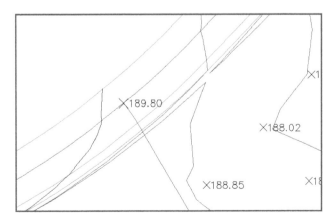

F I G U R E   4 . 1 8   Spot elevation label showing 189.80' (57.85 m) added where the new road meets the existing road

6. Pan to the south where the road centerline bends at a 90-degree angle. Note the steep slope to the south of the road in this area. You want to measure and label the slope in this area to determine whether homes can be built here and/or if guardrails will be required for the road.

7. If the Add Labels dialog box is already open, skip to the next step. If not, click one of the contours to select the surface, and then click Add Labels ➤ Add Surface Labels on the ribbon.

8. For Label Type, select Slope.

9. Verify that Slope Label Style is set to Percent-Existing, and click Add.

This creates a label that points downhill at the one point you select. With two-point labels, you control the direction.

10. When prompted at the command line, press Enter to accept the default of <One-point>.

11. Click a point to the south of the road to label the slope. Press the Esc key to end the command.

12. Click the label, and then click the square grip at the midpoint of the arrow. Move your cursor across the drawing, and note how the label changes.

This dynamic label behavior is consistent throughout Civil 3D.

13. If the Add Labels dialog box is already open, skip to the next step. If not, click one of the contours to select the surface, and then click Add Labels ➤ Add Surface Labels on the ribbon.

14. For Label Type, select Contour – Multiple. Verify that the names of all three label styles begin with Existing, and click Add.

15. Click two points in the drawing that stretch across several contours. Contour labels appear where contours fall between the two points you've selected (see Figure 4.19). You've actually drawn an invisible line that intersects with the contours.

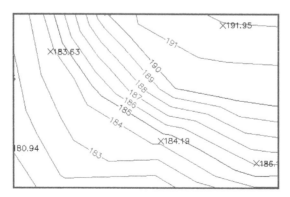

FIGURE 4.19   Contour labels

16. Press Esc to clear the previous command, and then click one of the newly created labels.

    Notice the line that appears. Click one of the grips, and move it to a new location to change the location of the line. The contour labels go where the line goes, even if you stretch it out and cause it to cross through more contours, in which case it will create more labels.

17. Continue placing contour labels until you've evenly distributed labels throughout the drawing.

18. Save and close the drawing.

You can view the results of successfully completing this exercise by opening `Labeling Surfaces - Complete.dwg`.

Now You Know

Now that you have completed this chapter, you understand the role of surfaces in land-development projects. You can create surfaces from survey data and perfect them by adding breaklines and boundaries. You can modify surfaces by deleting lines and editing points. You can get answers and tell stories about surfaces using analysis types such as elevation banding, slope banding, and slope arrows. Finally, you're able to provide additional information about a surface using several different types of labels.

Now that you've learned this major step in establishing the existing conditions of your project, you're ready to begin learning about the tools used to transform your project through design.

CHAPTER 5

Designing in 2-D Using Alignments

Now that the existing conditions of the project have been thoroughly established, you're ready to move on to designing the new work to be constructed on the site. A common way of beginning this design is to lay out a 2-D version of some of the key features of the project. If this were a commercial site project, you might start by drawing the outlines of buildings, sidewalks, and parking lots. For an environmental project such as wetland relocation, you might begin by drawing a 2-D outline of the new wetland boundary. Because our example project is a single-family residential development, the key features are the roads. Thus, you would begin your design by drawing a basic version of them in 2-D. As you're about to learn, alignments in AutoCAD® Civil 3D® are the best tool for establishing this basic geometry and then using it as the basis for additional design.

In this chapter, you'll learn to:

▶ **Understand alignments**

▶ **Create alignments from objects**

▶ **Create alignments using the Alignment Creation Tools**

▶ **Edit alignments**

▶ **Apply design criteria files and check sets**

Understanding Alignments

You can think of the basic road geometry discussed in the chapter introduction as a single-line form of the roads, as shown in Figure 5.1. The lines that you draw will typically represent the centerlines of the roads, and eventually you'll build the rest of each road around those centerlines.

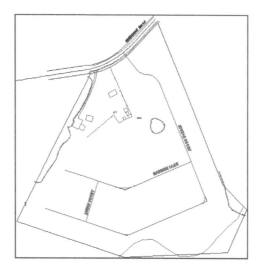

FIGURE 5.1   A single-line drawing of the subdivision roads (in red)

Civil 3D alignments are designed specifically for the task of representing the initial single-line version of a linear design feature. They are also used to establish the backbone of linear designs such as roads, railroads, channels, and pipelines. The lines, arcs, and spirals that make up an alignment have the ability to interact with one another. This enables you to edit part of the alignment and have the other parts fix themselves automatically. Also, other design objects such as profiles, sections, and corridors can be built around alignments. You'll learn more about these other design objects later in this book.

Creating Alignments from Objects

Certification
Objective

A common way of creating an alignment is to use the basic AutoCAD® software geometry that's already in the drawing. You may be using someone's "sketch," or maybe you've chosen to draw the initial version of the layout this way because of the simplicity of the AutoCAD tools. Whatever the case, Civil 3D makes it fairly easy to convert simple AutoCAD entities into alignments.

Exercise 5.1: Create Alignments from Objects

In this exercise, you'll create alignments from polylines in the drawing that represent road centerlines.

1. Open the drawing named Alignment from Objects.dwg located in the Chapter 05 class data folder.

   Because alignment design is strictly a 2-D type of design, the drawings in this chapter aren't set up with multiple viewports.

2. On the Home tab of the ribbon, click Alignment ➤ Create Alignment From Objects.

3. When the command line prompts you to select an object, click the longest magenta polyline, labeled Jordan Court.

4. Press Enter.

   A black arrow should appear on the polyline, indicating the program's guess at the direction of the alignment.

5. If the arrow is pointing toward the south, press Enter. If it's pointing north, press R and then press Enter.

   Believe it or not, the choice here is very important. The direction of the alignment will affect the configuration and labeling of many more components of this design as it progresses.

6. In the Create Alignment From Objects dialog box, do the following:

   ▶ For Name, enter **Jordan Court**.

   ▶ For Type, verify that Centerline is selected.

   ▶ For Site, verify that <None> is selected.

   ▶ For Alignment Style, verify that Proposed is selected.

   ▶ For Alignment Label Set, verify that _No Labels is selected.

   ▶ Uncheck the box next to Add Curves Between Tangents.

   ▶ Verify that the box next to Erase Existing Entities is checked.

   ▶ Click OK.

7. Click the newly created alignment, and then click one of the magenta polylines.

   Notice how the polyline grips are different from the alignment grips (see Figure 5.2).

If you haven't already done so, download and install the files for Chapter 5 according to the instructions in this book's Introduction.

Notice on the command line that the Create Alignment From Objects command accepts lines, arcs, and polylines and will even let you select objects from XREFs.

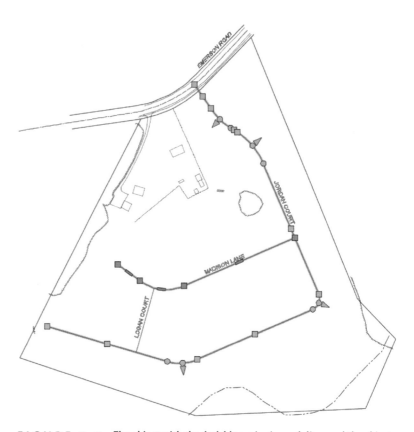

FIGURE 5.2   The object with the dark blue grips is a polyline, and the object with the light blue grips is an alignment. Alignments have more types of grips that enable more geometric editing functionality.

8. Experiment with moving the grips, and compare the behavior of a Civil 3D alignment with the behavior of a polyline.

9. Repeat steps 2 through 6 to create the Madison Lane and Logan Court alignments.

10. Save and close the drawing.

You can view the results of successfully completing this exercise by opening Alignment from Objects - Complete.dwg.

ALIGNMENTS ARE SMARTER

As you investigate the grip-editing behavior of the alignment versus the polyline, what do you find? You should notice that the alignment wants to follow a very basic geometric rule that the polyline doesn't worry about too much: maintaining tangency. Whether you move or stretch a straight line portion (aka tangent) or modify a curve, the adjacent lines and curves morph themselves to remain tangent (shown here). This is a good thing because driving your car down a road where the curves and lines aren't tangent could be hazardous to your health.

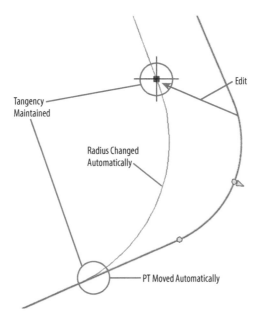

Creating Alignments Using the Alignment Creation Tools

Many times you won't have geometry in the drawing that you can simply convert to an alignment. In these cases, you can use the Civil 3D Alignment Creation Tools to create alignments from scratch. The Alignment Creation Tools

Certification
Objective

are housed in Civil 3D's version of a toolbar and consist of a comprehensive set of commands to create and edit the lines, curves, and spirals that make up an alignment.

ALIGNMENT TERMINOLOGY

Before jumping into the next exercise, you may want to review the following list of terms that you'll find throughout the Alignment Creation Tools commands as well as other places in Civil 3D:

Tangents (Alignment Segments)   The straight-line portions of an alignment

Tangent (Geometric Condition)

▶ Touching or passing through at a single point

▶ In the case of a line and arc: perpendicular to a line drawn from the intersection point to the center point of the arc

▶ In the case of two arcs: intersecting in such a way that a line drawn from the center point of one arc to the center point of the other arc passes through the intersection point

Curves   The curved portions of an alignment that have a constant radius

Spiral   The curved portions of an alignment that change in radius from one end to the other

PI (Point of Intersection)   The place where two tangents intersect or would intersect if they were extended

PC (Point of Curvature)   The place where the curve begins

PT (Point of Tangency)   The place where the curve ends

Free   A line, curve, or spiral that is dependent on another alignment segment at both ends

Floating   A line, curve, or spiral that is dependent on another alignment segment at one end

Fixed   A line, curve, or spiral that is not dependent on another alignment component at either end

Exercise 5.2: Create Alignments Using the Alignment Creation Tools

In this exercise, you'll create alignments using the Alignment Creation Tools. You'll draw the alignments according to reference geometry, dimensions, and other information that has been provided for you.

If you haven't already done so, download and install the files for Chapter 5 according to the instructions in this book's Introduction.

1. Open the drawing named `Alignment Creation Tools.dwg` located in the `Chapter 05` class data folder.

2. Examine the blue geometry and accompanying dimensions and notes.

    This geometry is described in detail in the sidebar "Using Temporary Geometry."

3. On the Home tab, click Alignment ➤ Alignment Creation Tools.

4. In the Create Alignment – Layout dialog box, enter **Jordan Court** for Name, and click OK.

5. On the Alignment Creation Tools toolbar, click the black triangle on the first button on the left to expand it downward (see Figure 5.3). Then click Tangent-Tangent (With Curves).

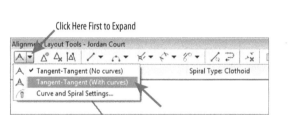

FIGURE 5.3 Selecting the Tangent-Tangent (With Curves) command

6. Snap to the center of the circle marked A.

7. Snap to the centers of circles B through E (skip over circles F and I), and press Enter. The Jordan Court alignment is created.

8. To create the Madison Lane alignment, repeat steps 3 through 7, entering **Madison Lane** for Name and using circles F through H.

9. To create the Logan Court alignment, repeat steps 3 through 7, entering **Logan Court** for Name and drawing it from circle I perpendicular to the Madison Lane alignment.

   10. Save and close the drawing.

You can view the results of successfully completing this exercise by opening
Alignment Creation Tools - Complete.dwg.

USING TEMPORARY GEOMETRY

Existing physical and legal boundary features almost always influence the layout
of any land-development design. In a residential project such as the example in
this book, the goal is to create as many optimally sized lots as possible within
the available area. Every lot must also be accessible from roads built through
the site. With these things in mind, along with the geometry of the existing
property boundaries, terrain, and other constraints, it's frequently helpful to
create some temporary geometry to guide you in the creation of the alignments.

In the drawing for this exercise, the blue linework is provided for you and represents geometry that references existing features of the site. Dimensions and
notes have also been provided to help explain the reasoning behind this geometry. The following list represents key points to consider when you're creating
this temporary geometry:

  ▶ 150' (45-m) offset from the road centerline to the backs of the lots to
    accommodate a 50' (15-m) right-of-way, an adequate front yard, a single-
    family residence, and an adequate rear yard.

  ▶ Perpendicular intersection with the existing road that is ideal for safety
    and accessibility.

  ▶ Avoidance of the steep area to the south.

  ▶ Uniform geometric properties where possible, such as 90° angles, parallel
    lines, and so on. This is recommended for simpler, more efficient stake-
    out and construction.

  ▶ Avoidance of the farmhouse and buildings, because that part of the
    property will be deeded back to the original owner.

In the real world, you'll need to come up with this temporary geometry on your
own. In fact, this is what design is all about: using your knowledge and creativity
to come up with a technical solution to a need or problem. Creating the alignment is the easy part. Coming up with the temporary geometry as described
here is the real challenge.

Editing Alignments

Of course, nobody gets it right the first time. As a general rule, you'll find your-self laying things out about 10 percent of the time and spending the remaining 90 percent making edits. That's totally OK; it's the way Civil 3D was designed to be used. In fact, it's highly recommended that you do a rough layout of the basic design elements at the beginning of a project and then spend the rest of the time adjusting, refining, and improving that initial layout until it's the way it needs to be. This is also a great approach because it matches up with the general nature of land-development designs, which typically change frequently through-out the life of the project.

Editing Alignments with Grips

As you learned in the first section of this chapter, alignments are different. They're smarter and more sophisticated than basic AutoCAD entities. They have more types of grips, and the way they respond to geometric changes is more intelligent. You can leverage this to make quick visual edits to your alignment without ever typing a number or entering a command.

Exercise 5.3: Experiment with Alignment Grips

In this exercise, you'll experiment with the different grips that can be used for editing alignments.

1. Open the drawing named Graphical Editing.dwg located in the Chapter 05 class data folder.

2. Click the Jordan Court alignment to display its grips. Click the upright triangular grip on the second curve, and move your cursor to a new location without clicking the new location.

    This grip is located at the PI. As you move it, the curve always remains tangent and the radius of the curve remains constant (see Figure 5.4).

If you haven't already done so, download and install the files for Chapter 5 according to the instructions in this book's Introduction.

This exercise goes more smoothly if Osnaps are turned off. If they are turned on, you can press F3 to turn them off.

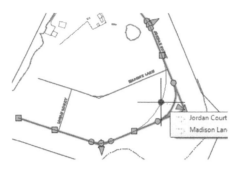

FIGURE 5.4   Moving a PI grip

3. Press Esc, and click the circular grip at either end of the curve. Move your cursor to a different location without clicking.

    These grips are located at the PC and PT. As you move them, the radius changes and tangency is maintained at both ends of the curve (see Figure 5.5). They can be used to graphically set the exact beginning point or ending point of a curve.

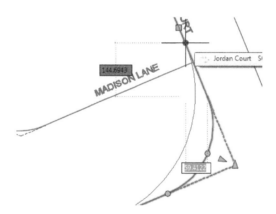

FIGURE 5.5   Moving a PC or PT grip

4. Press Esc, and click the circular grip at the midpoint of the curve. Move your cursor to a different location without clicking.

    This grip is located at a pass-through point, and it forces the curve to pass through that point while maintaining tangency at both ends. This is accomplished by changing the radius of the curve (see Figure 5.6). You can use this grip to make the curve pass through a specific point.

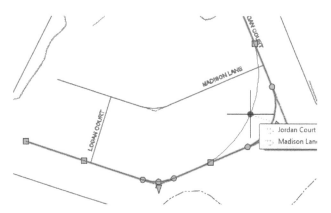

FIGURE 5.6   Moving the pass-through point grip

5. Press Esc, and click the triangular grip located near the midpoint of the curve. Move your cursor to a different location without clicking.

This grip controls the radius of the curve while maintaining tangency at both ends of the curve (see Figure 5.7).

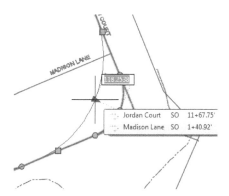

FIGURE 5.7   Moving the radius grip

6. Press Esc, and click the square grip at the end of the Jordan Court alignment. Move your cursor to a different location without clicking.

This type of grip is located at either the beginning or the end of the alignment. As it's moved, the geometry adjacent to it responds. In the case of this alignment, the curve just before the endpoint changes the locations of its beginning and ending points to remain tangent at both ends (see Figure 5.8).

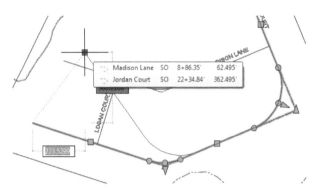

FIGURE 5.8   Moving the start point or endpoint grip

7. Press Esc, and click the square grip located at the midpoint of the last tangent in the alignment. Move your cursor to a new location without clicking.

    This grip moves the tangent while maintaining its orientation in the drawing. Adjacent geometry responds as needed to meet its geometric rules. In the case of this alignment, the PI to the left of this grip changes location, and the curve to the right changes its beginning and ending points to remain tangent (see Figure 5.9).

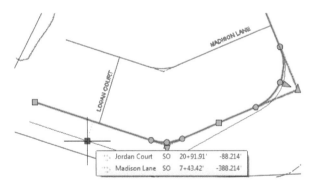

FIGURE 5.9   Moving the tangent midpoint grip

8. Close the drawing without saving.

Because this drawing was not changed, there is no "completed" version of the drawing.

Editing Alignments Using the Alignment Layout Tools

Grips are wonderful tools to edit geometry that is already there, but what if you need to add a PI or draw a curve? For that, you need the Alignment Layout Tools toolbar (see Figure 5.10). This toolbar is the same one you used initially to lay out the alignment.

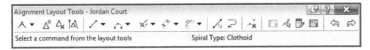

FIGURE 5.10   Alignment Layout Tools toolbar

Exercise 5.4: Apply the Alignment Editing Tools

In this exercise, you'll edit the Jordan Court alignment using the Alignment Editing Tools. The goal is to create a perpendicular intersection where Jordan Court meets Emerson Road.

1. Open the drawing named `Editing Tools.dwg` located in your `Chapter 05` class data folder.

2. Click the Jordan Court alignment, and then click Geometry Editor on the ribbon.
   This opens the Alignment Layout Tools toolbar.

3. On the Alignment Layout Tools toolbar, click Insert PI. Then snap to the center of the circle marked A.

4. Click Delete Sub-entity, and then click the curve at the PI marked B.

5. Click the tangent between A and B to remove it as well. The alignment should now look like Figure 5.11.

> If you haven't already done so, download and install the files for Chapter 5 according to the instructions in this book's Introduction.

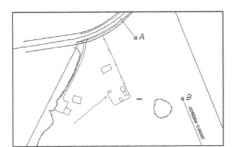

FIGURE 5.11   Alignment after removing a tangent and a curve

6. Expand the curve button, and click More Floating Curves ➢ Floating Curve (From Entity End, Radius, Length).

7. Click the tangent near point A.

8. Type O and press Enter to indicate a counterclockwise direction.

9. Type 100 (30) and press Enter to provide the radius.

10. Type 100 (30) and press Enter to provide the curve length.
    A short curve is placed at the end of the tangent.

11. On the Alignment Layout Tools toolbar, expand the curves button, and select Free Curve Fillet (Between Two Entities, Radius).

12. Click the curve you just created in the previous steps.

13. Click the red tangent that begins at point B.

14. Press Enter to indicate that the solution is less than 180 degrees.

15. Type R and then press Enter to indicate that it's a reverse curve.

16. Type 100 (30) and press Enter to provide the radius. Press Enter to end the command.
    The new curve is created in the drawing, as shown in Figure 5.12.

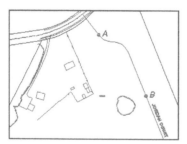

FIGURE 5.12   **Alignment after the addition of a reverse curve**

17. Save and close the drawing.

You can view the results of successfully completing this exercise by opening Editing Tools - Complete.dwg.

Editing Alignments Numerically

At times, you may want to adjust your design by telling Civil 3D the exact dimension of a portion of the alignment. This can be done in one of two different ways. The first is Alignment Grid View, which opens a tab in Panorama. This tab shows the geometry of the alignment in table form and enables you to edit some of the values to adjust the design.

Exercise 5.5: Edit Alignments Using Alignment Grid View

In this exercise, you'll edit the Jordan Court alignment using the Alignment Grid View command.

1. Open the drawing named Alignment Grid View.dwg located in the Chapter 05 class data folder.

2. Click the Jordan Court alignment, and then click Geometry Editor on the ribbon.

3. Click Alignment Grid View to open the Alignment Entities tab and display the tabular version of the alignment geometry, as shown in Figure 5.13.

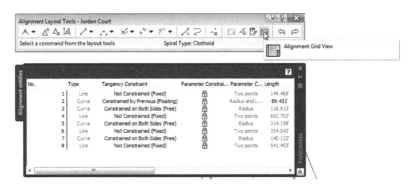

FIGURE 5.13 The Alignment Entities tab of Panorama showing the tabular data of the alignment

4. For the Radius values for items 2 and 3, type **150 (45)** and press Enter. Notice that the alignment updates automatically in the drawing.

5. Save and close the drawing.

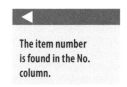

If you haven't already done so, download and install the files for Chapter 5 according to the instructions in this book's Introduction.

The item number is found in the No. column.

You can view the results of successfully completing this exercise by opening Alignment Grid View - Complete.dwg.

Another method for editing the alignment design numerically is referred to as *component-level editing*. With this approach, you open the numerical data for a piece of the alignment (such as a line, curve, or spiral) in a separate window. You do so by clicking the Sub-entity Editor button on the Alignment Layout Tools toolbar and then using the Pick Sub-entity tool to choose the part of the alignment you want to edit.

Exercise 5.6: Edit Alignments Using Component-Level Editing

In this exercise, you'll edit the Jordan Court alignment using component-level editing.

1. Open the drawing named Component Level Editing.dwg located in the Chapter 05 class data folder.

2. Close Panorama if it's open. Click the Jordan Court alignment, and then click Geometry Editor on the ribbon.

3. Click Sub-entity Editor on the Alignment Layout Tools toolbar to display the Alignment Layout Parameters dialog box. (This dialog box is blank when it first appears.)

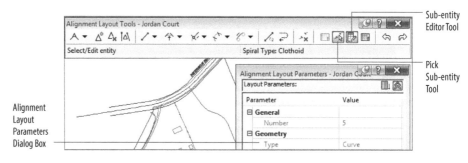

FIGURE 5.14 The Sub-entity Editor Tool, Pick Sub-entity Tool, and Alignment Layout Parameters dialog box

4. Click Pick Sub-entity (see Figure 5.14), and then click the curve at the 90° bend on Jordan Court.

5. Type 50 (15) for Radius, and press Enter.
   The curve in the drawing updates automatically.

6. Close the Alignment Layout Parameters dialog box and the Alignment Layout Tools toolbar.

7. Save and close the drawing.

You can view the results of successfully completing this exercise by opening `Component Level Editing - Complete.dwg`.

Applying Design Criteria Files and Check Sets

When you're laying out a design, how do you know whether you're doing it right? What should the curve radii be? Should there be a minimum tangent length between curves, or is it OK to have back-to-back curves? How does the expected speed of traffic affect the answers to these questions?

The answers to these types of questions can differ, depending on the project. For road design, the government entity that accepts responsibility for the road is most likely calling the shots when it comes to design standards. That may be the state Department of Transportation (DOT), county planning commission, or even the community homeowners association. In other cases, you may be designing roads or other linear features on private property that isn't governed by any official design standards. In this case, you'll have to utilize your knowledge and experience to create the best design. Whether the design standards come from you or someone else, it's helpful to have tools that ensure that your design meets the requirements assigned to it.

Design criteria and check sets are two ways of telling Civil 3D what your design standards are and asking Civil 3D to tell you when you've violated those standards by displaying a warning symbol (see Figure 5.15). These two features are customizable, so you can use them to represent any standard or combination of standards that is necessary.

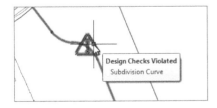

FIGURE 5.15 Tooltip relaying details about a design check set violation

Applying Design Check Sets

A *design check set* is a collection of one or more design checks. There are four types of design checks: line, curve, spiral, and tangent intersection. When a design check set is applied to an alignment, Civil 3D flags any violations with a triangular yellow shield marked with an exclamation point. You can hover over the shield to get more information about the violation, as shown previously in Figure 5.15.

PRELOADING YOUR DESIGN STANDARDS

If you work for a company that does projects in different jurisdictions that have different design requirements, it would be a good idea to talk with your CAD manager about separate templates, one for each jurisdiction. Not only can these templates establish graphical standards as discussed previously, but they also can be set up with preloaded design-criteria files and design check sets that represent applicable design standards. With this type of setup, you can simply choose the right template before starting your design and proceed with confidence that a warning symbol will pop up if you have not met a requirement of the county, state, or client for whom you're designing.

Exercise 5.7: Apply a Design Check Set

If you haven't already done so, download and install the files for Chapter 5 according to the instructions in this book's Introduction.

In this exercise, you'll apply a design check set to the Jordan Court alignment and then make edits based on the results.

1. Open the drawing named Design Check Set.dwg located in the Chapter 05 class data folder.

2. Click the Jordan Court alignment, and then click Alignment Properties on the ribbon.

3. In the Alignment Properties dialog box, click the Design Criteria tab.

4. For Design Seed, type **25 (40)**, and press Enter.

5. Check the box next to Use Criteria-Based Design.

6. Uncheck the box next to Use Design Criteria File.

7. Verify that Use Design Check Set is checked, and select Subdivision.

8. Click OK to close the Alignment Properties dialog box. Press Esc to clear the grips on the alignment. You should see three yellow warning symbols in the drawing, as shown in Figure 5.16.

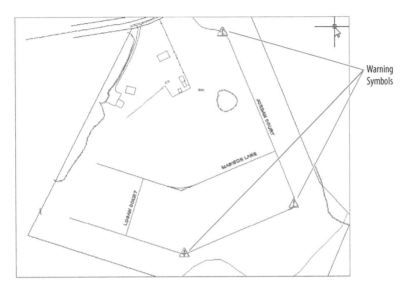

Warning Symbols

FIGURE 5.16 Warning symbols indicating design check set violations within the alignment

9. Zoom in to the curve farthest to the south. Hover your cursor over the yellow shield.
   A tooltip should appear, indicating that the Subdivision Curve design check has been violated.

10. Click the alignment to display its grips; then click the circular grip at the midpoint of the curve, and drag it northward to increase the radius of the curve. Repeat as necessary until the shield disappears.

11. Click the Jordan Court alignment, and then click Geometry Editor on the ribbon.

12. On the Alignment Layout Tools toolbar, click Alignment Grid View.
   Notice the yellow shields in the No. column as well as the bold values in the Radius column and several other columns (see Figure 5.17). This tells you which items have violations as well as which specific values are causing them.

If no tooltip appears, type **rollovertips** at the command line; then type **1**, and press Enter.

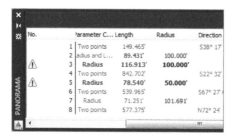

FIGURE 5.17 Warning symbols in Panorama indicate design check set violations.

The columns may not appear in the same order as shown here. You may need to scroll right to view one or more of the columns.

13. For the Radius value of item 3, type 150 (45), and press Enter.

     The shield should disappear, and the bold values for item 3 should now show in normal print. The Radius value for item 5 will remain at 50' (15 m).

14. Save and close the drawing.

You can view the results of successfully completing this exercise by opening Design Check Set - Complete.dwg.

Applying Design Criteria Files

Design criteria files are another way of having Civil 3D check your design as you go. From an end-user standpoint, there isn't much difference between a design check set and design criteria file: they're both something you assign to your alignment so that certain design parameters can be checked. From a setup standpoint, they're quite different. Design check sets are a group of design checks that are relatively simple and are managed through the Settings tab of the Toolspace. A design criteria file is a single file, and it's potentially much more sophisticated. There is a special tool for editing design criteria files called the Design Criteria Editor. Civil 3D comes with AASHTO design criteria files that can be used as is or copied and modified to meet local requirements. Autodesk also provides numerous country kits that include even more design criteria files that meet the requirements of various design authorities around the world.

AASHTO stands for the American Association of State Highway and Transportation Officials. It's the basis for many of the state DOT standards in the United States.

Exercise 5.8: Apply a Design Criteria File

In this exercise, you'll apply a design criteria file to the Jordan Court alignment and then make edits based on the results.

If you haven't already done so, download and install the files for Chapter 5 according to the instructions in this book's Introduction.

1. Open the drawing named Design Criteria Files.dwg located in the Chapter 05 class data folder.
   Note that currently only one warning symbol is shown for the Jordan Court alignment.

2. Click the Jordan Court alignment, and select Alignment Properties on the ribbon.

3. Click the Design Criteria tab. Check the box next to Use Design Criteria File.

4. Click the button to the right of the file path, and select the file named Autodesk Civil 3D Imperial (2011) Roadway Design Standards .xml (Autodesk Civil 3D Metric (2011) Roadway Design Standards.xml). Click Open.

5. Uncheck the box next to Use Design Check Set.

6. Click OK, and press Esc to clear the grips.
   New warning symbols appear on the first, second, and fourth curves (the one on the third curve was there previously). As you can see, the design criteria file is a bit more stringent than the design check set of the previous exercise.

7. Hover your cursor over the warning symbol farthest to the north.

The tooltip informs you that the required radius is 154' (47 m).

8. Select the alignment, and click Geometry Editor on the ribbon.

9. Click Alignment Grid View on the Alignment Layout Tools toolbar.

10. Note that the minimum radius is listed in Panorama. Change the radius of items 2, 3, and 7 to **155** (**48**).
    Do not edit item 5; it should remain set to 50' (15 m).

11. Close Panorama, and observe the change to the alignment.

12. Save and close the drawing.

With the exception of one curve, the alignment meets the requirements of both the design criteria file and the design check set.

You can view the results of successfully completing this exercise by opening Design Criteria Files - Complete.dwg.

You Have the Power

Design check sets and design criteria files don't change your design. They simply tell you when one of the rules has been broken. Depending on many factors, there will be times when you fix the issue to satisfy the rule and times when you don't. In the previous case of the 50' (15 m) radius, you know that Phase II of the project will create a T intersection at this location, which makes the sharp turn OK.

Now You Know

Now that you have completed this chapter, you have an understanding of alignments: their purpose, how to create them, and how to modify them. You're able to create alignments from objects already in the drawing or create them from scratch using the Alignment Creation Tools. You can edit alignments graphically and numerically using a number of approaches. These include grips, Alignment Editing Tools, Alignment Grid View, and component-level editing. You now know how to apply design check sets and design criteria files to enable Civil 3D to keep track of how well your design adheres to your standards. Generally speaking, having completed this chapter, you're ready to begin working with alignments in a production environment.

CHAPTER 6

Displaying and Annotating Alignments

As you'll find with nearly every design component you create for a land-development project, creating the design is only half the job—you must also address the graphical appearance and annotation of what you've created. Alignments serve as the basis for further design of a linear feature, but they also serve as a means of expressing the geometry of the feature to reviewers and contractors. The alignment by itself doesn't tell this story in enough detail and must therefore be stylized and annotated appropriately. In addition, alignments often serve as baselines used to express the location of other features within the project.

In this chapter, you'll learn how to use various styles and annotations to convey important information about alignments.

In this chapter, you'll learn to:

▶ **Apply alignment styles**

▶ **Apply alignment labels and label sets**

▶ **Create station/offset labels**

▶ **Create segment labels**

▶ **Apply tag labels and tables**

Using Alignment Styles

As with other styles you have learned about, alignment styles are, as their name implies, used to control the appearance and behavior of alignments. By applying different styles, you can graphically distinguish between existing centerlines, proposed centerlines, and so on. You can even use styles to display an alignment as something that is not a centerline at all, such as a property line or even a utility line. Figure 6.1 illustrates how styles enable alignments to represent many different things.

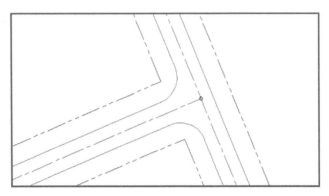

F I G U R E   6 . 1   Different alignment styles are used to represent the right-of-way, edges of pavement, and centerlines in this drawing.

Alignment styles have two major ways of affecting the appearance of alignments. First, they control which components of the alignment are visible, and second, they control the graphical properties such as layer, color, and linetype of the components that are displayed.

> If you haven't already done so, download and install the files for Chapter 6 according to the instructions in this book's Introduction.

Exercise 6.1: Apply Alignment Styles

In this exercise, you'll use alignment styles to control the appearance of alignments.

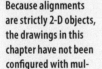

> Because alignments are strictly 2-D objects, the drawings in this chapter have not been configured with multiple viewports.

1. Open the drawing named Alignment Styles.dwg located in the Chapter 06 class data folder.

   The drawing contains a dozen different alignments that are intended to serve different purposes. Currently, all the alignments look the same because they have been assigned a style of Standard.

2. Zoom in to the alignment representing the centerline of Emerson Road. Select the alignment, right-click, and select Properties.

3. Change the style to C-ROAD-CNTR-E, as shown in Figure 6.2.

This displays the alignment as a simple series of lines and curves on the existing road centerline layer.

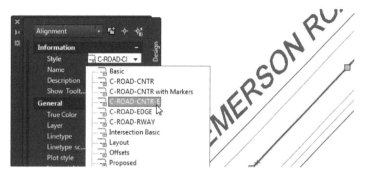

FIGURE 6.2   Assigning an alignment style in the Properties window

Press Esc each time you change a style so that you can see the true appearance of the alignment without the effect of being selected.

4. Press Esc to clear the selection of the alignment. Select the Jordan Court centerline alignment, and change its style to C-ROAD-CNTR.
   This displays this alignment as a simple series of lines and curves on the proposed road centerline layer.

5. Pan south so that you can see the curves in the Jordan court centerline alignment. Change the style of this alignment to C-ROAD-CNTR With Markers.
   With this style, markers are placed at the beginning, end, points of curvature (PCs), points of tangency (PTs), points of reverse curvature (PRCs), and points of intersection (PIs). In addition, line extensions are displayed with the tangents extending to the PI markers. You would use this style for the polished look of a final plan but probably not for design.

You would use this style for analysis purposes during design, not for the polished look of a final plan.

6. Pan south until you can see the Madison Lane alignment. Change the style of this alignment to Layout.

7. For the alignments that run parallel to the Jordan Court centerline and extend the full length of the centerline, assign the C-ROAD-RWAY style.
   This displays the alignments on the right-of-way layer, enabling them to take on the appearance of property lines.

You can select both right-of-way alignments and assign the C-ROAD-RWAY style to both of them at once using the Properties window.

8. For the remaining alignments that represent the edges of pavement, change the style to C-ROAD-EDGE.

    This displays the alignments on the edge-of-pavement layer.

9. Save and close the drawing.

You can view the results of successfully completing this exercise by opening `Alignment Styles - Complete.dwg`.

Applying Alignment Labels and Label Sets

Certification
Objective

Alignments (and, as you'll learn later, profiles) have a special kind of annotation that is applied either to the entire alignment at once or to a range of stations within the alignment. This annotation repeats at specified increments or when specific types of geometry are encountered. This type of annotation is very useful because it changes as the alignment changes, even if new geometry is added or the length of the alignment changes. In all, you can add seven types of alignment labels in this way. This chapter doesn't cover all seven types, but you'll learn about the following three alignment label types:

Major Station Labels   Placed at the major station increment, which is larger than the minor station increment. They typically include a tick mark along with a numerical label calling out the station.

Minor Station Labels   Placed at the minor station increment, which is smaller than the major station increment. These typically consist of tick marks.

Geometry Point Labels   Placed at key geometric points along the alignment, such as the beginning of the alignment, ending of the alignment, places where there are curves, and so on.

Exercise 6.2: Apply Labels to Alignments

In this exercise, you'll use the Add/Edit Station Labels command to add station labels, station ticks, and geometry labels to the Jordan Court alignment.

1. Open the drawing named `Alignment Labels.dwg` located in the `Chapter 06` class data folder.

2. Click the Jordan Court alignment. Then click Add Labels ➢ Add/Edit Station Labels on the contextual ribbon tab.

3. In the Alignment Labels dialog box, do the following:

   a. For Type, verify that Major Stations is selected.

   b. For Major Station Label Style, verify that Parallel With Tick is selected; then click Add.

   c. For Increment, enter 50 (20) to indicate the number of feet (meters) to increment, and then click OK.

Remember that values listed in parentheses are not conversions but values that would make sense in a metric environment. Although 50 feet and 20 meters aren't equal, each is a reasonable increment for stationing.

4. Zoom in, and examine the labels that have been created.
   Notice that a tick mark and label have been placed at 50-foot (20-meter) increments along the alignment.

5. Click the Jordan Court alignment, and launch the Add/Edit Station Labels command as you did in step 2.

6. In the Alignment Labels dialog box, do the following:

   a. For Type, select Minor Stations.

   b. For Minor Station Label Style, verify that Tick is selected; then click Add.

   c. Change Minor Station Increment to 10 (5) to indicate the number of feet (meters) to increment, and then click OK.

7. Examine the alignment once more.
   Now you should see tick marks at 10-foot (5-meter) increments, which means there are four (three) minor tick marks between the major tick marks and labels.

8. Launch the Add/Edit Station Labels command again, as you did in step 2. In the Alignment Labels dialog box, do the following:

   a. For Type, select Geometry Points.

   b. For Geometry Point Label Style, verify that Perpendicular With Tick And Line is selected; then click Add.

   c. In the Geometry Points dialog box, uncheck all boxes except Tangent-Curve Intersect, Curve-Tangent Intersect, and Reverse Curve-Curve Intersect.

You can use the button in the top-right corner of the dialog box to clear all the check boxes quickly. The boxes you check will take care of PCs, PTs, and PRCs, respectively.

   d. Click OK twice to dismiss the Geometry Points and Alignment Labels dialog boxes.

9. Press Esc to clear the selection. Examine the alignment labels, and note the labels at the PCs, PTs, and PRC, as shown in Figure 6.3.

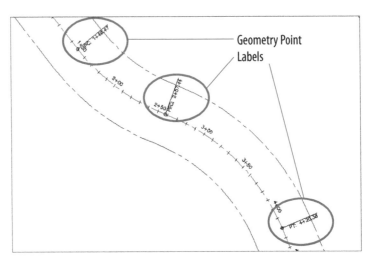

FIGURE 6.3 Geometry point labels displayed on the Jordan Court alignment

10. Save and close the drawing.

You can view the results of successfully completing this exercise by opening `Alignment Labels - Complete.dwg`.

Using Alignment Label Sets

As you might guess, the collection of labels used in the previous exercise is quite common: station and tick at the major station, just a tick at the minor station, and labels calling out key geometric features. What if you could gather those three label types together in a nice, neat package and apply them all at once? That's the exact purpose of a *label set*.

Exercise 6.3: Leverage Alignment Label Sets

If you haven't already done so, download and install the files for Chapter 6 according to the instructions in this book's Introduction.

In this exercise, you'll use an alignment label set to capture the label configuration for Jordan Court and make it available for easy transfer to Madison Lane.

1. Open the drawing named `Alignment Label Sets.dwg` located in the `Chapter 06` class data folder.

2. Click the Jordan Court alignment. Then click Add Labels ➢ Add/Edit Station Labels on the contextual tab of the ribbon.

3. In the Alignment Labels dialog box, click Save Label Set.

4. In the Alignment Label Set dialog box, on the Information tab, enter **M50 Stations & m10 Ticks & Geometry Points (M20 Stations & m5 Ticks & Geometry Points)** in the Name field.

5. Click OK twice to close the Alignment Label Set dialog box and the Alignment Labels dialog box.

6. Press Esc to clear the selection of the Jordan Court alignment. Click the Madison Lane alignment, and then click Add Labels ➤ Add/Edit Station Labels on the contextual tab of the ribbon.

7. In the Alignment Labels dialog box, click Import Label Set.

8. Select M50 Stations & m10 Ticks & Geometry Points (M20 Stations & m5 Ticks & Geometry Points), and then click OK.

9. Click OK to dismiss the Alignment Labels dialog box.

10. Press Esc to clear the selection. Examine the Madison Lane alignment (see Figure 6.4), and note that the label set applied here is the same as the label set that was applied to Jordan Court.

M50 stands for a major station increment of 50 feet, and m10 stands for a minor station increment of 10 feet in the imperial system. Similarly, M20 stands for a major station increment of 20 meters, and m5 stands for a minor station increment of 5 meters in the metric system.

Your CAD manager or other authorized person can create label sets and store them in your company template so they're always there for you to use.

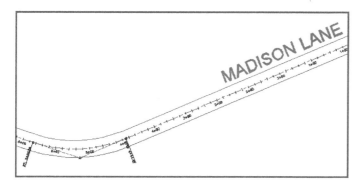

F I G U R E   6 . 4   The Madison Lane alignment after the label set has been applied

11. Save and close the drawing.

You can view the results of successfully completing this exercise by opening `Alignment Label Sets - Complete.dwg`.

Editing Alignment Labels

This Ctrl key trick works for many types of labels that exist in groups.

Working with alignment labels is a bit different than working with other labels because alignment labels exist in *groups*. If you click a major station label, for example, all the major station labels for the entire alignment will be selected. So, what if you want to change something about just one label? The answer is to use your Ctrl key when selecting individual labels in a group.

Another type of label edit that you'll be introduced to in this chapter is *flipping*. Flipping a label simply means switching it over to the other side of the line.

Exercise 6.4: Edit Alignment Labels

If you haven't already done so, download and install the files for Chapter 6 according to the instructions in this book's Introduction.

In this exercise, you'll edit the labels for Jordan Court such that the geometry labels are moved outside the right-of-way lines. You'll also flip a geometry point label and grip-edit an individual station label to resolve a labeling conflict.

1. Open the drawing named `Editing Alignment Labels.dwg` located in the `Chapter 06` class data folder.

2. Click one of the geometry point labels on the Jordan Court alignment. Then click Edit Label Group on the contextual ribbon tab that appears.

Notice that the right-of-way line is passing through the geometry point labels. These labels should be moved beyond the right-of-way line, which you'll do in the next few steps.

3. Click in the Style column to the right of Geometry Points. Select Perpendicular With Tick And Line – Offset, and click OK.

The labels are now shown outside the right-of-way line (see Figure 6.5).

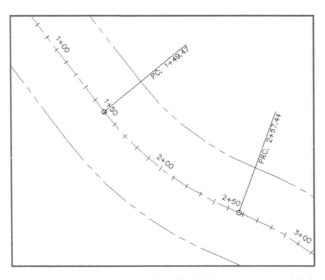

FIGURE 6.5 Changing the style of the geometry point labels improves their appearance and readability by moving them outside the right-of-way line.

4. Click OK to dismiss the Alignment Labels dialog box, and press Esc to clear the selection.

5. While holding down the Ctrl key, click the first PC label, and then click Flip Label on the ribbon. The label is flipped to the opposite side of the road.

6. Zoom to the intersection of Madison Lane and Jordan Court.

7. Click the 0+00 (0+000) station label of Madison Lane, and then click the square grip that appears above the label. Drag the grip to a clear area in the drawing.

   The station label is more readable in its new location, and a leader appears that indicates the actual location of the station.

8. Save and close the drawing.

You can view the results of successfully completing this exercise by opening `Editing Alignment Labels - Complete.dwg`.

Note how the 0+00 (0+000) station label for Madison Lane is conflicting with the centerline of Jordan Court.

Dragged State

In step 7, when you use a special grip on a label to drag it to a new location, a leader magically appears. This happens because the leader is turned on in the *dragged state* configuration of the label style. The dragged state of a label can dramatically change the look of that label when it's dragged to a new location. In addition to the appearance of a leader, you might see a change in text height or orientation, the appearance of a border around the text, and several other changes.

Creating Station/Offset Labels

As mentioned earlier, an alignment is often used as a baseline, enabling other features to express their locations in relation to that baseline. This is typically done with station offset notations, and, of course, the AutoCAD® Civil 3D® program provides you with labels to do just that. This type of label is referred to as a *station/offset label*.

Unlike the label groups you learned about earlier, station/offset labels stand alone instead of being part of a set. They are capable of reporting the station and offset of a point that you select as well as the alignment name, coordinates of the point, and other types of information.

You can create station/offset labels as either fixed or floating labels. If they are fixed, then they hold their positions and update the station and offset values when the alignment is edited. If they are floating, then they maintain their station and offset values and move with the alignment when it's edited. Like spot elevation labels, station/offset labels are paired with a marker.

Exercise 6.5: Create Station/Offset Labels

In this exercise, you'll add station/offset labels to define the road geometry at the intersection of Jordan Court and Madison Lane.

If you haven't already done so, download and install the files for Chapter 6 according to the instructions in this book's Introduction.

1. Open the drawing named Station Offset Labels.dwg located in the Chapter 06 class data folder.

This drawing is zoomed in to the intersection between Jordan Court and Madison Lane. Your task is to label the station and offset of either end of each curve that forms the intersection between the two roads.

2. Click the Jordan Court alignment, and then click Add Labels ➢ Station/Offset – Fixed Point on the contextual ribbon tab.

3. While holding down the Shift key, right-click and select Endpoint.

4. Click the northern end of the northern arc. A new label that references the Jordan Court alignment is created at this location.

5. While holding down the Shift key, right-click and select Endpoint. Then click the southern end of the southern arc.

6. Press Esc twice to end the command and clear the selection of the alignment. Click the Madison Lane alignment, and then click Add Labels ➢ Station/Offset – Fixed Point on the contextual ribbon tab.

7. While holding down the Shift key, right-click and select Endpoint. Click the western end of the northern arc.

This label and the one created in step 7 provide the station and offset in reference to the Madison Lane alignment.

8. While holding down the Shift key, right-click and select Endpoint. Then click the western end of the southern arc.

9. Press Esc twice to end the labeling command and clear the selection of the alignment.

10. Click one of the labels, and then click the square grip and drag it to a new location that is clear of other lines and text. Repeat this for the other labels to improve their appearance and readability.

The result should look similar to Figure 6.6.

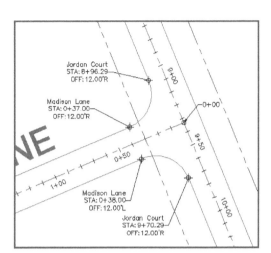

FIGURE 6.6 Station/offset labels applied to the edge-of-pavement arcs at the intersection of Madison Lane and Jordan Court

11. Save and close the drawing.

You can view the results of successfully completing this exercise by opening Station Offset Labels - Complete.dwg.

Creating Segment Labels

So far, you have seen label groups that label the entire alignment at once and station/offset labels that are typically used to label something other than the alignment. What about the individual parts of the alignment? How do you tell reviewers and contractors how to re-create those alignments in the field? The answer is segment labels. *Segment labels* allow you to label things such as bearings, distances, and curve data. By providing this information as text in the drawing, you give viewers of the drawing the information they need to stake out the alignment in the field. You're also sharing information about the geometric "performance" of the alignment that might answer questions such as these: Are the curves too sharp for the expected speed? Is the alignment parallel to other important features? Are intersecting roads perpendicular to one another?

Segment labels stand alone like station/offset labels; however, you can create them in bulk if you so desire. For example, all the tangents of an entire alignment can be labeled at once if you choose that option when creating the labels.

Exercise 6.6: Create Segment Labels

In this exercise, you'll add segment labels to define bearing, distance, and curve information for the Madison Lane and Jordan Court alignments.

1. Open the drawing named Segment Labels.dwg located in the Chapter 06 class data folder.

2. Click the Madison Lane alignment, and then click Add Labels ➢ Add Alignment Labels.

3. In the Add Labels dialog box, do the following:

    a. For Label Type, select Single Segment.

    b. For Line Label Style, verify that Bearing Over Distance is selected.

    c. For Curve Label Style, verify that Curve Data is selected, and then click Add.

4. Zoom in, and click one of the tangents of Madison Lane. Notice the bearing and distance label that is created.

5. Press Esc to end the labeling command. Click the newly created label, and then click Flip Label on the ribbon. This swaps the position of the bearing and distance.

6. Select the label again, and this time select Reverse Label.

7. Click Add in the Add Labels dialog box. Then click the curve and the other tangent of Madison Lane to create two more labels in the drawing.

8. Press Esc to end the labeling command. Click the curve label, and then click the label's square grip and drag it to a clear location in the drawing.

9. In the Add Labels dialog box, change Label Type to Multiple Segment. Change Curve Label Style back to Curve Data.

10. Click Add, and then click anywhere on the Jordan Court alignment. All tangents and curves are labeled at once.

If you haven't already done so, download and install the files for Chapter 6 according to the instructions in this book's Introduction.

Notice what happens to the bearing: It switches from SW to NE (or vice versa, depending on where you clicked in step 4), but the numbers don't change.

This improves the appearance and readability of the label and automatically creates a leader pointing back to the curve.

11. Move the curve labels for Jordan Court to open areas in the drawing so that they are easier to read (see Figure 6.7).

12. Save and close the drawing.

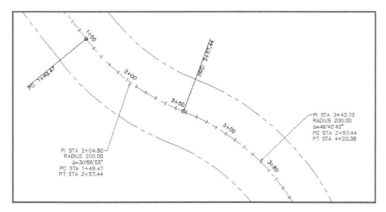

FIGURE 6.7   Curve labels added to the Jordan Court alignment. To improve readability, the labels have been dragged away from the alignment and into clear areas.

You can view the results of successfully completing this exercise by opening Segment Labels - Complete.dwg.

WHY BE A BEAR ABOUT BEARINGS?

If this is the first time you've seen bearings, you may not know what is going on here. A *bearing* is a way of expressing the direction of a line. In this exercise, the bearing of the eastern tangent of Madison Lane is S67°27'02.54"W. That means if you face south and then turn yourself toward the west about 67°, you'll be facing roughly in the direction that this line is pointing. Because there are 90° between south and west, you'll actually be facing more west than south.

When the bearing is reversed, it's like you've done an about-face and you're now facing 67° east of north. This doesn't change the appearance of the line, and it might seem picky to distinguish between SW and NE in this case. But when you think about it, the stationing of this road is increasing in a certain direction (west in the case of Madison Lane), which establishes the direction of the alignment. For consistency, it's a good idea for the direction of your bearing labels to agree with the direction of your alignment.

Using Tag Labels and Tables

Sometimes, it's better to put all the geometric data for an alignment in a table rather than labeling it right on the alignment itself. This can clear up a cluttered drawing and provide space for other types of annotations. You can accomplish this in Civil 3D by using tag labels and tables.

A *tag label* is a special kind of label that assigns a number to a curve, tangent, or spiral. Common examples are C1, S1, and L1 for a curve, spiral, and tangent, respectively. Tag labels can be created ahead of time if you know you're going to use a table, or you can convert regular labels to tag labels on the fly. In fact, you can convert just a few of the labels to tag labels and use a combination of a table and in-place labels to convey alignment information. This is common in cases where certain segments of an alignment are too short to have a label fit on them nicely.

As Murphy's Law would have it, the numbers you get when creating tag labels are almost never what you want them to be. This is no fault of the software; in fact, the reason for this happening so frequently is that the software is doing its job. Each time you create a tag label, Civil 3D bumps the next tag number up by one. Because most designs are laid out and labeled more than once (lots more, in most cases), your next tag number is likely to be set to something other than 1.

Fortunately, Civil 3D is quite good at enabling you to correct your tag labels. There is even a Renumber Tags command designed for that specific purpose.

Exercise 6.7: Create Tag Labels

If you haven't already done so, download and install the files for Chapter 6 according to the instructions in this book's Introduction.

In this exercise, you'll create and renumber tag labels for the Jordan Court alignment.

1. Open the drawing named Tag Labels.dwg located in the Chapter 06 class data folder.

2. Click the Jordan Court alignment, and then click Add Labels ➤ Add Alignment Labels on the contextual ribbon tab.

3. In the Add Labels dialog box, select Multiple Segment as the label type.

4. Verify that Circle Tag is selected for both Line Label Style and Curve Label Style.

5. Click Add, and then click anywhere on the Jordan Court alignment. Press Esc to end the labeling command.

   As you can see in Figure 6.8, curve and line tag labels have been created, but the numbering is not what it should be. You'll address this in the next few steps.

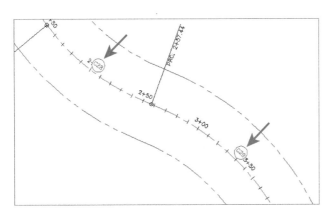

F I G U R E   6 . 8   Curve tag labels on the Jordan Court alignment

6. Close the Add Labels dialog box. Click the Jordan Court alignment, and then select Renumber Tags on the contextual ribbon tab.

7. On the command line, type **S** for settings, and press Enter.

8. Change all values to **1** in the Table Tag Numbering dialog box, and click OK.

9. Starting at the beginning of the Jordan Court alignment, click each tag label in order from start to end.

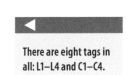

There are eight tags in all: L1–L4 and C1–C4.

10. Save and close the drawing.

You can view the results of successfully completing this exercise by opening Tag Labels - Complete.dwg.

Creating Tables

Once you have created all the tag labels and numbered them correctly, you're ready to create a table. Civil 3D provides four types of alignment tables that you can insert into your drawing: line, curve, spiral, and segment. A segment table is a combination of the other three tables.

When you create a table in your drawing, you have full control over which data is included in it. You can choose to provide table data for the entire alignment, you can tell Civil 3D to seek out certain label styles and include them in your table, or you can handpick the labels from the drawing by selecting them directly.

As you'll find with all Civil 3D tables, they are dynamically linked to the objects for which they display data. In the case of alignments, as the alignment is modified, the table updates automatically. There is even an option to create additional table entries as new tangents, curves, or spirals are created in the process of editing. Imagine how much time is saved by not having to go back and check all the numbers in a table each time an alignment is tweaked.

Exercise 6.8: Create a Table

If you haven't already done so, download and install the files for Chapter 6 according to the instructions in this book's Introduction.

In this exercise, you'll create a table for the tag labels you created and renumbered in the previous exercise.

1. Open the drawing named Create Table.dwg located in the Chapter 06 class data folder.

2. Click the Jordan Court alignment, and then click Add Tables ➢ Add Segments on the contextual ribbon tab.

3. In the Alignment Table Creation dialog box, click the Select By Label Or Style option.

4. If you're unable to read the label style names, click and drag the lower-right corner of the dialog box to the right to increase its size. Then click and drag the line between the Label Style Name and Selection Rule column headings to widen the Label Style Name column. Repeat these actions as needed until you can see the full names of the label styles listed.

5. Check the boxes in the Apply column for Alignment Curve: Circle Tag and Alignment Line: Circle Tag.

6. Click OK. Click a point in an open area of the drawing to insert the table. The table reflects the geometric data for the alignment (see Figure 6.9).

Jordan Court				
Number	Radius	Length	Line/Chord Direction	Start Station
L1		149.47	S38° 17' 44.49"E	0+00.00
C1	200.00	107.97	S53° 45' 42.11"E	1+49.47
C2	200.00	162.94	S45° 53' 18.59"E	2+57.44
L2		762.92	S22° 32' 57.46"E	4+20.38
C3	50.00	78.54	S22° 27' 02.54"W	11+83.29
L3		504.04	S67° 27' 02.54"W	12+61.83
C4	200.00	140.13	S87° 31' 23.49"W	17+65.88
L4		541.45	N72° 24' 15.56"W	19+06.01

FIGURE 6.9   An alignment segment table for Jordan Court

7. Save and close the drawing.

You can view the results of successfully completing this exercise by opening Create Table - Complete.dwg.

NOW YOU KNOW

Now that you have completed this chapter, you're able to annotate alignments. You can apply styles to change the appearance and content of alignment labels that already exist in a drawing. You can apply groups of labels to handle stationing, tick marks, and geometry points throughout an entire alignment. You know how to leverage label sets so that you can be more efficient when using the same label configurations with multiple alignments. You can label individual points of interest with station/offset labels and convey even more geometric information using segment labels. When drawings become too cluttered, you can use tag labels and tables to provide a clean and organized approach for displaying information about an alignment. Now that you have completed this chapter, you're ready to begin creating and modifying alignment labels and tables in a production environment.

Designing Vertically Using Profiles

Now that the paths of the roads have been established as alignments representing their centerlines, we'll look at the answers to these questions: What will it be like to travel along those paths? Will the terrain be steep or flat? Will it change much from one end of the road to the other? Will it require earth to be moved to smooth out the bumps in the road?

In Chapter 4, "Modeling the Existing Terrain Using Surfaces," you learned how existing ground surfaces can be used to analyze the shape of the ground. Although surfaces can be quite effective for this purpose, you're looking for something that tells you specifically what the terrain is like in relation to the road alignment. Once you have learned that, you'll be looking for an effective way to redesign the terrain to create a nice, smooth road.

Whether you're analyzing the terrain along an alignment or redesigning it, the tool that is most effective is the profile. Profiles allow you to show a slice through the ground along a specific alignment. This provides you with a clear and direct visualization of changes in terrain so that you can assess existing conditions and improve your design if necessary.

In this chapter, you'll learn to:

▶ **Create surface profiles**

▶ **Display profiles in profile views**

▶ **Create design profiles**

▶ **Edit profiles**

▶ **Apply design check sets and criteria files**

Creating Surface Profiles

Certification
Objective

One of the first steps in designing the vertical aspect of a linear feature is to analyze the shape of the existing terrain along that feature. You've learned how surfaces are used to create 3D models of the shape of the ground. You've also learned that there are many potential uses for surfaces other than displaying contours or labeling spot elevations. One of these uses is the creation of profiles from surface data, which helps with the design of linear features such as roads, channels, pipelines, and so on.

When a profile is created based on the data within a surface, it's aptly named a *surface profile*. A surface profile maintains a dynamic link to the surface it references. In fact, a surface profile is tied to both the alignment and the surface used to create it. If either one changes, the surface profile is updated.

> If you haven't already done so, download and install the files for Chapter 7 according to the instructions in this book's Introduction.

Exercise 7.1: Create a Surface Profile

In this exercise, you'll create a surface profile along the Jordan Court alignment.

> Because the majority of the work in this chapter is done in profile view, the drawings aren't configured with multiple viewports.

1. Open the drawing named Surface Profile.dwg located in the Chapter 07 class data folder.

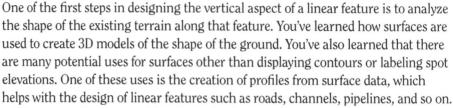

2. Click the Jordan Court alignment in the drawing, and then click Surface Profile on the contextual ribbon tab.

3. In the Create Profile From Surface dialog box, verify that Jordan Court is selected as the alignment.

4. Under Select Surfaces, select EG. Click Add, and then click OK.

5. In Prospector, expand Alignments ➤ Centerline Alignments ➤ Jordan Court ➤ Profiles. You should see EG – Surface (1) listed under Profiles.

   You should also notice a small orange triangle next to Jordan Court. This indicates that there are objects in the drawing that are dependent on this alignment. In this case, the dependent object is the profile you just created.

6. Right-click EG – Surface (1) and select Properties.

> EGCL stands for *existing ground centerline*.

7. On the Information tab of the Profile Properties dialog box, change Name to **Jordan Court EGCL**. Click OK.

   Although Prospector shows you that a profile has been created, you have nothing graphical to view. To display a graphical representation of the profile in your drawing, you need a profile view, which takes us to the next section.

8. Save and close the drawing.

You can view the results of successfully completing this exercise by opening Surface Profile - Complete.dwg.

Displaying Profiles in Profile Views

In the AutoCAD® Civil 3D® software, you must use a *profile view* to display a profile. A profile view is basically a grid that represents stations in the x direction and elevations in the y direction. The stations along the alignment and their corresponding elevations are plotted on this grid, and the resulting line represents changes in the terrain along the alignment. The profile view also includes various types of labels, such as axis labels and axis titles, to provide context to the display of the profile. Profile views can be further augmented with bands, which will be covered in Chapter 8, "Displaying and Annotating Profiles."

Certification Objective

If you haven't already done so, download and install the files for Chapter 7 according to the instructions in this book's Introduction.

Exercise 7.2: Create a Profile View

In this exercise, you'll create a profile view to display the surface profile that you created in the previous exercise.

1. Open the drawing named Profile View.dwg located in the Chapter 07 class data folder.

2. Click the Jordan Court alignment, and then click Profile View on the contextual ribbon tab.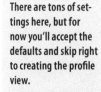

There are tons of settings here, but for now you'll accept the defaults and skip right to creating the profile view.

3. In the Create Profile View – General dialog box, click Create Profile View.

4. When prompted for the profile view origin, click a point in the open area to the east of the project.

A new profile view is inserted into the drawing, as shown in Figure 7.1.

The profile view origin is the lower-left corner of the profile view.

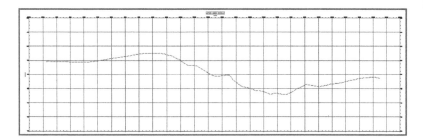

F I G U R E 7 . 1   **The newly created profile view**

5. Save and close the drawing.

You can view the results of successfully completing this exercise by opening
`Profile View - Complete.dwg`.

Now you have your first look at the nature of the terrain along the Jordan
Court alignment. As you study the profile, you see a relatively flat area at the
beginning, a fairly steep drop into a low area, and then a gradual rise for the
remaining third of the alignment. The appearance of the line is somewhat jag-
ged, which indicates moderately rough terrain. In just a short time, you have
created a graphical depiction of what it would be like to travel down the path of
the road as it exists right now. From this image, you can begin to visualize the
adjustments that will be needed to create a smooth and safe driving experience.

Creating Design Profiles

Certification
Objective
Earlier, you used a surface profile to determine the nature of the existing terrain along the path of Jordan Court. As the surface profile shows, the current
state of this path isn't suitable for driving, so it must be transformed into something with much more subtle geometry. In other words, a new profile must be
designed for the road. In Civil 3D, this type of profile is often referred to as a
design profile or *layout profile*.

Like alignments, design profiles consist of straight-line segments (called
tangents) and the curves that connect them. The curve geometry is a bit different, but essentially you can think of a design profile as an alignment turned
on its side. The process of laying out a profile is very similar to laying out an
alignment, right down to the Profile Layout Tools toolbar, which bears a strik-
ing resemblance to the Alignment Layout Tools toolbar.

If you haven't already
done so, download
and install the files for
Chapter 7 according to
the instructions in the
Introduction.

FGCL stands for *finished
ground centerline*.

Exercise 7.3: Design a Profile

In this exercise, you'll create a design profile representing the finished ground
centerline elevations for Jordan Court.

1. Open the drawing named `Design Profile.dwg` located in the
   `Chapter 07` class data folder.

2. Click one of the grid lines for the Jordan Court profile view, and then
   click Profile Creation Tools on the contextual ribbon.

3. In the Create Profile – Draw New dialog box, enter **Jordan Court FGCL**
   for Name.

PROFILE TERMINOLOGY

Familiarizing yourself with the following terms will be helpful as you work with design profiles:

Tangent   The straight-line portions of a profile.

PVI (Point of Vertical Intersection)   The location where two tangents intersect.

PVC (Point of Vertical Curvature)   The beginning of a vertical curve.

PVT (Point of Vertical Tangency)   The end of a vertical curve.

Parabolic Curve   A vertical curve that doesn't have a constant radius and follows the shape of a parabola.

Circular Curve   A vertical curve that has a constant radius.

Asymmetric Curve   A vertical curve that is created from two back-to-back parabolic curves.

Crest Curve   A vertical curve at the top of a hill where the grade leading into the curve is greater than the grade leading out. The PVI is located above the curve.

Sag Curve   A vertical curve at the bottom of a valley where the grade leading into the curve is less than the grade leading out. The PVI is located below the curve.

4. Verify that Profile Style is set to Design Profile and Profile Label set is set to _No Labels. Click OK.

5. On the Profile Layout Tools toolbar, click the small black triangle on the far-left button to expand it, and then click Draw Tangents With Curves (see Figure 7.2).

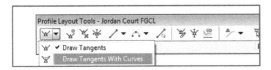

FIGURE 7.2   Invoking the Draw Tangents With Curves command

6. Press and hold the Shift key, and then right-click. Click Osnap Settings at the bottom of the context menu.

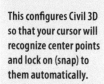

This configures Civil 3D so that your cursor will recognize center points and lock on (snap) to them automatically.

7. In the Drafting Settings dialog box, uncheck all boxes except Object Snap On (F3) and Center. Click OK.

8. Click the center of the circle marked A. Then click the remaining circles in order from left to right. Press Enter after clicking the circle marked G.

   The newly created profile consists of a PVI at each point you clicked. Because you used the Draw Tangents With Curves command, all PVIs (except for the begin and end points) also include a vertical curve.

9. Save and close the drawing.

   You can view the results of successfully completing this exercise by opening `Design Profile - Complete.dwg`.

Editing Profiles

As you learned in Chapter 5, "Designing in 2D Using Alignments," it is common (and often recommended) to lay out a rough version of a design and then apply a series of refinements to achieve the final design. This is especially true with profiles because the first pass is usually an attempt to match existing ground as closely as possible without creating too many of your own bumps in the road. Why try to match existing ground? Quite simply, it's cheaper. The closer your new road matches the existing terrain, the less earth will need to be moved to construct it. The cost of moving earth is measured by the volume of earth that is excavated, so less digging equals less cost.

After you create the initial profile that roughly matches existing ground, you must then refine the design based on various factors such as performance requirements for the road, avoiding overhead and underground obstacles, and ensuring that rainwater will drain properly. Many times, the adjustments you make are based not only on your own ideas but also on the input of others involved in the project. Whatever the case, a good set of tools for editing profiles is going to come in handy. Civil 3D provides a robust set of tools for editing profiles graphically and numerically.

Exercise 7.4: Edit a Profile with Grips

In yet another respect, profiles are similar to alignments in that they come equipped with specialized grips that enable editing to be done efficiently. In this exercise, you'll use grips to edit the Jordan Court design profile.

1. Open the drawing named Graphical Editing.dwg located in the Chapter 07 class data folder.

2. Click the blue Jordan Court FGCL profile to display its grips. Click the upright triangular grip located in the circle marked A1, and drag it to the center of the circle marked A2, as shown in Figure 7.3.

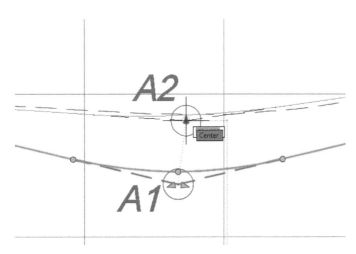

FIGURE 7.3   Moving a PVI grip

3. At the circle marked B1, click the triangle grip on the right and drag it to the center of the circle marked B2, as shown in Figure 7.4.

If you haven't already done so, download and install the files for Chapter 7 according to the instructions in the Introduction.

This is an example of moving the PVI grip, which changes the slope of both tangents, maintains the length of the curve, and keeps the curve tangent at both ends.

This type of grip moves the PVI along the slope of one of the tangents.

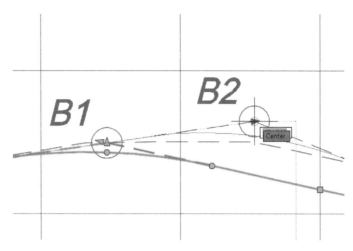

FIGURE 7.4   Moving a tangent slope grip

4. Click the square grip at the center of circle C1, and move it to the center of circle C2, as shown in Figure 7.5.

> This grip moves a tangent while keeping its slope constant. The result is that the PVIs at either end of the tangent are raised or lowered, and the curve geometry associated with them must update.

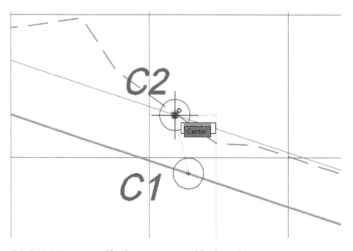

FIGURE 7.5   Moving a tangent midpoint grip

5. Click the circular grip located at the center of circle D1, and move it to the center of circle D2, as shown in Figure 7.6.

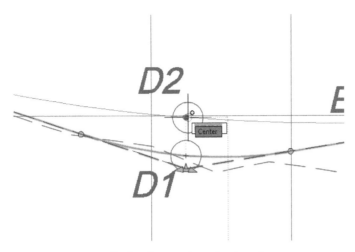

FIGURE 7.6   Moving the pass-through point grip

This is an example of moving the pass-through grip, forcing the curve to pass through a given point while adjusting the length of the curve.

6. Click the circular grip at the center of circle E1, and move it to the center of circle E2, as shown in Figure 7.7.

For vertical curves, the curve length refers to the horizontal distance from the beginning of the curve to the end.

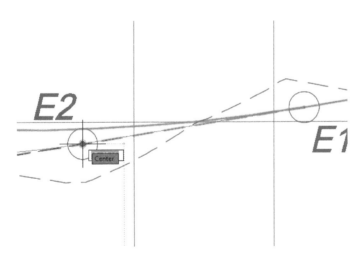

FIGURE 7.7   Moving the start point or endpoint grip

This is an example of moving the endpoint grip of the curve, which also moves the start point to adjust the length of the curve.

7. Save and close the drawing.

You can view the results of successfully completing this exercise by opening Graphical Editing - Complete.dwg.

PROFILE LOCKING

You may wonder what happens to a profile when the alignment is edited. For surface profiles, the answer is simple: the profile updates to match the new path of the alignment. For design profiles, the answer is a little more complicated due to a feature called profile locking. You'll find this feature as a tab on the Profile Properties dialog. With this feature, you can link profile geometry with alignment geometry, and Civil 3D will attempt to keep key features of both aligned.

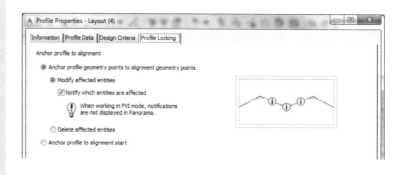

If you haven't already done so, download and install the files for Chapter 7 according to the instructions in the Introduction.

Exercise 7.5: Edit a Profile Using the Profile Layout Tools

Grips are wonderful tools for editing geometry that is already there, but what if you need to add a PVI or draw a curve? For that, you need the Profile Layout Tools toolbar (see Figure 7.8). This toolbar is the same one you would use to create a profile initially.

FIGURE 7.8   Profile Layout Tools toolbar

In this exercise, you'll use the Profile Layout Tools to edit the Jordan Court profile to better match existing ground and to simplify the design.

1. Open the drawing named Editing Tools.dwg located in your Chapter 07 class data folder.

2. Click the Jordan Court FGCL profile, and then click Geometry Editor on the ribbon.
   This opens the Profile Layout Tools toolbar.

3. On the Profile Layout Tools toolbar, click Insert PVI. While holding down the Shift key, right-click and select Endpoint.

4. Zoom in to the left end of the profile, and click the sharp break in the existing ground profile that is located at the center of the circle marked A.

   This sharp break is the edge of the existing road that the new road will tie into.

5. On the Profile Layout Tools toolbar, click Delete PVI. Then click in the circle marked B. Doing so deletes the PVI at this location and removes the slight bend in the profile.

6. On the Profile Layout Tools toolbar, click Insert PVIs – Tabular.

7. In the Insert PVIs dialog box, enter **19+10** (0+582) for Station and **174.00** (53.000) for Elevation.

8. Press the Enter key to create a new line. Then enter **21+55** (0+655) for Station and **173.5** (52.750) for Elevation. Click OK.

   This creates two new PVIs located near the centers of the circles marked C and D.

9. On the Profile Layout Tools toolbar, click the black triangle to the right of the curves button to view the curves menu. Select More Free Vertical Curves ≻ Free Vertical Parabola (PVI Based), as shown in Figure 7.9.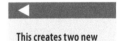

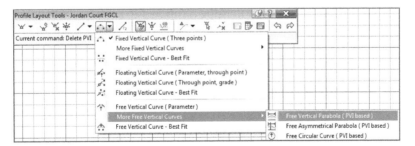

FIGURE 7.9 **Clicking the Free Vertical Parabola (PVI Based) command**

10. Click in the circle marked C. Type **150** (**45**), and press Enter to provide the curve length.

11. Click in the circle marked D. At the command line, type **200** (**60**) for the curve length, and press Enter.

12. Press Enter to end the command.

13. Save and close the drawing.

You can view the results of successfully completing this exercise by opening Editing Tools - Complete.dwg.

Exercise 7.6: Edit a Profile Using Profile Grid View

If you haven't already done so, download and install the files for Chapter 7 according to the instructions in this book's Introduction.

At times, you may want to adjust your design by telling Civil 3D the exact dimension of a portion of the profile. You can do this in one of two different ways. The first is using Profile Grid View, which opens a tab in Panorama. This tab shows the geometry of the profile in table form and enables you to edit some of the values to adjust the design. The second way, using component-level editing, will be covered in the next exercise.

In this exercise, you'll use Profile Grid View to make some edits to the PVI stations and elevations of the Jordan Court design profile.

1. Open the drawing named Profile Grid View.dwg located in the Chapter 07 class data folder.

2. Click the Jordan Court FGCL profile, and then click Geometry Editor on the ribbon.

3. Click Profile Grid View to open the Profile Entities tab and display the numerical version of the profile geometry.

4. Change the Station value for Item 3 to **2+70.00** (**0+080.00**) and the PVI Elevation value to **188.00** (**57.00**).

5. Change the remaining items as follows:

You don't have to type the plus signs in these entries. For example, instead of typing **8+55.00 (0+260)**, you can just type **855** (**260**), and Civil 3D will automatically fill in the required plus signs.

Item	Station	PVI Elevation
4	8+55.00 (0+260)	196.50 (60.0)
5	10+50.00 (0+320)	188.50 (57.5)
6	16+90.00 (0+515)	164.00 (50.0)

6. Close Panorama.

The drawing may not look very different than before because the changes you made were very subtle.

7. Save and close the drawing.

You can view the results of successfully completing this exercise by opening `Profile Grid View - Complete.dwg`.

KEEP IT SIMPLE

As you might have guessed, the main objective of Exercise 7.6 is simplification of the profile design. In most cases, the stations or elevations don't need to be located with a precision of 0.01, so why not round them off to nice, even numbers? The contractor and surveyor who are staking out the design in the field will appreciate this rounding because there will be fewer digits to keep track of and a bit less potential for error.

The PVIs of items 1, 2, and 9 were not rounded because these are specific locations and elevations that need to be met. Items 7 and 8 were already entered as round numbers when you used the Insert PVIs – Tabular command in the previous exercise.

Exercise 7.7: Edit a Profile Using Component-Level Editing

The second method for editing the profile design numerically is referred to as component-level editing. With this approach, you open the numerical data for a piece of the profile (such as a line or vertical curve) in a separate window. You do this by clicking the Sub-entity Editor button on the Profile Layout Tools toolbar and then using the Pick Sub-entity tool to choose the part of the profile you want to edit.

In this exercise, you'll use component-level editing to make some more changes to the Jordan Court design profile.

1. Open the drawing named `Profile Component Level Editing.dwg` located in the `Chapter 07` class data folder.

2. Click the Jordan Court profile, and then click Geometry Editor on the ribbon.

If you haven't already done so, download and install the files for Chapter 7 according to the instructions in this book's Introduction.

3. Click Profile Layout Parameters on the Profile Layout Tools toolbar to display the Profile Layout Parameters dialog box. (This dialog box is blank when it first appears.)

This populates the Profile Layout Parameters dialog box with data.

4. Click Select PVI, and then click near the curve at the lowest point on the Jordan Court FGCL profile.

5. Change Profile Curve Length to 275 (80). Close the Profile Layout Parameters dialog box and the Profile Layout Tools toolbar.

Again, the drawing doesn't appear to change much because the edit you made was so subtle.

6. Save and close the drawing.

You can view the results of successfully completing this exercise by opening Profile Component Level Editing - Complete.dwg.

Using Design Check Sets and Criteria Files

You first learned about design criteria files and check sets in Chapter 5. These two features enable you to check your design on the fly to catch any errors or design flaws as you work. Of course, what's considered right can differ from place to place and from design type to design type, so these checking tools are customizable. The task of setting them up is usually left to a CAD manager or one of the top CAD users in your company or organization. This is true of most Civil 3D customizations.

As discussed in Chapter 5, the actual details of how design criteria files and check sets are configured can be driven by government entities, such as a department of transportation or planning commission, or according to your own personal design standards or those adopted by your company. Whatever the case, you should be careful not to rely on them 100 percent. Even while using design criteria files and check sets, a solid understanding of design principles is a must. These tools are just a way of making sure you're applying what you already know, not a substitute for knowing it in the first place.

Exercise 7.8: Apply a Design Check Set

If you haven't already done so, download and install the files for Chapter 7 according to the instructions in this book's Introduction.

As you learned earlier, a design check set is a collection of one or more design checks. For profiles, there are two types of design checks: line and curve. When a design check set is applied to a profile, Civil 3D flags any violations with a triangular yellow shield marked with an exclamation point. You can hover over the shield to get more information about the violation.

In this exercise, you'll apply a design check set to the Jordan Court profile and then make some edits to address design violations.

1. Open the drawing named Design Check Set.dwg located in the Chapter 07 class data folder.

2. Click the Jordan Court FGCL profile, and then click Profile Properties on the ribbon.

3. In the Profile Properties dialog box, click the Design Criteria tab and check the box next to Use Criteria-Based Design.

4. Check the Use Design Check Set box, and select Subdivision.

5. Click OK to close the Profile Properties dialog box. Press Esc to clear the grips on the profile and note the two yellow shields near the right end of the profile, as shown in Figure 7.10.

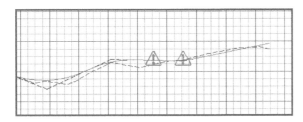

FIGURE 7.10   Warning symbols indicating design check set violations

6. Zoom in to the area where the warning symbols are displayed. Hover the cursor over the symbol on the left.

   The tooltip reports that the grade check is being violated for this tangent.

7. Click the profile to display its grips. Then click the PVI grip to the left of the warning symbol and move it upward.

8. Move the PVI down little by little until both tangent warning symbols disappear, indicating that you have satisfied the design check for both tangents.

9. Press Esc to clear the selection, and then hover your cursor over the remaining warning symbol.

This warning symbol disappears, but a new warning symbol may appear on the tangent to the left because the grade of this tangent now exceeds 5 percent.

This tooltip indicates that the minimum curve length of 3 (1) times the design speed isn't being met.

10. Click the profile to display the grips, and then click one of the circular grips at either end of the curve and move it outward to lengthen the curve. When you lengthen the curve enough, the warning symbol disappears.

11. Save and close the drawing.

You can view the results of successfully completing this exercise by opening Design Check Set - Complete.dwg.

Exercise 7.9: Apply a Design Criteria File

If you haven't already done so, download and install the files for Chapter 7 according to the instructions in this book's Introduction.

As you did with alignments, you can assign design criteria files to a profile. The general behavior of design criteria files is the same as it is for design checks: they display warning symbols when certain design parameters aren't met. However, behind the scenes, design criteria files are much more sophisticated than design check sets, and you can use them to check more types of geometric criteria.

In this exercise, you'll apply a design criteria file to the Jordan Court profile and then make some edits to address design violations.

1. Open the drawing named Design Criteria File.dwg located in the Chapter 07 class data folder.

2. Click the Jordan Court FGCL profile, and select Profile Properties on the ribbon.

3. Click the Design Criteria tab. Check the boxes next to Use Criteria-Based Design and Use Design Criteria File.

4. Click the button to the right of the file path, and select the file named Autodesk Civil 3D Imperial (2011) Roadway Design Standards .xml (Autodesk Civil 3D Metric (2011) Roadway Design Standards.xml). Click Open.

New warning symbols appear on several of the vertical curves.

5. Verify that the box next to Use Design Check Set is unchecked.

6. Click OK, and press Esc to clear the selection.

Because passing won't be allowed anywhere in the subdivision, you can ignore this warning.

7. Hover your cursor over the warning symbol farthest to the left.
   The tooltip reports that the minimum passing sight distance isn't being met (see Figure 7.11).

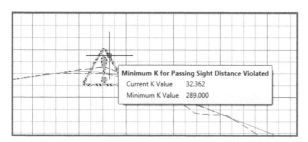

FIGURE 7.11   Warning symbol with a tooltip reporting that the passing-sight-distance criterion isn't being met

8. Hover your cursor over the warning symbol at the lowest point of the profile.

9. Click the Jordan Court FGCL profile, and then click Geometry Editor on the contextual ribbon tab.

10. On the Profile Layout Tools toolbar, click Profile Grid View.

11. In Panorama, scroll to the right until you can view the Minimum K For Headlight Sight Distance column.

    Note that a warning symbol appears in the row for Item 6 and that the required K value is 26.000 (9.000), as shown in Figure 7.12.

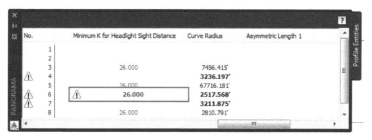

FIGURE 7.12   A warning symbol in Panorama indicating a violation of the headlight-sight-distance criterion

12. Scroll to the left until you can see the K Value column. Change the K value for Item 6 to **26** (**9**).

13. Change Profile Curve Length for Item 6 to **225** (**75**). This generates a K value of 27.193 (9.010), so the warning symbol is still suppressed.

14. Save and close the drawing.

You can view the results of successfully completing this exercise by opening Design Criteria File - Complete.dwg.

This curve isn't meeting the requirement for minimum headlight sight distance. This is a requirement that should be honored.

This removes the warning symbol and changes the curve length to 215.128 (74.914). To practice good design, you'll round that value in step 13.

What's So Special about K?

The K value is a way of expressing the abruptness of a vertical curve. If you've ever been driving on a country road and caught air at the top of a hill or smacked your head on the dashboard at the bottom of a hill, then you've experienced a K value that is too low for your speed. The K value is calculated as a ratio between the curve length and the change in grade. Longer, more subtle curves have a higher K value, which equates to greater safety because the change in grade is spread out over a longer distance.

Headlight sight distance is an important design parameter for all road designs. If the peaks and valleys of the road don't allow headlights to illuminate obstacles within an acceptable distance, then the road is considered unsafe. The acceptable distance varies based on design speed. Obstacles need to be detected much farther away at higher design speeds to allow the driver enough time to react.

Now You Know

Now that you have completed this chapter, you're able to create, display, analyze, and modify profiles—both existing and proposed. You can show the nature of the existing terrain along an alignment by creating a surface profile and showing it in a profile view. You can construct the proposed elevations of a road or other item by creating a design profile. Once the design profile is in place, you know how to edit it using a variety of tools—some graphical, some command driven, and some numerical. You can check your design by applying design check sets and design criteria files and then make edits to address violations reported by those features. You're ready to begin working with profiles on real projects in a production environment.

CHAPTER 8

Displaying and Annotating Profiles

Now that you have captured the nature of the existing ground along the road centerlines using surface profiles, and you have reshaped it using layout profiles, it's time to specify how you intend your design to be built. A wavy line in the drawing simply isn't enough information for a contractor to start building your design. You need to provide specific geometric information about the profile so that it can be re-created in the field. This is done with various types of annotations available in the AutoCAD® Civil 3D® software.

It's also important that the framework in which the profiles are displayed is properly configured. As you learned in the previous chapter, the grid lines and grid annotations behind your profiles form a profile view. In this chapter, you'll look at applying different profile view styles to control what information about your profiles is displayed and in what manner.

Finally, it's often necessary to show other things in a profile view that might impact the construction of whatever the profile represents. Pipe crossings, underground structures, rock layers, and many other features may need to be displayed so that you can avoid them or integrate your design with them. One way of showing these items in your profile view is through a Civil 3D function called object projection.

In this chapter, you'll learn to:

▶ **Change the display of profiles with profile styles**

▶ **Configure profile views using profile view styles**

▶ **Share information through profile view bands**

▶ **Add detail using profile labels**

▶ **Work efficiently using profile label sets**

▶ **Add detail using profile view labels**

▶ **Project objects to profile views**

Applying Profile Styles

As with any object style, you can use profile styles to show profiles in different ways for different purposes. Specifically, you can use profile styles to affect the appearance of profiles in three basic ways. The first is to control which components of the profile are visible. You might be surprised to know that there are potentially eight different components of a profile, and you can change a profile's appearance dramatically by changing the visibility of those components. The second is to control the graphical properties of the components, such as layer, color, linetype, and so on. Finally, a profile style enables you to control the display of markers at key geometric points along the profile. Once again, you might be surprised at the number of types of points that can be marked along a profile: there are 11 of them.

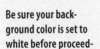

If you haven't already done so, download and install the files for Chapter 8 according to the instructions in this book's Introduction.

Exercise 8.1: Apply Profile Styles

In this exercise, you'll assign different profile styles to a profile and observe the different ways profiles can be represented.

1. Open the drawing named Profile Styles.dwg located in the Chapter 08 class data folder.

   Because the majority of the work in this chapter is done in profile view, the drawings aren't set up with multiple viewports.

Be sure your background color is set to white before proceeding with these steps.

2. In the Jordan Court profile view, click the red existing-ground profile, and then click Profile Properties on the ribbon.

3. On the Information tab of the Profile Properties dialog box, change the style to _No Display. Then click OK.

   The profile disappears from view.

USING A STYLE TO HIDE AN OBJECT

In step 3 of Exercise 8.1, you use the style _No Display to hide the profile—something you might normally do by turning off or freezing a layer. This method of making things disappear via style is used quite a bit in Civil 3D. In fact, if you look in the stock template that ships with Civil 3D, you'll see a _No Display style for nearly every object type.

(Continues)

USING A STYLE TO HIDE AN OBJECT *(Continued)*

Using this approach has a couple of advantages over turning layers on and off. First, many Civil 3D objects have multiple components that can be displayed on different layers. Changing one style is more efficient than changing several layers, so it becomes easier and quicker to control the visibility of components by style. Second, you may not know which layer or layers need to be turned off to make the object disappear from view. By simply applying the _No Display style, you make the items disappear without considering layers at all.

4. Press Esc to clear the selection of the existing ground profile. Then click the black design profile for Jordan Court. Right-click, and select Properties.

5. In the Properties window, change the Style property to Layout, and press Esc to clear the grips.

The profile now shows curves and lines as different colors and includes markers that clearly indicate where there are key geometry points (see Figure 8.1). This might be helpful while you're in the process of laying out the profile, but it may not work well when you're using the profile to create a final drawing.

You can also use the specific Profile Properties command to access the style assignment. To show it a different way, however, in step 5 you use the generic Properties command instead.

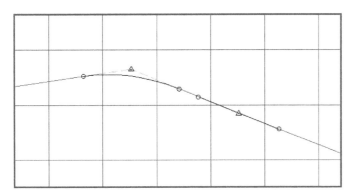

FIGURE 8.1　The Layout profile style displays lines and curves with different colors as well as markers at key geometric locations.

This is a very simple style that shows just the basic geometry with no markers or color differences.

6. Select the Jordan Court profile again. In the Properties window, change the style to Basic.

7. Change the style to Design Profile With Markers.

   This style is an example of how you might represent a profile in a final drawing. It displays lines and curves on the standard road profile layer, includes markers that are typically used for annotation, and shows the line extensions as dashed lines.

8. In Prospector, expand Alignments ➢ Centerline Alignments ➢ Jordan Court ➢ Profiles. Right-click Jordan Court EGCL and select Properties, as shown in Figure 8.2.

Remember that this profile was set to _No Display so we can't pick it in the drawing. One way to get to it is through the Prospector tab.

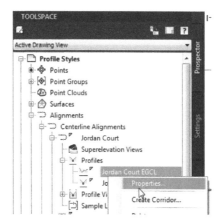

F I G U R E 8 . 2   Using Prospector to access the Properties command for the Jordan Court EGCL profile

9. Change the style to Existing Ground Profile, and click OK so the drawing it looks like it did when you started this exercise.

10. Save and close the drawing.

You can view the results of successfully completing this exercise by opening `Profile Styles - Complete.dwg`.

Applying Profile View Styles

Certification
Objective

Styles are especially important when you're working with profile views because of their potential to dramatically affect the appearance of the data that is being presented. Among other things, profile view styles can affect vertical exaggeration, spacing of the grid lines, and labeling.

Exercise 8.2: Apply Profile View Styles

In this exercise, you'll assign different profile view styles and observe how they can change the way profile information is presented.

If you haven't already done so, download and install the files for Chapter 8 according to the instructions in this book's Introduction.

1. Open the drawing named Profile View Style.dwg located in the Chapter 08 class data folder.

2. Click one of the grid lines of the Jordan Court profile view, right-click, and select Properties.

3. In the Properties window, change the style to Major & Minor Grids 10V. Press Esc to clear the selection.
   Note the additional grid lines that appear (see Figure 8.3).

10V refers to a vertical exaggeration that is 10 times that of the horizontal. Note that in the Properties window, the current profile view style is named Major Grids 10V.

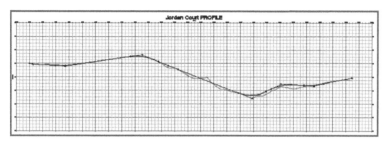

FIGURE 8.3   Additional grid lines displayed as a result of applying the Major & Minor Grids 10V profile view style

4. Select the profile view grid, and change the style to Major Grids 5V.
   With this change, the vertical exaggeration is reduced to 5. This makes the profile appear much flatter.

5. Change the style to Major Grids 1V.

This displays the profile in its true form, as it really exists in the field. Think about which profile would be easier to work with: the exaggerated one, where the peaks and valleys are obvious, or this one, which is true to scale but much more difficult to analyze?

IT'S OK TO EXAGGERATE SOMETIMES

Vertical exaggeration is a common practice used to display information in profile view. In most places, the earth is relatively flat, and changes in elevation are subtle. To make the peaks and valleys stand out a bit more, the elevations are exaggerated while the horizontal distances are kept the same. The result is a profile that appears to have higher high points, lower low points, and steeper slopes in between. This makes the terrain easier to visualize and analyze.

(Continues)

IT'S OK TO EXAGGERATE SOMETIMES *(Continued)*

When this technique is used, you'll likely see a pair of scales assigned to the drawing: one that represents the horizontal scale and one that represents the vertical scale. For example, a drawing that has a horizontal scale of 1" = 50' and a vertical scale of 1" = 5' is employing a vertical exaggeration factor of 10. For a metric example, a horizontal drawing scale of 1:500 and a vertical drawing scale of 1:50 also achieves a vertical exaggeration of 10.

The following three profile views have a vertical exaggeration of 10, 5, and 1, from left to right. The same existing ground profile is shown as a red line in all three.

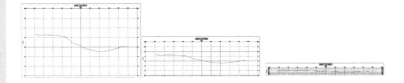

DOT stands for *Department of Transportation*, which in the United States is a common way of referring to government regulatory departments and other agencies that manage roads and other transportation infrastructure.

6. Change the style of the profile view to DOT.

   This is an example of how the graphical standards of a client or review agency can be built into your Civil 3D standard styles, making it easy to meet the requirements of others.

7. Save and close the drawing.

You can view the results of successfully completing this exercise by opening `Profile View Style - Complete.dwg`.

Applying Profile View Bands

Profile view bands can be added to a profile view along the top or bottom axis. You can use these bands to provide additional textual or graphical information about a profile. They can be configured to provide this information at even increments or at specific locations along the profile.

Exercise 8.3: Apply Profile View Bands

In this exercise, you'll configure bands for the Jordan Court profile view so that information about stations, elevations, and horizontal geometry can be displayed.

1. Open the drawing named Profile View Bands.dwg located in the Chapter 08 class data folder.

2. Click one of the grid lines of the Jordan Court profile view, and then click Profile View Properties on the contextual ribbon tab.

3. On the Information tab of the Profile View Properties dialog box, change Object Style to Major & Minor Grids 10V.

4. Click the Bands tab. Verify that Profile Data is selected as Band Type.

5. Under Select Band Style, choose Elevations And Stations. Then click Add.

6. In the Geometry Points To Label In Band dialog box, on the Profile Points tab, select Jordan Court EGCL as Profile 1, as shown in Figure 8.4. Click OK.

   A new entry is added to the list of bands.

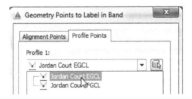

FIGURE 8.4   Assigning Jordan Court EGCL as Profile 1

7. In the Profile View Properties dialog box, scroll to the right until you see the Profile 2 column. Click the cell in this column, and select Jordan Court FGCL.

8. Click OK to dismiss the Profile View Properties dialog box and return to the drawing. Zoom in to the bottom of the profile view.

   Across the bottom of the profile view, there is now a band that labels the stations and elevations at even increments (see Figure 8.5).

If you haven't already done so, download and install the files for Chapter 8 according to the instructions in this book's Introduction.

Earlier, you used the Autodesk® AutoCAD® Properties window to change the profile view style. This is another way to do it.

You may have noticed the long list of geometry points in this dialog box. The band style you have selected doesn't include references to any of these points; therefore, no geometry point information will appear on the band.

This band is designed for two profiles, so there are two sets of elevations. The elevations on the left side of each line refer to the Jordan Court EGCL profile, and the ones on the right side refer to the Jordan Court FGCL profile.

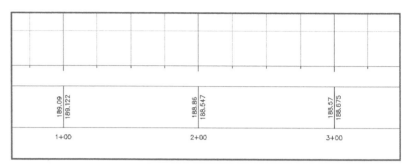

FIGURE 8.5 The newly added band showing stations, existing elevations (left), and proposed elevations (right)

9. Click the profile view, and select Profile View Properties from the ribbon again.

10. On the Bands tab, select Horizontal Geometry as Band Type.

Add>>

11. Under Select Band Style, choose Geometry, and click Add.

BAND SETS

Right after step 11 you could have clicked Save As Band Set and stored the two bands as a new band set. This band set could then be imported into another profile view at a later time. This feature is handy when you repeatedly use the same list of bands, enabling you to avoid rebuilding the list each time.

---

12. Click OK to dismiss the dialog box and return to the drawing.

The new band is a graphical representation of the alignment geometry. Upward bumps in the band represent curves to the right, and downward bumps represent curves to the left. The beginning and ending of each bump correspond with the beginning and ending of the associated curve. There are also labels that provide more specifics about the horizontal geometry.

13. Click the Jordan Court profile view; then click Profile View Properties on the ribbon.

14. On the Bands tab, click the Horizontal Geometry band entry, and then click the red X icon to remove it.

15. Click OK to return to the drawing.

16. Save and close the drawing.

   You can view the results of successfully completing this exercise by opening Profile View Bands - Complete.dwg.

The Horizontal Geometry band is removed from the bottom of the Jordan Court profile view.

Applying Profile Labels

Profile labels are similar to alignment labels. They're applied to the entire profile or to a range within the profile, and they show up wherever they encounter the things they're supposed to label. For example, if a vertical curve label is applied to a profile that has three vertical curves, then three vertical curve labels will appear. This approach offers two advantages. The first is that you can label multiple instances of a geometric feature with one command. This becomes significant when you're working on a long stretch of road with dozens of vertical curves. The other advantage is that labels appear as new geometric features are added. Continuing to use vertical curves as an example, if you apply a vertical curve label to a profile, curve labels will appear or disappear automatically whenever you create or delete vertical curves.

Certification Objective

If you haven't already done so, download and install the files for Chapter 8 according to the instructions in the Introduction.

Exercise 8.4: Apply Profile Labels

In this exercise, you'll configure the labels for the Jordan Court design profile so that tangent grades and curve data are labeled.

1. Open the drawing named Profile Labels.dwg located in the Chapter 08 class data folder.

2. Click the Jordan Court FGCL profile, and then click Edit Profile Labels on the ribbon.

3. In the Profile Labels – Jordan Court FGCL dialog box, select Crest Curves as Type.

4. Select Crest Only for Profile Crest Curve Label Style, and then click Add.

Refer to the sidebar "Profile Terminology" in Chapter 7 to review information about crest curves and sag curves.

Add>>

5. Click OK to return to the drawing. All the crest curves in the profile are labeled.

6. Click the Jordan Court FGCL profile, and then click Edit Profile Labels on the ribbon again. Add the following profile labels:

Type	Style
Sag Curves	Sag Only
Lines	Percent Grade
Grade Breaks	Station over Elevation

The list of labels should appear as shown in Figure 8.6.

The profile is now annotated with several types of labels. Some of the label positions need to be adjusted to improve readability, which you'll do next.

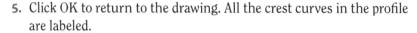
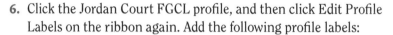
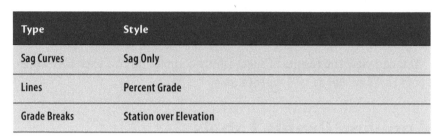

FIGURE 8.6   The list of labels to be applied to the Jordan Court FGCL profile

7. Click OK to close the Profile Labels – Jordan Court FGCL dialog box and return to the drawing. Press Esc to clear the selection in the drawing.

8. Zoom in to the third curve label from the left.

9. Click the label to show its grips. Then click the diamond-shaped grip at the base of the dimension text, and move it up until the label is more readable.

Notice how the curve-length dimension line is crossing through the profile.

10. Repeat step 9 for any other curve labels that need to be moved to improve readability.

11. Save and close the drawing.

You can view the results of successfully completing this exercise by opening `Profile Labels - Complete.dwg`.

Creating and Applying Profile Label Sets

In the previous exercise, you used several types of profile labels to annotate the design profile for Jordan Court. Each one had to be selected and added to the list of labels, making this a multistep process. A profile *label set* enables you to store a list of labels for use on another profile. The settings for each label—such as weeding, major station, minor station, and so on—can also be stored in the label set. This is quite helpful if you use the same profile labels for multiple profiles. A label set can even be stored in your company template so it's always there for you to use.

Exercise 8.5: Apply Profile Label Sets

In this exercise, you'll use a label set to capture the label configuration for Jordan Court and apply it easily to Logan Court.

If you haven't already done so, download and install the files for Chapter 8 according to the instructions in this book's Introduction.

1. Open the drawing named Profile Label Set.dwg located in the Chapter 08 class data folder.

2. Click the Jordan Court FGCL profile, and click Edit Profile Labels on the ribbon.

3. In the Profile Labels – Jordan Court FGCL dialog box, click Save Label Set to open the Profile Label Set – New Profile Label Set dialog box.

4. Click the Information tab, and enter **Curves-Grades-Breaks** for Name. Click OK twice to return to the drawing.

5. Press Esc to clear the selection of the Jordan Court FGCL profile. Zoom to the Logan Court profile view. Click the Logan Court FGCL profile, and select Edit Profile Labels on the ribbon.

6. In the Profile Labels – Logan Court FGCL dialog box, click Import Label Set.

7. Select Curve-Grades-Breaks in the Select Label Set dialog box, and then click OK. Click OK to dismiss the Profile Labels dialog box and return to the drawing.

   Two grade-break labels and a grade label have been added to the Logan Court FGCL profile (see Figure 8.7).

No curve labels appear on the profile because there are no curves. However, if a curve were added, a curve label would appear.

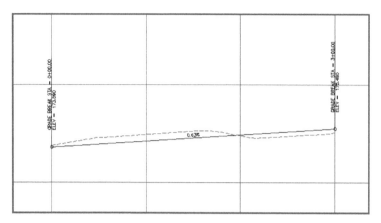

FIGURE 8.7 Logan Court FGCL profile after the newly created profile label set has been applied

8. Save and close the drawing.

You can view the results of successfully completing this exercise by opening Profile Label Set - Complete.dwg.

Creating Profile View Labels

You have just seen how useful profile labels can be because they are applied to the entire profile and continuously watch for new geometric properties to label. However, this dynamic nature may not be ideal in certain situations, or you may need to provide annotation in your profile view that isn't related to any profiles in that view. Profile view labels are the solution in this case.

Profile view labels are directly linked to the profile view: the grid, grid labeling, and bands that serve as the backdrop for one or more profiles. Because of this, you can use labels that are independent of any profiles. For example, you might use a station and offset label to call out the location of an underground obstruction crossing through the profile view. Because this object isn't directly affected by any profile in the drawing, it wouldn't make sense to associate this label with a profile. Instead, you would use a profile view label that is specifically intended for this object.

Three types of profile view labels are available in Civil 3D: station elevation, depth, and projection. You'll work with the first two in the next exercise, and the third will be covered later in this chapter.

Exercise 8.6: Apply Profile View Labels

In this exercise, you'll use profile view labels to label the location where Jordan Court ties in to Emerson Road, including the identification of the ditch area.

If you haven't already done so, download and install the files for Chapter 8 according to the instructions in this book's Introduction.

1. Open the drawing named Profile View Labels.dwg located in the Chapter 08 class data folder.

   This drawing is zoomed in to the left end of the Jordan Court FGCL profile. At this location, there is a PVI where the new road ties to the edge of the existing road. There is also a V-shape in the existing ground profile that shows the existence of a roadside drainage ditch (see Figure 8.8).

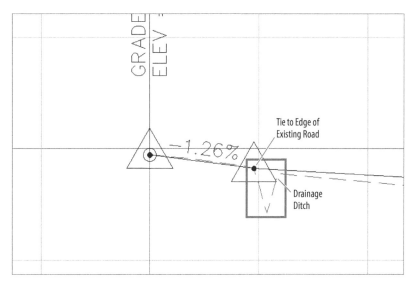

F I G U R E 8 . 8   The beginning of the Jordan Court FGCL profile, where there is a tie to the edge of the existing Emerson Road as well as a V-shaped drainage ditch

2. Click one of the grid lines for the Jordan Court profile view. On the ribbon, click Add View Labels ➤ Station Elevation.

3. While holding down the Shift key, right-click and select Endpoint from the context menu.

4. Click the center of the black-filled circle at the second PVI marker.

5. Repeat the previous two steps to specify the same point for the elevation.

   A new label appears, but it's overlapping the grade label to the left.

You must provide the location in two separate steps: first you specify the station (step 4), and then you specify the elevation (step 5).

6. Press Esc twice to clear the selection of the profile view and end the command. Then click the newly created label, and drag the square grip up and to the right. Click a point to indicate the new location of the label.

Nearly all Civil 3D labels can be edited in this way using the Edit Label Text command.

7. With the label still selected, click Edit Label Text on the ribbon.
   This opens the Text Component Editor.

8. In the text view window on the right, click just to the left of STA to place your cursor at that location. Press Enter to move that line of text down and provide a blank line to type on.

9. Click the blank line at the top, type **TIE TO EDGE**, and press Enter.

10. Type **OF EXIST ROAD**.
   The Text Component Editor dialog box should now look like Figure 8.9.

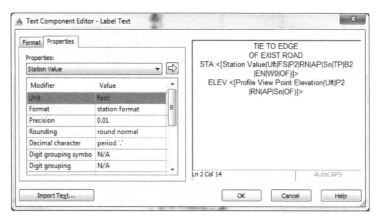

FIGURE 8.9   Additional text added to a label in the Text Component Editor dialog box

Invert is a term referring to the lowest elevation of the ditch. It's also used to refer to the lowest elevation of a pipe or a structure, such as a manhole or inlet.

11. Click OK to return to the drawing.
   The label now clearly calls out the station and elevation where the new road should tie to the existing road.

12. Press Esc to clear the current label selection. Click one of the grid lines of the profile view, and then click Add View Labels ➢ Depth.

13. Pick a point at the invert of the V-shaped ditch, and then pick a point just above it approximating the top of the ditch.

14. Press Esc twice to end the command and clear the selection of the profile view.

15. Click the newly created depth label, and then click one of the grips at the tip of either arrow. Move the grip to a new location, and note the change to the depth value displayed in the label.

   Both the station-elevation label and the depth label can be seen in Figure 8.10.

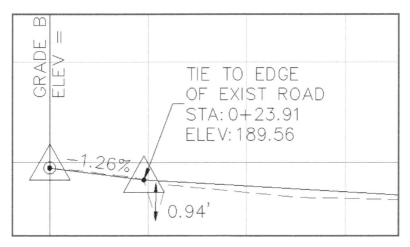

FIGURE 8.10   The station-elevation label and depth label added to the Jordan Court profile view

16. Save and close the drawing.

You can view the results of successfully completing this exercise by opening `Profile View Labels - Complete.dwg`.

REMEMBER EXAGGERATION?

The roughly 1-foot (0.3-meter) depth shown by the label might seem small to you, based on the dramatic plunge of the V in the profile. Remember that this profile view is exaggerated in the vertical aspect by a factor of 10. If you were to measure this same depth using the DISTANCE command, you would get about 10 feet (3 meters). Profile view labels automatically factor in the vertical exaggeration of your profile view.

Projecting Objects to Profile Views

At times, it may be necessary or helpful to show more in a profile view than just the existing and finished profiles of your design. Features such as underground pipes, overhead cables, trees, fences, and so on may be obstacles that you need to avoid or features that you need to integrate into your design. Whatever the case, Civil 3D object projection enables you to quickly represent a variety of objects in your profile view and provide the accompanying annotation.

Projecting Linear Objects

When you project an object to a profile view, different things can happen depending on the type of object you have chosen. For linear objects such as 3D polylines, feature lines, and survey figures, the projected version of the object is still linear, but it will appear distorted unless it's parallel to the alignment. This can be a bit tough to envision, but just imagine a light being shone from behind the object in the direction of the alignment. The projection of this object seen in a profile view would be somewhat like the shadow cast by the object. The parts of it that are parallel to the alignment would appear full length, and the parts that aren't parallel would appear shortened.

Based on the settings you choose, the elevations that are applied to a projected linear object can vary. For linear objects that are already drawn in 3D, you can choose to use the object elevations as they are. For 2D objects that need to have elevations provided, the elevations can be derived from a surface or profile.

Projecting Blocks and Points

Objects that indicate location—such as AutoCAD points, Civil 3D points, and blocks—are handled a bit differently than linear objects. They are represented with markers or as a projected version of the way they are drawn in plan view. This can lead to a distorted view of such objects because of the common practice of applying a vertical exaggeration to the profile view. The options for assigning elevations to these types of projections are the same as the options for linear objects, with one addition: the ability to provide an elevation manually. This allows you to specify the elevation graphically or numerically, independent of a surface, a profile, or the actual elevation of the object you've selected.

Exercise 8.7: Project Objects to Profile View

In this exercise, you'll use object projection to show a water line and some test borings on the Jordan Court profile view.

1. Open the drawing named Object Projection.dwg located in the Chapter 08 class data folder.

2. Click one of the grid lines of the Jordan Court profile view, and then click Project Objects To Profile View on the ribbon.

3. Zoom in to the eastern property line, and click the blue 3D polyline representing the water pipe that runs parallel to the eastern property line. Press Enter.

4. In the Project Objects To Profile View dialog box, verify that Style is set to Basic and Elevation Option is set to Use Object.

5. Click OK. Pan and zoom to the profile view, and press Esc to clear the selection of the profile view.

   The projected version of the water line is shown in the profile view (see Figure 8.11). Note the strange bends in the line around station 12+00 (0+360). These are caused by the alignment turning away from the water pipe at this location, which produces some odd projection angles and distorts the projected appearance of the water pipe.

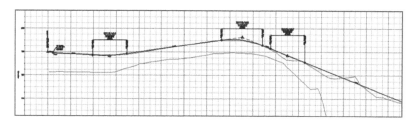

FIGURE 8.11   A 3D polyline representing a water pipe has been projected into the Jordan Court profile view.

6. Select the profile view grid for Jordan Court, and click Project Objects To Profile View on the ribbon.

7. Click three of the points labeled BORE that appear along the Jordan Court alignment. Press Enter.

The type of style referred to here is a Civil 3D *point style*. A few steps later, you'll use a different type of style for a block.

8. In the Project Objects To Profile View dialog box, verify that Test Bore is selected as Style and Use Object is selected as Elevation Option for all three points.

9. Click OK, and view the projected points in the profile view.

   As you can see, the points are inserted with a marker and a label that indicates the station and ground-surface elevation of the test boring (see Figure 8.12).

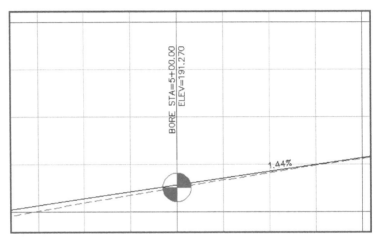

FIGURE 8.12   A Civil 3D point projected to the Jordan Court profile view

This is an AutoCAD block, not a Civil 3D point.

10. Press Esc to clear the previous selection. Zoom in near the midpoint of Logan Court, and note the red test-boring symbol shown there.

11. Click the profile view for Logan Court, and then click Project Objects To Profile View on the ribbon.

Feature lines and Civil 3D points have projection built into their styles, but for AutoCAD entities like this block, an *object projection style* is used.

12. Click the red test-boring symbol, and press Enter. Verify that Style is set to Basic, and change Elevation Options to Surface ➢ EG.

13. Click OK, and examine the new projection added to the profile view.

    It looks similar to the projected Civil 3D points, even though the source object in this case is a block with no elevation assigned to it.

14. Save and close the drawing.

You can view the results of successfully completing this exercise by opening `Object Projection - Complete.dwg`.

Now You Know

Now that you have completed this chapter, you can configure and label profiles so that they display information the way you need it to be displayed. You can apply profile styles and profile view styles to change the appearance of the graphical information. You can add bands to show additional information about the design in profile view. You're now able to add labels to convey detailed information about your profile design. And finally, you can project objects to your profile views, placing them in a useful context so their proximity with other objects in the design model can be assessed. You're ready to begin configuring, annotating, and enhancing profiles in a production environment.

CHAPTER 9

Designing in 3D Using Corridors

Long before AutoCAD® Civil 3D® objects, CAD, or even computers existed, engineers were designing roads and other linear features in three stages: alignment, profile, and cross section. I suspect the reason for this is that it's much easier to think of a design one dimension at a time rather than think of all three dimensions at once. This was especially true before designs could be visualized in 3D on a computer screen. This approach to linear design has carried right through to the present day and is still evident, even with cutting-edge technology such as Civil 3D.

You have already learned about the alignment and profile stages of this design approach. In this chapter, you'll learn how assemblies are used to provide the third stage of the design process: the cross section. Then you'll combine all three elements (alignments, profiles, and assemblies) to take this three-stage design process to the next level: a dynamic three-dimensional model.

In this chapter, you'll learn to:

▶ **Understand corridors**

▶ **Create an assembly**

▶ **Create a corridor**

▶ **Apply corridor targets**

▶ **Create corridor surfaces**

Understanding Corridors

A *corridor* consists of hundreds or even thousands of individual Civil 3D objects that are dynamically linked to one another. A good way to begin understanding how corridors work is to study how these different components come together to become a 3D representation of your design.

Understanding the 3D Chain

In Chapter 5, "Designing in 2D Using Alignments," you used alignments to design the 2D path of a linear feature, in this case a road. In Chapter 7, "Designing Vertically Using Profiles," you designed the vertical path of the road using profiles. When combined, the alignment and profile form a three-dimensional pathway called a *3D chain*. The 3D chain serves as the backbone of your design.

3D chains can actually be seen in your drawing, but only if you view the drawing from a 3D perspective, as shown in Figure 9.1.

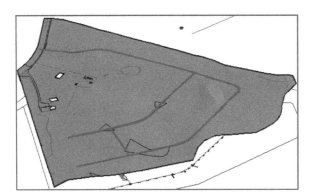

FIGURE 9.1   The blue lines represent 3D chains formed by combining alignments with profiles to form a three-dimensional pathway.

Because the 3D chain is dynamically linked to both the alignment and profile, a change to either one will automatically prompt a change to the 3D chain and subsequently update the corridor.

Understanding the Assembly

An *assembly* is a representation of the cross-sectional geometry of the feature you're designing. It establishes the overall shape of the cross section and distinguishes the areas within it. For example, a typical road cross section can have areas of asphalt pavement, base material, curbs, and sidewalks, as shown in Figure 9.2.

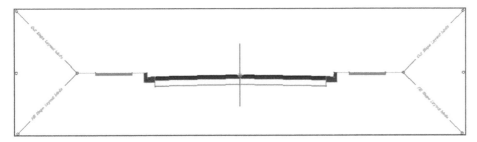

F I G U R E 9 . 2   A Civil 3D assembly that establishes lanes, curbs, sidewalks, and grading

The parts of an assembly are called *subassemblies*. They are dynamically linked to one another and therefore have the potential to affect one another. For example, if a curb subassembly is located at the edge of a lane subassembly, the curb subassembly will automatically move outward if the lane width is increased.

Understanding Assembly Insertions

To create a corridor, Civil 3D inserts instances of an assembly along a 3D chain at regular intervals. These assembly insertions can be thought of as the ribs of the 3D model, providing shape to the road one assembly at a time (see Figure 9.3).

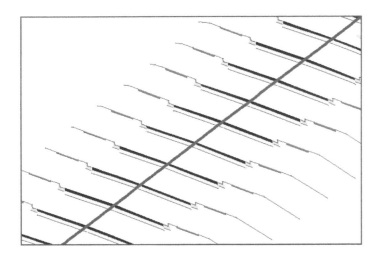

F I G U R E 9 . 3   Assemblies inserted at intervals along a 3D chain

Because the assembly insertions are dynamically linked to the 3D chain, any change to the alignment or profile will prompt a change in the corridor. The assembly insertions are also dynamically linked to the assembly itself, so any change to the assembly will also prompt an update to the corridor.

Understanding Corridor Feature Lines

To provide a framework in the longitudinal direction, Civil 3D draws feature lines from assembly to assembly (see Figure 9.4). The feature lines employ a coding system to determine which points they are drawn through each time they cross an assembly.

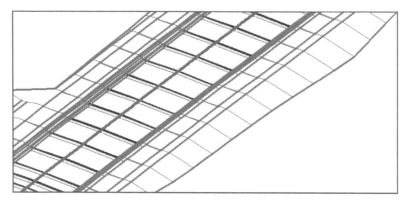

FIGURE 9.4 The red lines are feature lines that connect like points on each assembly insertion.

The feature lines are linked to the assembly insertions, which are linked to the 3D chain, and so on. I'll stop calling out relationships specifically and cover it all by saying that everything within a corridor is essentially related.

Understanding the Corridor Surface

As you view the assembly insertions along the 3D chain previously shown in Figure 9.3, imagine this as the structural framework of a ship or an airplane. With the framework in place, now imagine the hull or fuselage being installed on the vessel. This is a great way to envision the role of a *corridor surface* (see Figure 9.5).

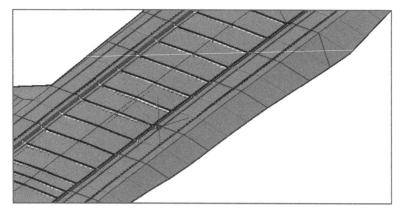

FIGURE 9.5 A corridor along with its corridor surface, shown in 3D view

Although they appear in Prospector like other surfaces, *corridor surfaces* are built directly from the corridor and maintain a link to the corridor. They can be displayed as contours, used to create surface profiles, and perform every other function normally associated with surfaces.

Creating an Assembly

As mentioned previously, an assembly consists of smaller components called *subassemblies*. To create an assembly, you begin by creating an assembly baseline, which is represented by a simple vertical line with a single base-point marker at its midpoint. Then you proceed by inserting individual subassemblies that represent elements such as lanes, curbs, ditches, and so on.

Before building an assembly, it's a good idea to have at least a sketch of the typical cross section of your design so you have something to reference as you work. Having detailed dimensions is helpful but not critical—the subassemblies can be changed with relative ease, even after the corridor has been built.

Exercise 9.1: Create an Assembly

In this exercise, you'll create an assembly that represents the cross section of the road for the proposed residential development.

1. Open the drawing named Creating an Assembly.dwg located in the Chapter 09 class data folder.

2. On the Home tab of the ribbon, click Assembly ➢ Create Assembly.

3. In the Create Assembly dialog box, enter **Subdivision Road** as the name. For Code Set Style, select All Codes With Hatching. Click OK.

4. Click a point near the center of the top-right viewport to insert the assembly baseline.

5. On the Home tab of the ribbon, click the Tool Palettes icon.

6. In the Tool Palettes window, right-click the gray strip labeled Tool Palettes, and select Civil Imperial (Metric) Subassemblies.

If you haven't already done so, download and install the files for Chapter 9 according to the instructions in this book's Introduction.

A vertical red line appears in your drawing.

7. Click the stack of tabs at the bottom of the Tool Palettes window, and then click Basic, as shown in Figure 9.6.

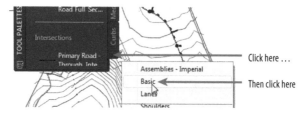

F I G U R E   9 . 6   Selecting the Basic tool palette

> The Properties window appears, and you're prompted on the command line to select a marker point.

8. On the Basic tool palette, click BasicLane.

9. In the Properties window, verify that Side is set to Right, and then click the marker at the midpoint of the assembly baseline.
   A lane subassembly is attached to the assembly baseline.

> You may need to zoom in to see the circle markers on the lane subassembly.

10. On the Basic tool palette, click BasicCurbAndGutter. In the Properties window, change the value for Curb Height to 0.50 (0.15).

11. Click the upper-right circle marker on the lane subassembly you inserted earlier.
    A subassembly representing a curb and gutter is now attached to the lane.

12. Press Esc to end the assembly-insertion command. Click the lane subassembly and the curb subassembly, and then click Mirror on the ribbon.

> This isn't the same Mirror command that AutoCAD® software uses for mirroring lines, arcs, and circles. This is a special command for subassemblies, and it must be used instead of the AutoCAD version.

13. Click the vertical red assembly baseline.
    Both sides of the assembly now display a lane and curb subassembly.

14. Save and close the drawing.

You can view the results of successfully completing this exercise by opening `Creating an Assembly - Complete.dwg`.

WHAT ARE SUBASSEMBLIES MADE OF?

Subassemblies are made up of three fundamental components: points, links, and shapes. A point is self-explanatory, a link is a line that is drawn between two points, and a shape is the result of three or more links forming a closed shape, as shown in the following diagram. Each point, link, and shape in a subassembly has at least one code. These codes are used to identify the purpose of a component and control its style, behavior, and relationship to other parts of the design. A collection of styles that apply to multiple codes is called a *code set style*.

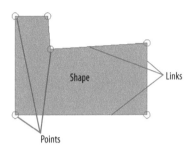

Creating a Corridor

Considering the complexity and sophistication of a corridor, the process of creating one is actually quite simple. Once the alignment, profile, and assembly are in place, it's just a matter of telling these three objects that they belong together. Of course, the design is far from complete at this point, but as you'll see in the next exercise, creating the initial version of a corridor involves only a few steps.

Certification
Objective

Exercise 9.2: Create a Corridor

In this exercise, you'll create the initial corridor for Jordan Court.

1. Open the drawing named Creating a Corridor.dwg located in the Chapter 09 class data folder.

2. On the Home tab of the ribbon, click Corridor.

If you haven't already done so, download and install the files for Chapter 9 according to the instructions in this book's Introduction.

3. In the Create Corridor dialog box, do the following:

   a. For Name, enter **Jordan Court**.

   b. For Alignment, verify that Jordan Court is selected.

   c. For Profile, select Jordan Court FGCL.

   d. For Assembly, select Subdivision Road.

   e. Uncheck the box next to Set Baseline And Region Parameters.

   f. Click OK.

4. Zoom in to the bottom-right viewport, and notice the corridor that has been created there (see Figure 9.7).

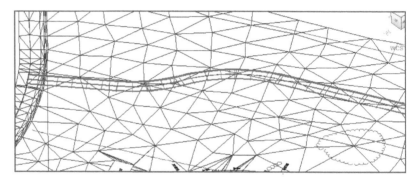

FIGURE 9.7 A portion of the newly created corridor shown in a 3D perspective

5. Save and close the drawing.

You can view the results of successfully completing this exercise by opening Creating a Corridor - Complete.dwg.

Applying Corridor Targets

One thing that makes corridors so powerful is their ability to interact with other objects in the drawing. Corridors are able to morph themselves into different shapes and sizes in order to respond to existing features or components of newly designed features. This is made possible through the use of special

> Normally you would also make a choice for Target Surface, but for now, leave this setting set to <None>.

subassemblies that can be stretched, twisted, and reconfigured as the design progresses along the corridor. What makes these subassemblies special is that they utilize corridor targets.

Three types of targets can be applied to a corridor: *surface targets*, *width or offset targets*, and *slope or elevation targets*.

Understanding Surface Targets

Surface targets are used in a number of cases where the corridor needs to interact with a surface, such as when a slope is projected from a design elevation to the point where it intercepts an existing ground surface. This is referred to as *daylighting*. For example, in a section of road design that is above existing ground, daylighting can be used to create the embankment from the elevation of the road to the original ground elevation (see Figure 9.8).

FIGURE 9.8   A cross-section view of a road that shows the daylighting of a 3:1 slope on either side

Although daylighting is the most common example of surface targeting, there are other examples such as establishing the cross slope of an existing road, setting the top elevation of a retaining wall, setting the depth of a pipe, and many others.

Understanding Width or Offset Targets

Another type of target used in corridor design is referred to as a *width or offset target*. As the name suggests, this type of target is used to vary the width of an object or the distance between a point and the centerline (also known as *offset*). For example, an alignment can be used as a target that controls the outside edge of a lane. As the path of the alignment moves away from the road centerline, the lane widens. As the path of the alignment moves toward the road centerline, the lane narrows (see Figure 9.9).

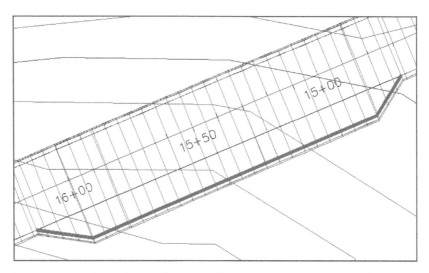

FIGURE 9.9   A width or offset target (in red) applied to a corridor to widen the lane and create a pull-off area

In addition to alignments, you can use feature lines, survey figures, and polylines as width or offset targets. Lane widening is probably the most common use of a width or offset target, but there are many other uses. For example, you can use a width or offset target to control the location of a ditch, the width of a shoulder, or the distance between a shoulder and a guardrail.

Understanding Slope or Elevation Targets

Slope or elevation targets are used to control the elevations of one or more components of a corridor. For example, these targets can control the elevations of a roadside ditch to ensure that it drains to a specific point, regardless of the slope of the adjacent road (see Figure 9.10). Profiles, feature lines, survey figures, and 3D polylines can be used as this type of target.

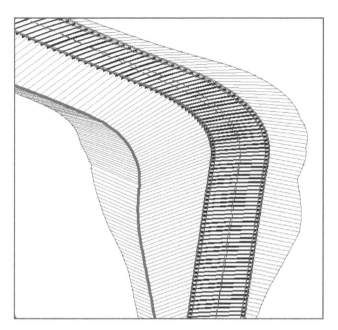

F I G U R E   9 . 1 0   The use of a profile (3D chain shown in red) to control the elevations of a ditch

TYING PROPOSED ELEVATIONS TO EXISTING ELEVATIONS

The concept of daylighting is found throughout all types of land development. As I've mentioned, one of the fundamental activities of land development is changing the shape of the land. This means portions of the development will have new elevations that are above or below the existing elevations. Because things such as roads and parking lots aren't much good underground and can't simply float in midair, there must be some way of transitioning between new elevations and existing elevations. The most economical material that can be used to construct that transition is soil, but soil isn't stable on steep slopes. Therefore, the transition between new and existing elevations is done with relatively mild slopes such as 3:1 (three units horizontal to one vertical). One of the most important components of your land-development design will be this tie-in between proposed elevations and existing elevations.

Enabling Target Behavior

Before you can use targets within your corridor, you must apply subassemblies that have targeting capabilities. Civil 3D comes with hundreds of subassemblies, each designed for a different purpose or application. Some of these subassemblies can use targets, and some can't. For example, the BasicLane subassembly that you used earlier doesn't have the ability to target anything. So if you would like to use a width or offset target to incorporate a turning lane, a pull-off area, or some other feature into your corridor, you'll have to use a different subassembly.

Exercise 9.3: Apply Subassemblies That Can Use Targets

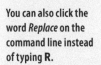
If you haven't already done so, download and install the files for Chapter 9 according to the instructions in this book's Introduction.

In this exercise, you'll add subassemblies that will enable the corridor lane width to vary and the corridor to tie to an existing ground surface.

1. Open the drawing named Adding Target Subassemblies.dwg located in the Chapter 09 class data folder.

2. Open the Tool Palettes window, and click the Basic tool palette.

You can also click the word *Replace* on the command line instead of typing **R**.

3. Click BasicLaneTransition. On the command line, type **R** and press Enter to invoke the Replace option.

4. In the upper-right viewport, click the right-lane subassembly. When prompted to select an attachment point for the highlighted subassembly, click the upper-left point of the curb and gutter, as shown in Figure 9.11

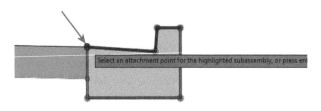

FIGURE 9.11   Choosing the attachment point for the curb and gutter subassembly

5. Repeat the previous two steps for the left-lane subassembly. This time, pick the upper-right corner point of the left curb and gutter subassembly.

6. Press Esc to clear the current selection. Click the assembly baseline (the vertical line to which the subassemblies are attached), and then click Assembly Properties on the ribbon.

7. In the Assembly Properties dialog box, do the following:

   a. Click the Construction tab. Click Group (1) twice to edit the name. Type **Right**, and press Enter. Use the same procedure to change the name of Group (2) to **Left**.

   b. Under the group now named Right, rename the two subassemblies **Right Lane** and **Right Curb**. Do the same for the Left group, naming the subassemblies **Left Lane** and **Left Curb**.

   c. Click Right Lane. Then, under Input Values, scroll down and find the Transition value. Change it to Hold Grade, Change Offset.

   d. Repeat step c for Left Lane.
      Figure 9.12 shows the Assembly Properties dialog after you complete all the tasks in this step.

As the name implies, the Hold Grade, Change Offset setting maintains the cross grade of the lane (which happens to be 2 percent) while widening or narrowing it to the specified distance.

FIGURE 9.12 The Assembly Properties dialog box after the groups and subassemblies have been renamed and the properties for the lanes have been set properly

8. Click OK to close the Assembly Properties dialog box and return to the drawing.

The assembly now contains two BasicLaneTransition subassemblies in place of the BasicLane subassemblies. This enables targeting so that you can create a turning lane in the next exercise.

9. On the Basic tool palette, click BasicSideSlopeCutDitch.

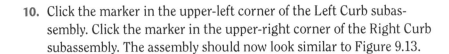

Notice that you didn't have to set the Side property to Left or Right. Civil 3D has a special feature that automatically guesses which side of the assembly you're on.

10. Click the marker in the upper-left corner of the Left Curb subassembly. Click the marker in the upper-right corner of the Right Curb subassembly. The assembly should now look similar to Figure 9.13.

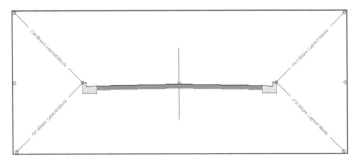

F I G U R E   9 . 1 3   The assembly with newly added BasicSideSlopeCutDitch subassemblies on either side

11. Press Esc to end the current command. Click the right BasicSideSlopeCutDitch subassembly, and then click Subassembly Properties on the ribbon.

12. On the Information tab of the Subassembly Properties dialog box, change the name to **Right Daylight**.

13. Repeat the previous two steps for the same subassembly on the left, this time naming it **Left Daylight**.

14. Save and close the drawing.

Take the time to rename your subassemblies using logical, easy-to-remember names. This not only makes it easier to keep track of these things as you continue to work on your corridor, it also helps if you have to pass your work on to someone else.

You can view the results of successfully completing this exercise by opening `Adding Target Subassemblies - Complete.dwg`.

Assigning Targets

You use the Target Mapping dialog box to assign targets within a corridor. This dialog box lists the three types of targets (surfaces, width or offset targets, and slope or elevation targets) along with subassemblies within your corridor that are able to use each type of target (see Figure 9.14). Targets don't have to be used whenever they are available. In fact, for many corridors, the majority of the targets are set to <None>.

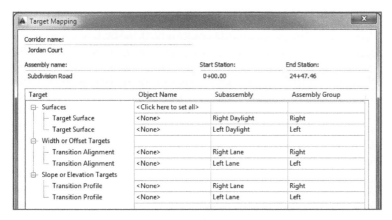

FIGURE 9.14 The Target Mapping dialog box showing the three types of corridor targets along with the subassemblies that can use each type of target

To assign a target, you click the cell in the Object Name column that corresponds to the subassembly you would like to set up. This displays a dialog box where you can select objects in the drawing graphically or by name.

Exercise 9.4: Assign Targets

In this exercise, you'll assign targets to the corridor to provide daylighting and a turn lane for Jordan Court.

1. Open the drawing named Applying Corridor Targets.dwg located in the Chapter 09 class data folder.

2. Click the corridor in the drawing, and then click Edit Targets on the ribbon.

3. When prompted to select a region, click inside the left viewport anywhere within the corridor.

If you haven't already done so, download and install the files for Chapter 9 according to the instructions in this book's Introduction.

CORRIDOR REGION

In step 3, you're prompted to select a *region* to edit. A region is essentially a part of your corridor that begins at one station and ends at another. All corridors start out with a single region that extends the full length of the corridor. As a design evolves, however, you'll typically break up the corridor into multiple regions.

This opens the Set Width Or Offset Target dialog box.

4. In the Target Mapping dialog box, under Width Or Offset Targets, click <None> in the Object Name column next to the Left Lane subassembly.

5. In the Set Width Or Offset Target dialog box, under Select Object Type To Target, select Feature Lines, Survey Figures, and Polylines.

6. Click Select From Drawing. Then, in the left viewport, zoom in to the beginning of Jordan Court where it intersects with Emerson Road.

7. Click the red polyline that represents the desired path of the left lane's edge, and then press Enter.

It may seem that the red polyline is on the right side of the road, but remember that left and right are defined while looking in the direction in which the stations increase.

8. Click OK twice to return to the drawing. The corridor is widened near the entrance, as shown in Figure 9.15. By widening the left lane this way, you make extra room for a turning lane.

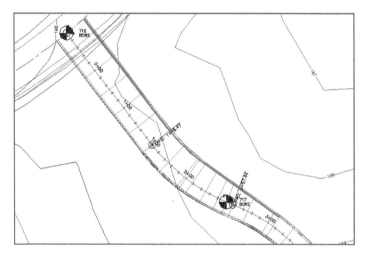

FIGURE 9.15   The corridor is wider where the lane-edge polyline was targeted.

9. Click within the corridor to reopen the Target Mapping dialog box.

10. In the Target Mapping dialog box, click the cell next to Surfaces that reads <Click Here To Set All>.

11. Select EG, and click OK. Then click OK to dismiss the Target Mapping dialog box. Pan around in the lower-right viewport to view the 3D representation of the corridor.

You should now see additional geometry along the edges of the corridor (see Figure 9.16). This represents the daylighting that has been applied. The daylighting geometry is noticeably wider in some areas than in others. These are areas that are below existing ground through which a ditch has been constructed. This automatic creation of ditches is a function of the BasicSideSlopeCutDitch subassembly.

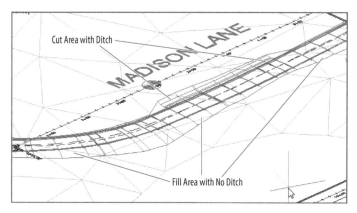

FIGURE 9.16 **Areas of daylighting along the corridor**

12. Save and close the drawing.

You can view the results of successfully completing this exercise by opening `Applying Corridor Targets - Complete.dwg`.

Creating Corridor Surfaces

In Chapter 4, "Modeling the Existing Terrain Using Surfaces," you learned about the benefits of using a surface to model the existing terrain. A surface provided a model of the land and enabled you to do things like display contours, label elevations, and create surface profiles. Imagine having all those capabilities with a corridor as well. This is made possible through the creation of a corridor surface.

CUT AND FILL

The terms *cut* and *fill* are used quite a bit in relation to land-development activities. For example, in the BasicSideSlopeCutDitch subassembly, the word *cut* refers to a condition where the road is below existing ground and therefore has to project a slope upward in order to daylight. Another way to envision this is that earth must be cut away in order to construct the road in these areas. The opposite of cut is *fill*, which refers to conditions where an area must be filled in with earth to create a design feature. *Cut* and *fill* can also be used to refer to quantities of earth, where *cut* represents the volume of earth that must be removed to build something and *fill* represents the volume of earth that must be brought in to build something.

Corridor surfaces are unique in that they exist as an integrated part of the corridor, although they show up in Prospector like any other Civil 3D surface. You use the Corridor Surface dialog box to create the initial corridor surface, and then you choose the data within the corridor that is to be added to this surface. You can choose links and feature lines based on the codes assigned to them. You can also click the Boundaries tab and add a boundary to the surface. Often, the simplest way to apply a boundary is to use the corridor extents as the outer boundary. You can also create boundaries *automatically* based on coded feature lines within a corridor, *interactively* by selecting individual feature lines within the corridor, or manually by selecting a polyline that already exists in the drawing.

If you haven't already done so, download and install the files for Chapter 9 according to the instructions in this book's Introduction.

Exercise 9.5: Create a Corridor Surface

In this exercise, you'll create a finished ground surface for the Jordan Court corridor.

1. Open the drawing named Creating a Corridor Surface.dwg located in the Chapter 09 class data folder.

It's easier to select the corridor if you zoom in and click one of the blue lines representing an assembly insertion.

2. Click the Jordan Court corridor, and then click Corridor Surfaces on the ribbon.

3. In the Corridor Surfaces dialog box, click the leftmost icon to create a new corridor surface.

4. Edit the name of the new surface so it reads **Jordan Court FG**.

5. Verify that Data Type is set to Links and that Code is set to Top and then click the plus sign to add the Top coded links to the surface.

6. Click OK. If the Corridor Properties – Rebuild dialog box opens, click Rebuild The Corridor.

   You should now see contours in the left viewport and TIN lines in the bottom-right viewport; however, a large area in the center of the site contains incorrect surface information (see Figure 9.17).

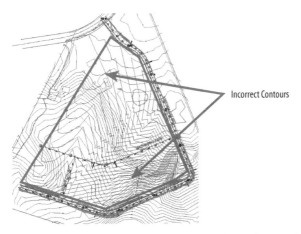

Incorrect Contours

FIGURE 9.17 Contours displayed for the newly created corridor surface. Note the incorrect contours in the center of the site.

7. If the corridor is no longer selected, click the corridor in the drawing, and then click Corridor Surfaces again. Click the Boundaries tab of the Corridor Surfaces dialog box.

8. Right-click Jordan Court FG, and select Corridor Extents As Outer Boundary, as shown in Figure 9.18.

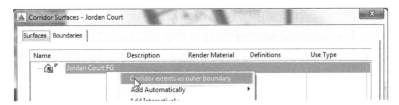

FIGURE 9.18 Selecting the corridor extents as the basis for creating a surface boundary

9. Click OK to return to the drawing. If the Corridor Properties – Rebuild dialog box opens, click Rebuild The Corridor.

    The surface has been contained within the extents of the corridor, as it should be. Now contours appear only where valid surface data exists.

10. Save and close the drawing.

You can view the results of successfully completing this exercise by opening `Creating a Corridor Surface - Complete.dwg`.

ALTERNATE CORRIDOR SURFACES

In this example, you created a surface that represents the top (finished) ground elevations of the corridor. You could have selected any one of the codes contained within the corridor, such as pave, datum, curb, and so on. Although most of these codes aren't particularly useful for creating surfaces, several are. The datum code, for example, is used to represent links that form the underside of the materials that make up the road. Why is this important? These links represent the trench, or *roadbed*, that must be excavated to accept road materials such as stone, concrete, and asphalt. The excavation of the roadbed often represents one of the most important aspects of constructing the project: earthmoving.

Certification
Objective

INTERSECTIONS

One of the most sophisticated applications of targets and regions is the design of an intersection. Here you'll find multiple baselines, regions, and targets that are necessary to tie two roads together as well as provide a smooth transition between them. For this reason, Civil 3D provides the Create Intersection command that automates the creation and management of these relationships.

After launching the Create Intersection command, you're presented with the Intersection Wizard, which contains the following series of dialog boxes that request information about the design:

General   In this dialog, you specify general information about the intersection such as its name, description, and associated styles. Most important, you choose from one of two types of intersection designs: Primary Road Crown Maintained and All Crowns Maintained, as shown here.

(Continues)

INTERSECTIONS *(Continued)*

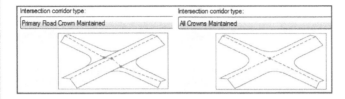

Geometry Details   In this dialog, you choose a profile for each alignment, which will drive the centerline elevations of each road. You also define important horizontal geometry specifications by modifying the Curb Return Parameters and Offset Parameters settings. You provide vertical design specifications by addressing the Lane Slope Parameters and Curb Return Profile Parameters settings. A portion of the Geometry Details dialog box is shown here.

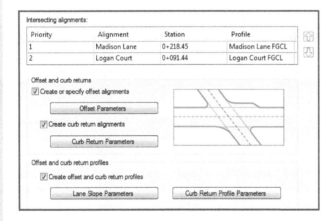

Corridor Regions   In this dialog box, you specify the different assemblies that will be assigned to different portions of the intersection design. This group of assemblies and their assignments is called an *assembly set*. Assembly sets are typically set up by a CAD manager or lead CAD person and will most likely be provided for you, at least for your first few designs.

Corridor Region Section Type	Assembly to Apply
⊟ Warp All Turn Lanes	
─ Curb Return Fillets	Curb Return Fillets ···
─ Primary Road Full Section	Primary Road Full Section ···
─ Primary Road Half Section – Daylight Left	Primary Road Half Section - Daylight Left ···
─ Primary Road Half Section – Daylight Right	Primary Road Half Section - Daylight Right ···
─ Secondary Road Full Section	Secondary Road Full Section ···
─ Secondary Road Half Section - Daylight Left	Secondary Road Half Section - Daylight L... ···
└ Secondary Road Half Section - Daylight Right	Secondary Road Half Section - Daylight ... ···

(Continues)

INTERSECTIONS *(Continued)*

After you complete the Create Intersection command, your drawing contains a full, 3D representation of the intersection, as shown in the following image. The intersection design consists of new baselines, regions, and targets. As you make changes to your design, the relationships between the many intersection components will be honored, keeping the design in sync within itself as well as with adjacent portions of the corridor.

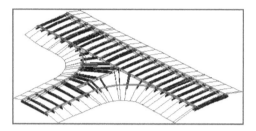

NOW YOU KNOW

Now that you have completed this chapter, you understand the anatomy of a corridor and how alignments, profiles, and assemblies are combined to build a 3D corridor model. You can create an assembly representing a typical road cross section and then create a corridor using that assembly along with an alignment and a profile in the drawing. You can utilize target-capable subassemblies and configure the corridor to use the available targets to provide daylighting and changes in lane width. And finally, you're able to create corridor surfaces so that important surface information can be used elsewhere in the design.

You're now ready to begin creating and working with corridors in a production environment.

CHAPTER 10

Creating Cross Sections of the Design

One of the requirements for a successful and efficient design process is the ability to visualize the design in many different ways. So far, you have explored how profiles can give you more insight into your design by providing you with an alternate way to see and interact with it. In this chapter, you'll examine the use of cross sections to visualize and display your design in yet another way: by slicing through it in a perpendicular direction.

In the AutoCAD® Civil 3D® software, there are two primary approaches to viewing and documenting your design in cross-section view. For design purposes, you use a Civil 3D feature called the Section Editor that enables you to analyze and modify your design section by section. For documentation purposes, you use sample lines, sections, and section views. The section view, just like the profile view, is the backdrop that houses the sections while providing a grid and annotations to go with them. There are also some things that sections can do that profiles can't, such as slice through corridors and create multiple section views at once.

In this chapter, you'll learn to:

▶ **Use the Section Editor**

▶ **Create sample lines**

▶ **Create section views**

▶ **Sample additional sources**

Using the Section Editor

To understand what the Section Editor is and how it works, let's review how a corridor is built. An alignment and a profile are combined to create a 3D chain, and then an assembly is repeatedly inserted along that 3D chain to create the full model. As you construct the assembly, you're looking at a static version of the cross-sectional geometry of the road. This version doesn't reflect the way in which the subassemblies interact with the targets you have assigned to them. However, the Section Editor enables you to view each assembly insertion in cross-section view, including any interactions involving targets. In addition, you can use the Section Editor to make edits to each corridor section and perfect your design down to the smallest detail.

When you click Section Editor on the ribbon, a Section Editor tab provides you with the tools you need to configure and navigate in the editor (see Figure 10.1). It can be very helpful to divide your drawing area into two or three viewports so you can see the section viewer alongside the "normal" view of your drawing. In fact, a great feature of the tool is that it displays a marker on the alignment and profile that indicates the location of the section you're viewing. Thus, with three viewports available (plan, profile, and section), you can view your design from three different perspectives at once.

FIGURE 10.1   The Section Editor ribbon tab

As the name implies, you can also use the Section Editor to *edit* your corridor design. This is done with the Parameter Editor command found on the Section Editor ribbon tab. This command shows all the subassemblies and their associated settings at a specific location on the corridor. These settings can be overridden one corridor section at a time, or the overrides can be applied to a range of stations. The changes you make here are stored as overrides within the corridor.

Exercise 10.1: View and Edit with the Section Editor

If you haven't already done so, download and install the files for Chapter 10 according to the instructions in the this book's Introduction.

In this exercise, you'll use the Section Editor to view the corridor design for Jordan Court in section view and then remove unwanted ditches from the design.

1. Open the drawing named Using Section Editor.dwg located in the Chapter 10 class data folder.

2. In the left viewport, click one of the blue corridor lines to select the corridor. Then click in the upper-right viewport, and click Section Editor on the ribbon.

   The view shown in the upper-right viewport changes to display a cross section of the corridor at the location you picked before launching the Section Editor command (see Figure 10.2).

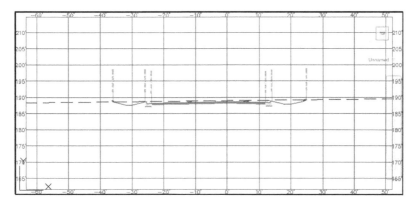

FIGURE 10.2   A section view shown by the Section Editor command

Notice the line markers that indicate your location in plan and profile view.

3. In the left viewport, zoom out until you can see the plan view of the site as well as the Jordan Court profile view. On the ribbon, click the Go To Next Station icon to advance to the next corridor section. Continue advancing to view several different corridor sections.

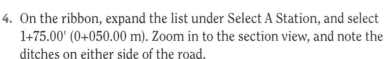

4. On the ribbon, expand the list under Select A Station, and select 1+75.00' (0+050.00 m). Zoom in to the section view, and note the ditches on either side of the road.

   The ditches were added automatically because the road is in a cut condition; however, the amount of cut is so small that the ditches can be omitted. You'll make this change in the next few steps.

5. Click Parameter Editor on the ribbon. This opens the Corridor Parameters window.

6. In the Corridor Parameters window, scroll down to Left Daylight and change the value for Backslope Width and Foreslope Width to 0.000. Repeat for the Right Daylight subassembly.

The Backslope Width and Foreslope Width values define the width of the ditch. When you set them to zero, the ditch will disappear.

7. Click Close on the ribbon to close the Section Editor and return the drawing to its normal state. If you zoom in to the plan view, you'll notice that the ditch has been omitted, but only at one location in the corridor (see Figure 10.3).

   You need to apply this change across a number of corridor sections.

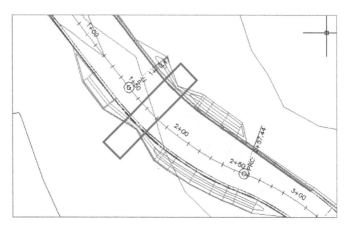

FIGURE 10.3   The ditches have been removed, but only at a single station within the corridor.

 8. Click one of the blue corridor lines, click in the upper-right viewport, and then click Section Editor on the ribbon. Select station 1+75.00' (0+050.00 m) again.

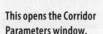
This opens the Corridor Parameters window.

 9. On the ribbon, click Parameter Editor.

 10. On the ribbon, click Apply To A Station Range.

 11. In the Apply To A Station Range dialog box, click the Pick button next to Start Station. Pick a point in the left viewport just northwest of the ditches.

Your start station should be around 0+80 (0+020), and your end station should be around 3+00 (0+090). You can type in these stations if you're not sure that you've picked the right points.

 12. Repeat the previous step for the End Station value, this time picking a point to the southeast of the ditches.

 13. Click OK to dismiss the Apply To A Station Range dialog box, and then click Close to close the Section Editor.

 14. Click the corridor, and then click Rebuild Corridor on the ribbon. The ditches have been removed from the corridor, as shown in Figure 10.4.

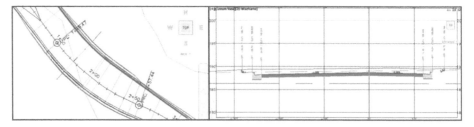

FIGURE 10.4   A plan view (left) and section view (right) of the corridor after the ditches have been removed

15. Save and close the drawing.

You can view the results of successfully completing this exercise by opening Using Section Editor - Complete.dwg.

What's In a Name?

Think back to the previous chapter when you spent some time in Exercise 9.3 renaming the individual subassemblies that made up the composition of the road. You should recognize the names Left Daylight and Right Daylight here in Exercise 10.1. This is an example of how spending a few extra seconds on bookkeeping helps things go much more smoothly when you're further along in the design process. It's an even bigger help when you're working on a team; your teammates will thank you when your good bookkeeping makes their jobs easier and saves them time.

Creating Sample Lines

With a profile, the alignment serves as the path along which the profile is cut. For a cross section, the sample line assumes this role. When sample lines are created, they are associated with an alignment. Multiple sample lines are typically created simultaneously, so Civil 3D requires that sample lines be placed in a *sample line group*. An alignment can host multiple sample line groups if necessary. So the placement of sample lines in the alignment hierarchy is Alignment ➢ Sample Line Groups ➢ Sample Lines.

After launching the Sample Lines command on the ribbon, you're prompted to select the parent alignment. Then you're asked to name and stylize the sample lines and choose the sources that will be sampled to create cross sections. You can sample four types of objects: surfaces, corridors, corridor surfaces, and pipe networks. Finally, you're presented with the Sample Line Tools toolbar, which contains an array of commands for creating and modifying the sample lines in a sample line group.

On the Sample Line Tools toolbar, a pull-down menu provides several methods for placing sample lines along the alignment (see Figure 10.5). A description of each method is as follows:

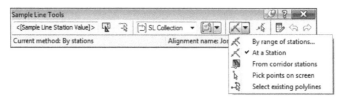

FIGURE 10.5   The Sample Line Tools toolbar showing the different methods available for sample line placement

By Range Of Stations   This method creates multiple sample lines with predetermined swath widths at a specified increment along the alignment. It's great for creating large numbers of sample lines that are evenly distributed along the alignment. These sample lines are perpendicular to the alignment.

At A Station   This method is probably the simplest. You supply the station value, left swath width, and right swath width for each sample line you want to place. You can specify the station value graphically by clicking a point in the drawing or numerically by typing the value at the command line. This method is good if you only need to draw a few sample lines at odd locations. These sample lines are perpendicular to the alignment.

> *Swath width* is the distance from the alignment to either the left or right end of the sample line.

From Corridor Stations   This method creates a sample line wherever there is an assembly insertion on the corridor. This is a great solution when you would like to create and display cross sections for design purposes. Of course, one of the sources for your sample lines must be a corridor.

Pick Points On Screen   As the name suggests, with this method you click points on the screen, in effect drawing the sample line. This is ideal for irregularly shaped sample lines that have multiple vertices and/or aren't perpendicular to the alignment.

Select Existing Polylines   This method yields the same result as Pick Points On Screen, but you use it when you have already drawn a polyline representing the path of the sample line.

Exercise 10.2: Create Sample Lines

In this exercise, you'll create sample lines along the Jordan Court alignment.

1. Open the drawing named Creating Sample Lines.dwg located in the Chapter 10 class data folder.

2. On the Home tab of the ribbon, click Sample Lines. When prompted to select an alignment, press Enter and select Jordan Court in the Select Alignment dialog box. Click OK.

3. In the Create Sample Line Group dialog box, do the following:

   ▶ For Name, enter **Design**.

   ▶ For Sample Line Style, verify that Road Sample Line is selected.

   ▶ For Sample Line Label Style, verify that Section Name is selected.

   ▶ Under Select Data Sources To Sample, uncheck all but the second check box.

   ▶ Verify that the settings in the dialog box match Figure 10.6, and click OK.

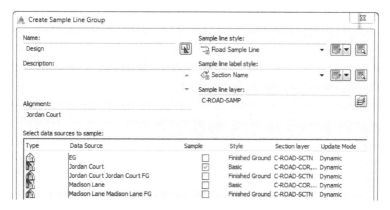

FIGURE 10.6 **The Create Sample Line Group dialog box**

4. On the Sample Line Tools toolbar, expand the button that lists creation methods, and select From Corridor Stations.

If you haven't already done so, download and install the files for Chapter 10 according to the instructions in the this book's Introduction.

The Create Sample Line Group dialog box opens because no sample line groups exist for this alignment. If one had existed, step 4 would have been skipped completely.

You're selecting only the Jordan Court corridor to be sampled.

5. In the Create Sample Lines – From Corridor Stations dialog box, click OK to accept the defaults and create the sample lines.

6. Press Esc to end the command. Zoom in to the left viewport, and examine the sample lines that have been created (see Figure 10.7).

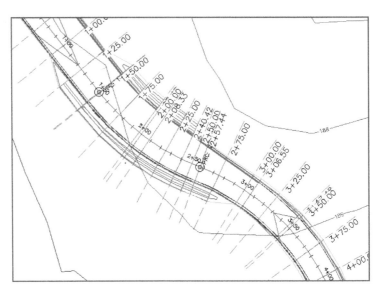

F I G U R E 1 0 . 7 Sample lines created at corridor stations

7. Save and close the drawing.

You can view the results of successfully completing this exercise by opening `Creating Sample Lines - Complete.dwg`.

Creating Section Views

Certification
Objective

Now that you have sample lines in the drawing that have captured section data from the sources you've chosen for them, you need a means by which to display that data in your drawing. Just as a profile needs a profile view to make it visible, a cross section needs a section view. Section views are similar to profile views. They usually display a grid and some grid labels as a backdrop to the data they house. The section view is dynamically linked to the sample line and associated data sources. This means, as with other Civil 3D objects, that if the sample or source data is modified, the section view will update automatically.

Creating Individual Section Views

As mentioned previously, one extra consideration with section views is that they often are created in large numbers. You'll learn how to address that challenge in the next section. For now, let's focus on creating individual section views.

Exercise 10.3: Create Individual Section Views

In this exercise, you'll create an individual section view to use for close inspection of your design at a key location.

1. Open the drawing named Creating Single Section Views.dwg located in the Chapter 10 class data folder.

2. In the left viewport, zoom in to the sample line labeled 13+25.00 (0+405.00). Click the sample line, and then click Create Section View ➤ Create Section View on the ribbon.

3. In the Create Section View – General dialog box, verify that the following items are selected:

   ▶ Select Alignment: Jordan Court

   ▶ Sample Line Group Name: Design

   ▶ Sample Line: 13+25.00 (0+405.00)

   ▶ Station: 13+25.00' (0+405.00 m)

   ▶ Section View Style: Design

4. Click Next to advance to the Create Section View – Offset Range dialog box.

5. Click Next to advance to the Create Section View – Elevation Range dialog box.

6. Click Next to advance to the Section Display Options dialog box. Verify that the style selected for the Jordan Court corridor section is Design.

7. Click Next to advance to the Data Bands dialog box. Verify that Design Offsets is selected under Select Band Set. Click Create Section View.

If you haven't already done so, download and install the files for Chapter 10 according to the instructions in the this book's Introduction.

Note that you can change the width of the section view by modifying the offset range.

Note that you can change the height of the section view by modifying the minimum and maximum elevations.

This section view could be helpful in assessing the design at a specific location. Note how the information is displayed in a way that aids in the design of the road. You could create additional section views at other key locations along the design of the road.

8. When prompted to identify the section-view origin, pick a point near the center of the upper-right viewport.

 A new section view is created in the drawing, as shown in Figure 10.8.

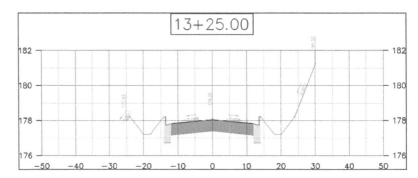

FIGURE 10.8 A newly created section view

9. Save and close the drawing.

You can view the results of successfully completing this exercise by opening Creating Single Section Views - Complete.dwg.

STYLE BY DESIGN

You may have noticed that many of the styles that were selected while creating this section view had the word *design* in their names. The significance of this is that the styles you chose were set up to aid the designer during the design process but may not be appropriate for final documents such as construction drawings. For example, the elevation and slope labels on the section would be much too small to read if this drawing were plotted. For design, however, they come in handy—enabling the designer to zoom in and quickly get information about key geometry. Leveraging styles by having some for design and others for documentation can be very useful.

Creating Multiple Section Views

For some projects, you may be required to provide documentation of cross sections at regular intervals along your design. This is especially common for road design projects, because a cross-section view is traditionally used to construct the road. Although newer techniques and technologies have replaced the use of cross sections to some extent, the creation of cross-section sheets is still a common practice for these types of designs.

For most projects, there are too many section views to fit on a single sheet, so multiple sheets are required. This means the section views must be created in groups that each fit efficiently in the printable area of a typical sheet. This "per sheet" arrangement is handled through a group plot style.

Exercise 10.4: Create Multiple Section Views

In this exercise, you'll use a new sample line group configured for section sheets to create multiple sheets containing section views.

1. Open the drawing named Creating Multiple Section Views.dwg located in the Chapter 10 class data folder.

2. On the Home tab of the ribbon, click Section Views ➤ Create Multiple Views.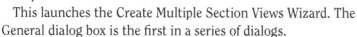
   This launches the Create Multiple Section Views Wizard. The General dialog box is the first in a series of dialogs.

3. In the Create Multiple Section Views – General dialog box, select Section Sheets for Sample Line Group Name. Click Next.

4. In the Create Multiple Section Views – Section Placement dialog box, verify that Production is selected under Placement Options.

5. Click the ellipsis next to the path to open the Select Layout As Sheet Template dialog box.

6. Click the ellipsis in the Select Layout As Sheet Template dialog box to browse for a template file.

7. Browse to the Chapter 10 class data folder, select Sections.dwt, and click Open.

8. Select ARCH D Section 20 Scale (ISO A0 Section 1 To 200), and click OK. Verify that Group Plot Style is set to Plot By Page.

9. Click Next in each of the remaining dialogs in the Create Multiple Section Views Wizard, and examine the settings for each one. Click Create Section Views.

If you haven't already done so, download and install the files for Chapter 10 according to the instructions in the this book's Introduction.

This drawing contains a new sample line group named Section Sheets that distributes the sample lines along the alignment at a consistent interval.

This is an important step because it configures the layout of the section views by establishing the size of a sheet, how much space should be allowed between section views, and so on.

WHY MORE SAMPLE LINES?

As you may recall, the first sample line group you created used the From Corridor Stations method to create the sample lines. This creates a sample line and the potential for a section view at each assembly insertion of the corridor. This configuration is specifically for design purposes so the designer can see a section view at any key point in the design if desired. Now you need to create section views that meet the requirements for construction drawings. For this application, you're often required to show cross sections at regular intervals. Here, the intent is related not to the design process but to documentation. Because you can create multiple sample line groups for any given alignment, you could set up one sample line group for design purposes and one for documentation purposes. In fact, if you use Prospector to browse to the sample line groups of Jordan Court in this example, you'll find that the Design sample line group still exists but that the styles have been set to hide the sample lines and their labels.

10. Click a point in the upper-right viewport in the open area to the north of the project. Three new section sheets should be created (see Figure 10.9).

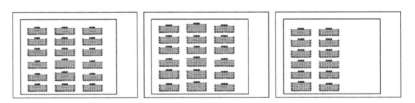

FIGURE 10.9   Newly created section views configured by sheet

11. Save and close the drawing.

You can view the results of successfully completing this exercise by opening `Creating Multiple Section Views - Complete.dwg`.

Sampling More Sources

So far, you have seen that corridors can be sampled and shown in a cross-section view, but what about other sources of data? It turns out that sample lines can also slice through surfaces and pipe networks. In this section, you'll learn how to sample and display data from these sources. In addition, you'll learn how to add more sources of data to an established set of sample lines and section views so you don't have to start over when new data becomes available.

Exercise 10.5: Sample More Sources

In this exercise, you'll add more data sources to your drawing, sample them, and show them in section views.

1. Open the drawing named Sampling More Sources.dwg located in the Chapter 10 class data folder.

2. Click one of the section views in the upper-right viewport, and then click Sample More Sources on the ribbon.

3. In the Section Sources dialog box, click EG under Available Sources. Then click Add.

4. Under Sampled Sources, verify that the style for EG is set to Existing Ground.

5. Verify that the Section Sources dialog box looks like Figure 10.10, and then click OK.

   After a pause, a red dashed line is added to each section view. This line represents the surface of the existing ground. In addition, a default label set has been applied to the existing ground line, which isn't appropriate for this application. You'll remove the labels in the next several steps.

If you haven't already done so, download and install the files for Chapter 10 according to the instructions in the this book's Introduction.

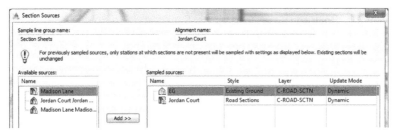

FIGURE 10.10 Sampling additional sources using the Section Sources dialog box

This opens the Section View Group Properties dialog box.

6. With the section view still selected, click View Group Properties on the ribbon.

The labels should be removed.

As you do this, try to visualize traveling down the road and experiencing the changes in the road geometry that you see from section to section.

The scenario here may be that an engineer has asked you to check the waterline design against your road design to see if there are any problems.

As you look at the section views, do you see any problems with the location of the waterline?

7. On the Sections tab, click <Edit> in the Label Set column next to EG.

8. Select _No Labels, and click OK. Click OK again to close the Section View Group Properties dialog box and return to the drawing.

9. In the top-right viewport, zoom in to the first section view at 0+50 (0+010) in the lower-left corner of the first sheet. Pan upward, and examine each section view. When you get to the top of the column, move to the bottom of the next column and pan upward to continue viewing the sections in order.

10. On the Insert tab of the ribbon, click LandXML. Browse to the Chapter 10 class data folder, and select Preliminary Waterline.xml. Click Open.

11. Click OK to dismiss the Import LandXML dialog box.

    A new pipe network representing the preliminary design of the waterline along Jordan Court has been created in the drawing. If you zoom in to the plan view of Jordan Court, you can see the double blue line along the right side of the road.

12. Click one of the section views, and then click Sample More Sources on the ribbon.

13. In the Selection Sources dialog box, click Preliminary Waterline and then click Add. Click OK to close the dialog box.

14. Press Esc to clear the selection of the section view. Zoom in, and examine the section views to verify that the waterline is being shown.

15. Use the LandXML command to import Subsurface Rock.xml. Use the Sample More Sources command to add the new surface named Rock to the section views. Set its style to Rock.

16. Once again, you need to clear the labels. Click a section view, and then click View Group Properties on the ribbon.

17. Click <Edit> in the Label Set column next to Rock. Select _No Labels, and click OK. Click OK again to return to the drawing.

18. Study the section views again.

    In a real-life situation, you may need to inform the engineer that the waterline design requires the excavation of a significant amount of rock. Also notice that around station 9+00 (0+270), the rock layer is very close to the surface—you may want to consider raising the road a bit in this area to avoid costly rock excavation.

19. Save and close the drawing.

You can view the results of successfully completing this exercise by opening `Sampling More Sources - Complete.dwg`.

WHAT DO YOU SEE?

As you pan from section view to section view, what story are you being told about the construction of this road? Which section views do you feel represent areas that require more time, effort, and money to build as opposed to others? In the first section views, you can see that the road cross section is much wider on the left side to account for the turning lane that you built into the corridor. As you progress further, you see sections that are very close to existing ground elevations, sections that are some distance above existing ground (a fill condition), and sections that are some distance below existing ground (a cut condition). How will the relationship of the road elevation to the existing ground elevation affect drainage for the homes that will be built along the road? Did you notice that ditches have been created in places where the road is in a cut condition? The amount of information and the number of additional questions generated by these simple pictures of the design are remarkable. The following images show some of the highlights of the design.

Station 1+50 (0+050) showing the widened left lane.

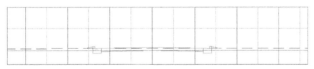

Station 4+50 (0+140), which is in an area that is very close to existing ground.

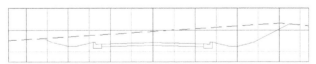

Station 13+50 (0+410) is in an area that is in cut. Note the ditches that are created.

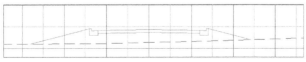

Station 19+50 (0+600) is in an area that is in fill.
Note that no ditches are created in this condition.

NOW YOU KNOW

Now that you've completed this chapter, you're able to use the Section Editor to view and edit corridors in section views. You can create sample lines and choose the information that will be captured and presented in the section views. You know how to create section views, individually and in groups that are arranged in sheets. And finally, you can add more sources to section views in the drawing to show additional information that supplements the road.

Now that you've completed this chapter, you're ready to begin working with sections and section views in a production environment.

CHAPTER 11

Displaying and Annotating Sections

As you have learned, creating a design is only part of the story—you also have to display and annotate it in ways that effectively represent your design for its intended purpose. This also applies to sections. As you'll see in this chapter, there are styles that control the appearance of the sections themselves as well as the section views that house them. There are labels that attach themselves to the sections and labels that can float in the section views. In fact, the methods you used to stylize and annotate sections and section views are very similar to those used for profiles and profile views.

Of course, there are also differences. For instance, you have to address the stylization and labeling of a corridor section, which you don't need to do with profile views. Another difference is that section views typically are created in bulk, so their arrangement and grouping into sheets must also be managed.

In this chapter, you'll learn to:

▶ **Apply section styles**

▶ **Apply section labels**

▶ **Control corridor section display with code set styles**

▶ **Apply labels with code set styles**

▶ **Apply section view styles**

▶ **Apply section view bands**

▶ **Apply group plot styles**

▶ **Create section view labels**

Applying Section Styles

Certification
Objective

Before I jump into section styles, I'll discuss the difference between sections and corridor sections. *Sections* are derived from surfaces, and they can be thought of as a very close relative to surface profiles. Like surface profiles, they are typically represented by a single line and can be annotated using a label set. Corridor sections are something quite different. You can think of a *corridor section* as an assembly superimposed on a section view. It consists of subassemblies, points, links, and shapes. Because of the differences between sections and corridor sections, the methods you use to stylize and label them are different.

With that out of the way, let's look at section styles. *Section styles* are used to change the appearance of a section either directly or by displaying it on a different layer. The most common application of a section style is the differentiation between sections that represent existing and proposed ground surfaces. You can also use section styles to show point markers at each vertex in the section line.

> If you haven't already done so, download and install the files for Chapter 11 according to the instructions in this book's Introduction.

Exercise 11.1: Apply Section Styles

In this exercise, you'll apply section styles to differentiate between sections that represent finished ground, existing ground, and rock surfaces.

> Because you're working exclusively with section views in this chapter, the drawings are set up with a single viewport rather than the multiple viewports used in prior chapters.

1. Open the drawing named `Applying Section Styles.dwg` located in the `Chapter 11` class data folder.

    Here, you see three section views that were plotted to investigate the shallow rock layer. The section views show a corridor section, existing ground surface section, and rock section.

2. Click the lowest section in the 8+50.00 (0+260.00) section view, and then click Section Properties on the Section: Rock ribbon tab.

> You may need to click the Section: Rock ribbon tab to see the Section Properties icon.

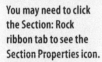

3. On the Information tab of the Section Properties dialog box, change Object Style to Rock. Click OK to close the dialog box. Press Esc to clear the selection.

    The rock section now appears as a gray dashed line.

> Using the Section Properties command to change the style is only one of three ways you can do this. You'll try out the other two later in this exercise.

4. Repeat the previous two steps for the section that appears above the rock layer, this time assigning a style of Existing Ground.

    The section representing existing ground now appears as a red dashed line along with the rock section from the previous step (see Figure 11.1).

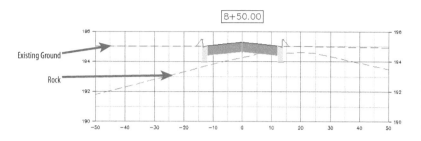

FIGURE 11.1   **The sections have been stylized to differentiate between rock and existing ground.**

5. Click the lower section in the 9+00.00 (0+270.00) section view, right-click, and select Properties.

6. In the Properties window, change Style to Rock. Keep the Properties window open.

7. Press Esc to clear the selection of the rock section. Click the existing ground section, and use the Properties window to change its style to Existing Ground.

8. Press Esc to clear the previous selection, and then click one of the grid lines for the 9+25.00 (0+280.00) section view. Click Section View Properties on the ribbon.

9. On the Sections tab of the Section View Properties dialog box, in the Style column, change the style of the section named EG to Existing Ground, and for the section named Rock, change the style to Rock. Click OK to dismiss the Section View Properties dialog box. Press Esc to clear the selection.

   All three section views should now properly display the existing ground and rock sections.

10. Save and close the drawing.

   You can view the results of successfully completing this exercise by opening Applying Section Styles - Complete.dwg.

If the section view grid obscures the red dashed line, select the section view, right-click, and select Display Order ➢ Bring To Front.

Using the Properties window to change the style is the second of three methods available to you. This method is a bit quicker because both sections can be changed in the same window.

Using the Section View Properties command to change the style is the third of three methods available to you. This method shows all the sections that are present in the section view.

Applying Section Labels

Certification
Objective

At times, you may need to annotate sections with information about their elevations, slopes, offsets, and so on. As you learned in Chapter 8, "Displaying and Annotating Profiles," label sets enable you to apply multiple labels at once as well as apply important configuration settings to the labels such as increment, weeding, and so on. For sections, the AutoCAD® Civil 3D® software environment provides the following four types of labels that can be compiled into a label set:

Major Offset Labels   These labels are placed at constant increments along the section. You can use this label type to label offset, elevation, instantaneous grade, and many other properties.

Minor Offset Labels   These are the same as major offset labels except they are created at a smaller increment and must exist as children of the major offset labels.

Segment Labels   You use this label type to label the grade, length, and other properties of the line segments that make up the section.

Grade Break Labels   You use this label type to label the offset, elevation, and other properties of grade breaks—the locations where segments meet.

The first two types are created at increments, so they are spaced evenly across the section. The last two are created at individual components of the section, so they are placed wherever these components exist. Because sections sometimes have many short segments, you can configure the label sets to skip points that are close together to prevent labels from overlapping.

If you haven't already done so, download and install the files for Chapter 11 according to the instructions in this book's Introduction.

Exercise 11.2: Apply Section Labels

In this exercise, you'll configure labels to show information on the elevations of the rock layer in each section view.

Here you see the same three section views from the previous exercise. The section view styles have been modified to create some extra space beneath the sections.

1. Open the drawing named Applying Section Labels.dwg located in the Chapter 11 class data folder.

2. Click the rock section on the lowest section view, and then click Edit Section Labels on the ribbon.

3. In the Section Labels – Rock dialog box, do the following:

    a. For Type, select Grade Breaks.

    b. For Section Grade Break Label Style, select Rock.

    c. Click Add.

    d. For Dim Anchor Opt, select Graph View Bottom.

    e. For Dim Anchor Val, enter 0.

    f. Click OK.

You should see three labels along the bottom of the section view with lines extending upward from each one.

With the options you have selected, only three labels appear. It would be better to increase the number of labels to include more points along the section. In steps 4 and 5, you'll adjust the Weeding setting to provide more labels.

ANCHORS AWEIGH

In step 3 of Exercise 11.2, you adjusted two settings relating to anchors. The concept of anchors is unique to certain types of labels that appear in section views and profile views. As a label style is composed, certain key points can be located at an anchor point whose location will be determined at the time the label is applied. This gives you some additional control over the placement of the labels. For example, in the previous steps, you specified that the labels should be aligned to the bottom of the grid by assigning Graph View Bottom as the Dim Anchor Opt setting. The Dim Anchor Val setting is an offset from the anchor point, which enables you to fine-tune the position of the label even more. An easy way to find out whether a label style that you have selected can respond to anchors is to look for a second grip. When initially created, this grip will be located where the anchor options specify. The grip can be moved to a location of your choice, providing even more flexibility with label placement.

4. Press Esc to clear the selection from the previous step. Click one of the labels, and then click Edit Label Group on the ribbon.

5. In the Weeding column, change the value to **5 (2)**. Click OK. Press Esc to clear the selection.

As shown in Figure 11.2, more labels appear because the Weeding setting allows the space between the labels to be as small as 5 feet (2 meters) rather than 100 feet (25 meters).

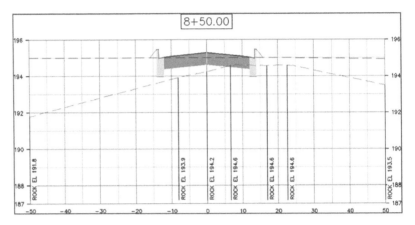

FIGURE 11.2   A label set has been applied to the rock section to provide information about the elevations of the rock layer.

6. Apply the same labels to the rock section in the other two section views.

THERE ARE LABEL SETS FOR SECTION VIEWS TOO

You learned about label sets in Chapter 6 and Chapter 8 when dealing with alignment and profile labels. The same label set functionality is available for section views too. Try it for step 6 in Exercise 11.2. Instead of manually setting up the rock labels, use the Save Label Set function to save the first configuration, and then use Import Label Set to apply it to the other section views.

7. Save and close the drawing.

You can view the results of successfully completing this exercise by opening `Applying Section Labels - Complete.dwg`.

Controlling Corridor Section Display with Code Set Styles

You have already seen how section styles can be used to change the appearance of sections, but what about corridor sections? As stated earlier, the way this is handled is different and is done through the use of a *code set style*. The setup of code set styles is complicated, and it's often left to the expertise of a CAD manager or very experienced Civil 3D user. However, once code set styles are created and made available to you, the task of assigning them to a corridor section is fairly simple.

Certification
Objective

CODE SET STYLES

Let's take a closer look at code set styles. First, it will be easier if you think of a corridor section as an assembly. You have already learned that assemblies are made up of smaller parts called *subassemblies*. You have also learned that subassemblies are made up of smaller parts called *points*, *links*, and *shapes*. Points, links, and shapes all have at least one *code* assigned to them, and this little string of text is the key to how code set styles work.

For example, one code that is used quite often is Pave. The BasicLaneTransition subassembly in your corridor uses a rectangular shape to represent the lane, and the Pave code is assigned to this shape as a property of the subassembly.

Shapes have styles just like all the other Civil 3D objects you have studied. For example, you can create a shape style called Hatched Pavement that displays the outline of the shape and fills it with a dot hatch to represent the pavement material. Another shape style might be Basic Pavement, which shows just an outline and no hatching.

Even for a simple assembly, the number of codes that are involved can grow quickly. And the number of styles can grow quickly as well—for example, you may want to apply a different style to each code to visually differentiate pavement from curbing from sidewalk, among other things. One job of a code set style is to match up multiple codes with multiple styles and store them all under one name. So, for example, you may have a code set style called Basic that uses the Basic Pavement style for any shape coded Pave. This might be only one of several or even dozens of match-ups between style and code in this code set style. Then, in another code set style named Detailed, you may decide to use the Hatched Pavement style for any instances of the Pave shape code. Again, this might be one of many code-style match-ups.

(Continues)

CODE SET STYLES *(Continued)*

Now, with both code set styles in place, you can quickly change the appearance of your corridor section to take on either a Basic or Detailed appearance by simply switching the code set style, as shown in the following diagrams.

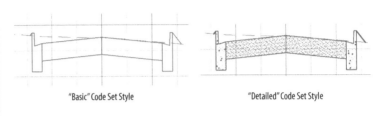

"Basic" Code Set Style   "Detailed" Code Set Style

If you haven't already done so, download and install the files for Chapter 11 according to the instructions in this book's Introduction.

Exercise 11.3: Apply Code Set Styles

In this exercise, you'll apply different code set styles to corridor sections and observe the changes that can occur. You'll explore code set styles for an individual section and for a section view group.

The drawing is zoomed in to the same three section views from the previous exercise.

The appearance of the corridor section changes to a more basic outline.

You now see the top surface of the corridor section highlighted in red.

1. Open the drawing named `Applying Code Set Styles.dwg` located in the `Chapter 11` class data folder.

2. Click the corridor section in the bottom section view, and then click Section Properties on the ribbon.

3. On the Information tab of the Corridor Section Properties dialog box, change Object Style to Road Sections and click OK. Press Esc to clear the selection.

4. Using the same procedure, change the style to Road Sections – Top Highlighted.

5. In the lower-right corner of your screen, click the icon for the customization menu. If there is no check mark next to LineWeight, click LineWeight to activate the button on the status bar.

6. Click the Lineweight icon on the status bar to turn on the display of lineweights.
   The icon turns blue if the feature is on.

7. Change the style of the corridor section to Presentation.

   With this style, the pavement is hatched with a different pattern than the curbs.

8. Press Esc to clear the previous selection. Zoom out, and pan to the north where the sheets of section views are located. Click one of the section views, and select View Group Properties on the ribbon.

   This opens the Section View Group Properties dialog box.

9. Click the Sections tab. In the Style column, change the style for Jordan Court to Presentation.

10. Click OK to dismiss the Section View Group Properties dialog box and return to the drawing. Zoom in, and study the change to the section views.

    The code set style has been assigned throughout the entire section view group (see Figure 11.3).

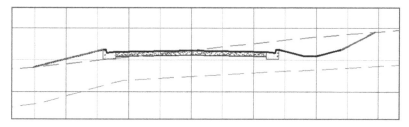

FIGURE 11.3 The Jordan Court corridor section with the Presentation code set style applied

11. Save and close the drawing.

You can view the results of successfully completing this exercise by opening `Applying Code Set Styles - Complete.dwg`.

Applying Labels with Code Set Styles

As you have seen, code set styles are very effective at assigning styles based on point, link, and shape codes. They can also be used to apply labels to corridor sections, and just as with styles, codes are the key to automating the placement of labels.

Certification
Objective

Exercise 11.4: Apply Labels with Code Set Styles

In this exercise, you'll use a code set style to add labels to a corridor section. You'll then modify the code set style to add a label at the crown.

1. Open the drawing named Labeling with Code Set Styles.dwg located in the Chapter 11 class data folder.

2. Click the corridor section in the bottom section view, and then select Section Properties on the ribbon.

3. Change Object Style to Design With Labels, and click OK. Press Esc to clear the selection.

   The corridor section now includes labels for slopes, elevations, and shape codes. Next, you'll modify the code set style to add an elevation label at the crown of the road.

4. Open the Tool Palettes window by clicking the Tool Palettes icon on the Home tab of the ribbon. Click the Basic tab in the Tool Palettes window to make the Basic palette come to the forefront.

   You're taken directly to the Help window for this subassembly.

5. Right-click BasicLaneTransition, and select Help.

   You're taken directly to the Help window for this subassembly. Note that point P1 is coded Crown (see Figure 11.4)—this is the code you'll use.

Point, Link, or Shape	Codes	Description
P1	Crown	Crown of road on finish grade
P2	ETW	Edge-of-traveled-way on finish grade
P3	Crown_Subbase	Crown of road on subbase
P4	ETW_Subbase	Edge-of-traveled-way on subbase
L1	Top, Pave	Paved finish grade
L3	Datum, Subbase	Subbase
S1	Pave1	

Coding Diagram

F I G U R E 11.4 Coding diagram for the BasicLaneTransition subassembly

6. Scroll to the bottom of the Help page, and study the coding diagram.

7. Close the Help window. Click the corridor section, and then click Section Properties ➤ Edit Code Set Style on the ribbon.

8. On the Codes tab of the Code Set Style dialog box, expand the Point section and locate the Crown code beneath it.

9. Click the icon to the right of <None> in the Label Style column across from Crown. Select Crown Elev, and click OK.

10. Click OK to dismiss the Code Set Style dialog box. Press Esc to clear the selection of the section.

   A marker and label are now displayed at the crown of the road. The code set style recognized the use of the Crown code in the corridor section and applied the label accordingly (see Figure 11.5).

Normally, editing a style would be considered outside the scope of this book; however, this simple exercise will help you understand the link between the code and the label.

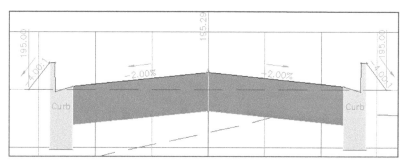

FIGURE 11.5   A code set style that includes labels has been applied to the Jordan Court corridor section.

11. Save and close the drawing.

You can view the results of successfully completing this exercise by opening Labeling with Code Set Styles - Complete.dwg.

Applying Section View Styles

Now that you have studied the display and annotation of sections, let's take a look at the appearance of the section view that provides the backdrop for the sections. Once again, there are many similarities between section views and profile views. Both have the capability to display a grid, both can apply a vertical

Certification Objective

exaggeration, and both can use bands to provide supplemental information along the bottom or the top of the view. In fact, the only significant difference between profile views and section views is that profile views display stations (read along the alignment) whereas section views display offsets (read perpendicular to the alignment).

Exercise 11.5: Apply Section View Styles

In this exercise, you'll experiment with changing the section view style for an individual section view as well as for a group of section views.

1. Open the drawing named Applying Section View Styles.dwg located in the Chapter 11 class data folder.

2. Click the lowest section view, and then click Section View Properties on the ribbon.

3. On the Information tab of the Section View Properties dialog box, change the style to Design 10V Major And Minor – No Padding. Click OK. Press Esc to clear the selection.

> If you haven't already done so, download and install the files for Chapter 11 according to the instructions in this book's Introduction.

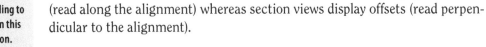

> Once again, you're viewing the three design cross sections that you have been working with in previous exercises.

> One way you might use this section view style is for close inspection and detailed editing of the section, because the grid lines appear very frequently and the vertical dimensions of the sections are exaggerated even more.

ALL THAT WITH ONE STYLE?

In step 3 of Exercise 11.5, when you changed the section view style from Design 5V Major And Minor to Design 10V Major And Minor – No Padding, the following changes were made to the section view:

▶ The vertical exaggeration changed from 5 to 10, causing the elevation changes in the sections to be much more dramatic.

▶ The elevation grid interval changed to increase the frequency of both the major grids and minor grids along with their associated labels.

▶ The space beneath the sections (padding) was removed.

▶ The minor interval of the offset grid lines was increased.

This is a classic example of the power of styles. To make these changes manually would have taken several minutes to figure out—even for an experienced user. Instead, all you have to do is assign a different style, and all the changes are applied instantaneously.

4. Use the Section View Properties command to change the style to Design 1V Major And Minor – No Padding.

   This view is similar to the previous one, but this time there is no vertical exaggeration.

5. Use the Section View Properties command to change the style to Design 1V – No Grid.

   Because this section view style excludes the grid and labels, you might use it to create illustrations for a report.

6. Use the Section View Properties command to change the style to Design 5V Major Only.

   This view is similar to the other views immediately above it, except the minor grids aren't displayed.

7. Press Esc to clear the previous selection. Zoom out, and pan north to the three sheets of section views. Click one of the section views, and select View Group Properties on the ribbon.

   This opens the Section View Group Properties dialog box.

8. On the Section Views tab, click in the Style column in the first row across from Section View Group – 1.

   The new section view style applies a vertical exaggeration of 2, so the section views take up more space top to bottom. In the next step, you'll rearrange the views on the sheet so they're easier to read.

9. Select Road Section Type 2, and click OK. Click OK again to dismiss the Section View Group Properties dialog box.

10. With one of the section views still selected, click Update Group Layout on the ribbon.

    The sections are rearranged, and the new layout must include an additional sheet (an additional two sheets for the metric drawing) to accommodate the extra space that is now taken up by the section views (see Figure 11.6).

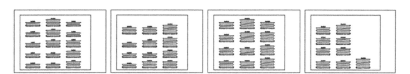

FIGURE 11.6 A fourth sheet is created as a result of changing the section view style applied to the section view group.

11. Save and close the drawing.

You can view the results of successfully completing this exercise by opening `Applying Section View Styles - Complete.dwg`.

Applying Section View Bands

You may need to display additional information about the sections to accompany what is conveyed by the section view. Bands can be a useful tool for this purpose, enabling you to display information both graphically and textually. There are two types of section view bands, as described here:

Section Data Bands   You use this type of band for labeling offset and elevation data at regular increments along the section view.

Section Segment Bands   You use this type of band to label length and slope information about individual segments. Because the individual labels are created segment by segment, they aren't evenly spaced across the band as you see in a section data band. Weeding can be applied to improve situations where segments are short and labels overlap.

Exercise 11.6: Apply Section View Bands

If you haven't already done so, download and install the files for Chapter 11 according to the instructions in this book's Introduction.

In this exercise, you'll apply section view bands to an individual section to display information for stations, elevations, and rock depth. You'll then apply bands to a group of section views and update the layout of the section views to account for the additional space taken up by the bands.

1. Open the drawing named `Applying Section View Bands.dwg` located in the `Chapter 11` class data folder.

2. Click the grid of the bottom section view, and select Section View Properties on the ribbon.

3. On the Bands tab of the Section View Properties dialog box, do the following:

    a. For Band Type, verify that Section Data is selected.

    b. Under Select Band Style, verify that Design – EG Elev is selected.

    c. Click Add.

      d. Change the Gap value for the newly added band to 0.

      e. Scroll right, and select EG in the Section1 column.

      f. Click OK.

    The band is added, but there are values with lines through them at either end of the band.

4. With the section view still selected, click Section View Properties on the ribbon again.

5. On the Bands tab of the Section View Properties dialog box, uncheck the boxes in the Label Start Offset and Label End Offset columns. Click OK.

    The labels at either end of the band are now omitted.

6. Add a band showing the depth of the rock surface beneath the existing ground surface by applying these settings:

    ▶ Type: Section Data

    ▶ Style: Rock Depth

    ▶ Gap: 0

    ▶ Label Start Offset: Unchecked

    ▶ Label End Offset: Unchecked

    ▶ Section1: EG

    ▶ Section2: Rock

7. Add a band showing offset values by applying these settings:

    ▶ Type: Section Data

    ▶ Style: Design – Offsets

    ▶ Gap: 0

    ▶ Label Start Offset: Checked

    ▶ Label End Offset: Checked

8. Access the Bands tab of the Section View Properties dialog box again. Click Save As Band Set.

9. Enter **Off-Elev-Rock Depth** in the Name field, and click OK. Click OK to close the Section View Properties dialog box.

10. Press Esc to clear the previous selection. Click the section view to the north, and then click Section View Properties on the ribbon.

11. On the Bands tab of the Section View Properties dialog box, click Import Band Set. Select Off-Elev-Rock Depth, and click OK.

12. Select EG for Section1 of the first two bands. Select Rock as Section2 of the second band. Click OK.

    The bands for this section view now match the bands of the section view that you modified in steps 2 through 7 (see Figure 11.7).

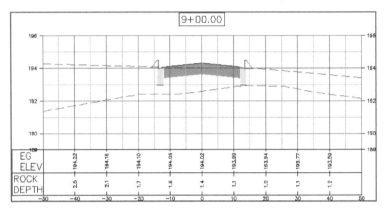

FIGURE 11.7 A section view with bands added for existing ground elevations, rock depth and offsets

13. Repeat steps 10 through 12 to add the same band set to the third design section view.

14. Press Esc to clear the previous selection. Zoom out, and pan north to the sheets of section views. Click one of the section views, and then click View Group Properties on the ribbon.

15. On the Section Views tab, click the ellipsis in the first row of the Change Band Set column.

16. Click Import Band Set, and select Section Sheets. Click OK until you have dismissed all dialog boxes and returned to the drawing.

    The bands have been added to the section views, but the section views must now be rearranged to account for the additional space they occupy. You'll address this in the next step.

17. With one of the section views still selected, click Update Group Layout on the ribbon.

    Civil 3D automatically creates a fourth sheet as a result of this update (see Figure 11.8).

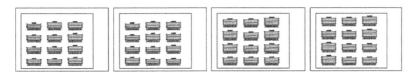

FIGURE 11.8 A fourth sheet is created to accommodate the extra area taken up by the section view bands.

18. Save and close the drawing.

You can view the results of successfully completing this exercise by opening `Applying Section View Bands - Complete.dwg`.

Applying Group Plot Styles

Certification
Objective

Throughout this chapter, you have been working with several sheets' worth of section views all neatly arranged within predefined sheet borders. You may be wondering what controls this behavior, and if you guessed that it's some sort of style, you're correct. The arrangement of multiple section views is accomplished by a *group plot style*.

A group plot style uses an assortment of settings to configure the layout of multiple section views. When section view groups are created, there are two placement options: Production and Draft. When a section view group is created using the Production placement option, the layout of section views is made to fit on individual sheets. The size and shape of the individual sheets come from a template (`.dwt`) file. When the Draft placement option is used, the section views are laid out as a single group and aren't bound within a given area.

Another function of group plot styles is to overlay a grid on the sections. With this approach to sheet creation, the section views don't typically have their own grid but are superimposed on a grid that covers the entire sheet.

Exercise 11.7: Apply Group Plot Styles

If you haven't already done so, download and install the files for Chapter 11 according to the instructions in this book's Introduction.

In this exercise, you'll experiment with applying different group plot styles to change the arrangement of the section views.

1. Open the drawing named Applying Group Plot Styles.dwg located in the Chapter 11 class data folder.

2. Click one of the section views displayed on the three sheets, and then click View Group Properties on the ribbon.
   The Section View Group Properties dialog box opens.

3. On the Section Views tab, click the first row in the Group Plot Style column (see Figure 11.9). Select Left To Right – Top Down, and click OK.

Click here.

FIGURE 11.9 Where to click to change the group plot style for the section view group

4. Click OK to dismiss the Section View Group Properties dialog box.

5. Click one of the section views, and click View Group Properties again. This time, do the following:

   a. Click the top row in the Group Plot Style column, and select Bottom Up – Left To Right With Grid.

   b. Click the top row in the Style column, and select Design 1V – No Grid.

   c. Click the ellipsis in the Change Band Set column.

   d. Select the Section Data band listed in the Section View Group Bands dialog box, and then click the red X to remove it. Click OK.

   e. Click OK to close the Section View Group Properties dialog box.

Notice that the section views shift toward the top left of the sheet and that they are arranged with the stations increasing from left to right.

6. Zoom in, and study the newly configured sheets.

   With this configuration, the section views are superimposed on a grid provided by the sheets. Because the grid is already there, the section view styles don't show the individual grids. These styles also have their own offset labels across the bottom, so the section view bands have been removed.

7. Click one of the section views, and then click Update Group Layout on the ribbon.

   With the newly applied section view styles and group plot style, the section views now all fit on two sheets (see Figure 11.10).

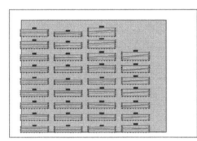 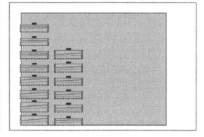

F I G U R E   1 1 . 1 0   **A section view group with a new group plot style applied**

8. Save and close the drawing.

You can view the results of successfully completing this exercise by opening `Applying Group Plot Styles - Complete.dwg`.

Creating Section View Labels

So far in this chapter, you have seen how to create many different types of annotations. There are label sets that are applied to sections, labels applied to corridor sections through code set styles, labels applied to section views and bands, and even labels attached to objects that have been projected to section views. One limitation of these labels is that they're all connected to something and therefore get their information and location from another object. What if you need to create a basic, all-purpose label that can be used to convey offset and elevation on a section view? To do this, you create a *section view label*.

Section view labels are attached to the section view itself. They can be placed anywhere in the section view and used to label just about anything.

Exercise 11.8: Create Section View Labels

In this exercise, you'll create a section view label that calls out the location of the curb flowline in a section view.

1. Open the drawing named Creating Section View Labels.dwg located in the Chapter 11 class data folder.

    The drawing is zoomed in to the first section view on Jordan Court where the road is widened to accommodate a turn lane. The scenario for this exercise is that you have been asked to include offset and elevation information for the curb flowline so that the contractor knows exactly where to place the curb in the widened area.

2. On the Annotate tab of the ribbon, click Add Labels. In the Add Labels dialog box, do the following:

    a. For Feature, select Section View.

    b. For Label Type, select Offset Elevation.

    c. For Offset Elevation Label Style, verify that Offset Over Elevation is selected.

    d. For Marker Style, verify that Basic is selected.

    e. Click Add.

3. Click one of the grid lines of the section view. Right-click while holding down the Shift key, and then select Endpoint. Click the flowline of the left curb.

4. Press Esc to clear the current command. Click the newly created label, and drag its square grip up and to the left to improve its readability.

5. Click the label, and then click Edit Label Text on the ribbon. This opens the Text Component Editor dialog box.

6. In the window on the right, click just to the left of the word *Offset* to place your cursor in the position before it. Type **CURB FLOWLINE**, and press Enter.

    The result should look like Figure 11.11.

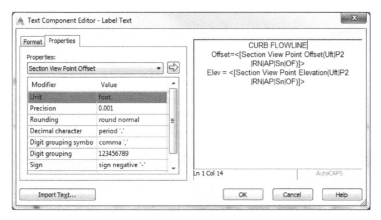

FIGURE 11.11 Customizing the label contents for a section view label

7. Click OK to close the Text Component Editor dialog.
   The label should now appear as shown in Figure 11.12.

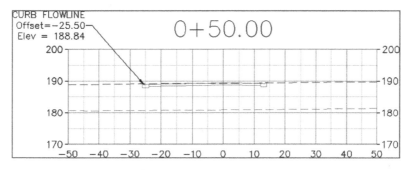

FIGURE 11.12 A label has been added that indicates the offset and elevation of the curb flowline.

8. Save and close the drawing.

You can view the results of successfully completing this exercise by opening `Creating Section View Labels - Complete.dwg`.

BE CAREFUL

Although the label in Exercise 11.8 is pointing to the curb, it isn't attached to it. If a change in the design causes the curb to move, the label might not be pointing to the right spot and will need to be updated manually. This isn't a difficult thing to do, but it's something that could easily be overlooked. A more permanent solution would be to incorporate the label into a code set style.

NOW YOU KNOW

Now that you have completed this chapter, you're able to apply section styles, code set styles, and section view styles to change the appearance of cross sections for your designs. You're also able to add labels through code set styles, section labels, and section view labels. You can display additional information in your section views using bands. Finally, you know how to use group plot styles to configure an array of section views that are formatted to fit on various sheets for easy documentation.

You're now ready to begin displaying and annotating sections and section views in a production environment.

CHAPTER 12

Designing and Analyzing Boundaries Using Parcels

In the previous chapter, you completed the road-design portion of the example project by creating and displaying cross sections. With the roads in place, it's now time to look at another aspect of the design: the layout of real-estate lots. Although the road design and lot layout are very different types of designs, they are still dependent on one another because the roads determine the front boundaries of the lots. In the example project, you won't return to road design, but in a real project, there are often adjustments to the road layout that can affect the lots as well as other design aspects.

As the designer in this project, you'll be asked to design the layout of the single-family lots as well as open space areas, community areas, utility easements, and so on. The developer makes money by selling the lots, so the more lots there are to sell, the more profit there is to be had. So why not make a thousand tiny little lots? Well, of course, if a lot is too small to fit a house, it will be nearly useless and won't sell. In addition, other aspects determine minimum size requirements for lots, such as the market the developer is targeting and/or zoning laws. Your job as the designer will be to create as many lots as possible while meeting these minimum size requirements.

In this chapter, you'll learn to:

▶ **Understand parcels**

▶ **Create parcels from objects**

▶ **Create parcels by layout**

▶ **Edit parcels**

Understanding Parcels

Quite often, a land-development project involves the purchase, consolidation, or subdivision of a piece of real estate. Even if this isn't the case, the boundary of the developed property must be accurately depicted in the design drawings. It must also be marked in the field to ensure that neighboring properties aren't encroached on. Yet another potential aspect of a land-development project is accurately determining the location of rights-of-way and easements, whether existing or proposed. Through parcel objects and their associated commands and annotations, the AutoCAD® Civil 3D® software environment provides you with tools for creating, analyzing, and displaying legal boundaries efficiently and accurately.

Understanding Parcel Objects

As you have seen with other Civil 3D features, Civil 3D makes use of specialized objects to perform specific tasks. Creating parcels is no different. It involves the use of specialized objects whose behavior makes the process of creating and modifying parcels as efficient as possible. The objects that are applied in this case are called *parcel segments*. You can think of parcel segments as lines and curves that have been identified as sides of a parcel. They can be drawn from scratch using a special toolbar, or they can be created by converting lines, arcs, and polylines. Parcel segments must be assigned to a *site* so Civil 3D understands that they should react to one another. When parcel segments in the same site form a closed shape, that shape becomes a *parcel object*. This is a unique arrangement because you can't directly create a parcel object; instead, you create other objects to form a closed area, and then Civil 3D creates the parcel object for you (see Figure 12.1).

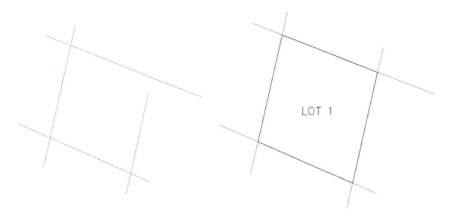

F I G U R E 1 2 . 1 The four parcel segments on the left don't form a closed shape; therefore, no parcel is created. On the right, a parcel object is created automatically, as shown by the black outline and the LOT 1 label.

In the same manner, any modifications to the fundamental objects that make up a parcel will result in an automatic update to the parcel itself. This is most evident when parcels are labeled with area, bearing, and distance information.

Understanding Sites

Placing objects within the same *site* is how you tell Civil 3D that you want these objects to "see" each other and interact. You can also prevent objects from interacting by placing them in different sites. The sites are listed in Prospector, and you can create as many as you need in a given drawing (see Figure 12.2).

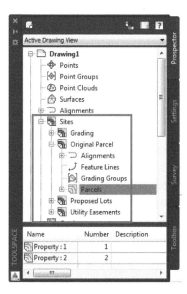

FIGURE 12.2   Sites listed in Prospector, with the contents of one site expanded

When parcel segments are placed in the same site in such a way that they create one or more closed shapes, the closed shapes automatically become parcels. Alignments, feature lines, grading groups, and survey figures can also occupy sites. These objects are able to interact with parcels and with one another. For example, if an alignment crosses through a parcel, the alignment automatically subdivides the parcel to create two parcels. For this to take place, the parcel and the alignment must be in the same site. By the same token, you can prevent the alignment from subdividing the parcel by placing the alignment and parcel in separate sites. In the left image of Figure 12.3, the alignment and parcel are in different sites and therefore don't interact to create two parcels from one. In the right image of Figure 12.3, the alignment has been moved to the same site as the parcel, causing it to be subdivided automatically.

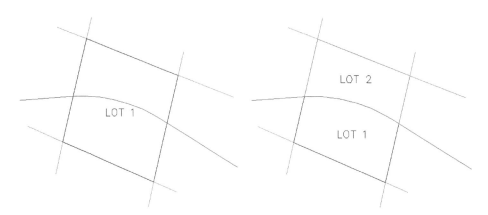

F I G U R E   1 2 . 3   The effect of sites on the interaction between an alignment and a parcel

Creating Parcels from Objects

One way you can create parcels is to select lines, arcs, and polylines that already exist in your drawing and convert them into parcel segments. This technique is often used when the parcel geometry is especially complex or must be drawn based on other geometry in the drawing. Civil 3D provides a few tools for drawing parcel segments directly, but many more drawing and editing commands are available in the AutoCAD part of Civil 3D. For this reason, you may find it easier to create the necessary geometry using the AutoCAD drafting commands rather than the Civil 3D commands.

Converting basic AutoCAD entities to parcel segments is relatively simple. You launch the command from the ribbon; select the lines, arcs, and/or circles that you would like to convert; and then provide some information about the parcel segments you're about to create. If the selected objects intersect to create closed shapes, Civil 3D takes care of the rest. You'll know the parcels have been created when the labels appear in the drawing area and the parcels are listed in Prospector.

Exercise 12.1: Create Parcels from Objects

If you haven't already done so, download and install the files for Chapter 12 according to the instructions in this book's Introduction.

In this exercise, you'll create parcels from geometry provided for you. You will first create the overall project parcel, then the right-of-way parcel, and finally, large parcel areas that will be subdivided into individual lots at a later time.

1. Open the drawing named Creating Parcels from Objects.dwg located in the Chapter 12 class data folder.

2. On the Home tab of the ribbon, click Parcel ➤ Create Parcel From Objects.

3. Click the green polyline representing the overall parcel boundary. Click the magenta polyline representing the southern right-of-way of Emerson Road. Press Enter.

4. In the Create Parcels From Objects dialog box, click OK to accept the default settings.

5. Open Prospector, and expand Sites ➤ Lot Layout. Right-click Parcels, and select Refresh.

    A plus sign appears next to Parcels, and a parcel named Basic : 1 should be listed in the item view area of Prospector (see Figure 12.4).

Because parcel layout is a 2D design, the drawings in this chapter aren't set up with multiple viewports, as in other chapters.

The hatching is a function of the parcel style that has been applied by default. The area is hatched, and a parcel label appears near the center of the property, indicating that a new parcel has been created.

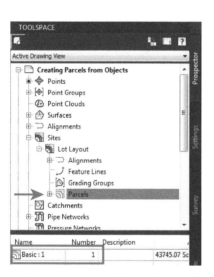

FIGURE 12.4   The newly created parcel shown in Prospector

6. If the item preview icon at the top left of Prospector isn't depressed, click it.

7. Right-click Parcels, and verify that there is a check next to Show Preview. If there isn't, click Show Preview.

8. Expand Parcels, and then click Basic : 1 listed beneath it.
    A preview of the shape of the parcel is shown in the item view area.

The red polylines represent the backs of the parcels. Selecting them subdivides the property into several large pieces. These pieces will be subdivided further to create individual lots. You may need to zoom in closely to pick one of the red polylines among the hatch lines.

9. Click one of the red polylines in the drawing, right-click, and choose Select Similar.

10. On the Home tab of the ribbon, click Parcel ➤ Create Parcel From Objects.

11. In the Create Parcels – From Objects dialog box, change Parcel Style to Property and click OK.

    Two new parcels are created, as shown by the areas where the hatching has been carved away.

12. In Prospector, right-click Parcels and select Refresh. Preview the parcels in the item view window as you did earlier with the Basic : 1 parcel.

13. Click one of the dashed right-of-way lines, right-click, and then pick Select Similar.

14. Again, on the Home tab of the ribbon, click Parcel ➤ Create Parcel From Objects. Click OK to dismiss the Create Parcel – From Objects dialog box with the default settings.

15. Refresh, and preview the parcels in Prospector again. Now there are seven parcels in all (see Figure 12.5).

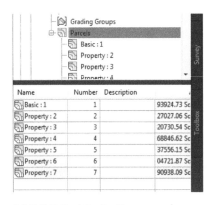

FIGURE 12.5   Seven parcels are now listed in the Prospector item view.

16. Save and close the drawing.

You can view the results of successfully completing this exercise by opening `Creating Parcels from Objects - Complete.dwg`.

Creating Parcels by Layout

Earlier in this chapter, you read about the advantage of using basic AutoCAD drafting commands to produce parcel geometry. As mentioned, these commands are great for drawing lines and curves based on general geometric principles. But what if you need to create parcels that occupy a certain area, parcel segments that are perpendicular to a road frontage, or parcels that meet a minimum depth requirement based on zoning laws? These are all criteria that are specific to property boundaries, and they are all built into the Civil 3D *Parcel Layout Tools* toolbar. When you launch the parcel layout tools from the ribbon, they appear on a specialized toolbar similar to what you have seen for alignments and profiles.

Certification
Objective

PARCEL TERMINOLOGY

Certain terms are unique to property boundary design. Here are a few that you'll want to become familiar with:

Parcel or Lot   This is a piece of land delineated by a legal boundary.

Bearing   This is a horizontal direction expressed in degrees east or west of a north or south direction. For example, N 25° E means to face north and then rotate to the right 25°. Bearings are often combined with distances to mathematically define a parcel line.

Right-of-way   This is a strip of land used for transportation purposes. It's commonly expressed as a constant width on either side of a road centerline.

Frontage   For lots along a road, this is the length of the front line that is coincident with the edge of the right-of-way. Increased frontage typically increases the value of a piece of land.

Setback   This is the required distance between a property line and a building. Often the front, rear, and side setbacks are expressed separately.

Easement   This is a strip of land that someone is given the right to use for a certain purpose, but not to own. For example, a utility easement might give a utility company the right to install and maintain a utility line within a certain area of a person's property.

Zoning   Zoning is a way of dividing large areas of land into zones and dictating different land-use requirements for each zone. For example, in one zone, the minimum lot size might be 5 acres (2 hectares), whereas in another, it might be 0.25 acres (0.10 hectares). Zoning boundaries and regulations are typically determined by a local government entity.

Using the Lot Line Tools

The first few buttons on the Parcel Layout Tools toolbar are used for basic parcel-segment drafting that is similar to using basic AutoCAD line and curve commands, as shown in Table 12.1. You can use these tools to draw parcels freehand or to retrace geometry that already exists in the drawing.

TABLE 12.1   Important lot-line tools

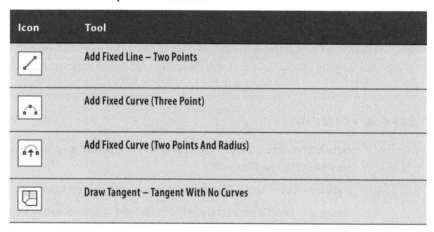

Icon	Tool
	Add Fixed Line – Two Points
	Add Fixed Curve (Three Point)
	Add Fixed Curve (Two Points And Radius)
	Draw Tangent – Tangent With No Curves

Exercise 12.2: Create Parcels Using the Lot Line Tools

If you haven't already done so, download and install the files for Chapter 12 according to the instructions in this book's Introduction.

In this exercise, you'll draw new parcel geometry using the Parcel Creation Tools command. You'll create a common area parcel near the entrance to the development as well as a parcel representing land that is to remain the property of the individual owner.

1. Open the drawing named Using the Lot Line Tools.dwg located in the Chapter 12 class data folder.

2. On the Home tab of the ribbon, click Parcel ➤ Parcel Creation Tools.

3. On the Parcel Layout Tools toolbar, click Add Fixed Line – Two Points. Click OK to accept the defaults in the Create Parcels – Layout dialog box.

4. Zoom in to Jordan Court near station 4+00 (0+100). Hold down the Shift key, and right-click to open the Object Snap context menu.

5. Click Endpoint. Then click the end of the magenta curve at station 4+20.38 (0+128.13), as shown in Figure 12.6.

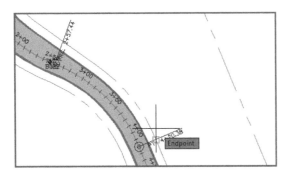

FIGURE 12.6 **Snapping to the end of the curve to begin creating a new parcel line**

6. Hold down the Shift key, and right-click. Select Perpendicular.

7. Click the magenta back-lot line, as shown in Figure 12.7. Press Esc twice to end the command.

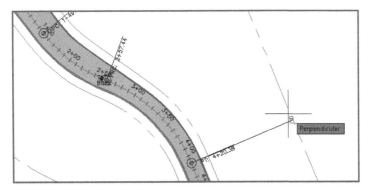

FIGURE 12.7 **Snapping to a location that is perpendicular to the eastern lot line**

You have created a new parcel near the front entrance that will be used for a community clubhouse and administrative offices.

8. Click Parcel ➤ Parcel Creation Tools on the Home tab of the ribbon.

9. Click Draw Tangent – Tangent With No Curves, and then click OK to dismiss the Create Parcels – Layout dialog box.

10. Using the Endpoint object snap, trace the fence line that surrounds the existing farm buildings. Begin at the north end of the fence, and work toward the south and west.

11. Once you have selected the last point on the fence, use the Perpendicular object snap to select the western boundary line, as shown in Figure 12.8.

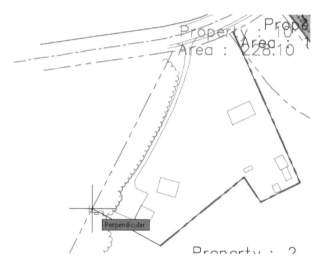

FIGURE 12.8 Completing the farm property boundary by clicking a point perpendicular to the west property boundary

In an actual project, to delineate this boundary properly, you would probably offset it a short distance behind the fence so the fence is entirely on the landowner's property. You have created a new parcel that will remain the property of the original landowner.

12. Press Esc twice to exit the Parcel command.

13. Save and close the drawing.

You can view the results of successfully completing this exercise by opening Using the Lot Line Tools - Complete.dwg.

Using the Parcel Sizing Tools

The next set of tools on the Parcel Layout Tools toolbar that you'll learn about is by far the most powerful: the parcel sizing tools. These tools enable you to lay out multiple lots within a predetermined area, with each lot meeting the size parameters you specify. These tools will create the bulk of the lots in a residential land-development design such as the example project you're working on.

You can use the following three tools to create new lots based on size:

Slide Line – Create   This tool creates one or more lots by sliding a line along the frontage until all size and dimension requirements are met.

Swing Line – Create   This tool creates one or more lots by rotating a line around a fixed swing point and intersecting it with a lot line across from the swing point. The result is one or more lots that radiate outward from the swing point.

Free Form Create   This tool creates a lot by attaching one end of a line to a parcel segment and extending that line along a specified angle (usually perpendicular) until it intersects another parcel segment.

Exercise 12.3: Create Parcels Using the Parcel Sizing Tools

In this exercise, you'll create several new parcels using the parcel sizing tools on the Parcel Layout Tools toolbar.

If you haven't already done so, download and install the files for Chapter 12 according to the instructions in this book's Introduction.

1. Open the drawing named Using the Parcel Sizing Tools.dwg located in the Chapter 12 class data folder.

2. On the Home tab of the ribbon, click Parcel ➢ Parcel Creation Tools.

3. On the Parcel Layout Tools toolbar, expand the button containing the parcel sizing tools, and click Slide Line – Create.

4. Click OK to dismiss the Create Parcels – Layout dialog box. When you're prompted to select a parcel, click the label that reads Property : 25 at the southwest end of the project.

5. When you're prompted to select the first point on the frontage, click the western endpoint of the lot line you previously created at station 4+20.38 (0+128.13), as shown in Figure 12.9.

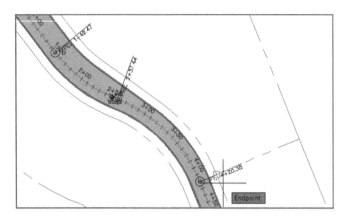

FIGURE 12.9   Selecting the beginning point of the frontage

6. Move your cursor in a southeastern direction along the frontage line. Note the orange "highlighter" that follows your cursor. Snap to the endpoint of the curve at station 11+83.29 (0+360.67), as shown in Figure 12.10.

> This "highlighter" is called a *jig line*, and it serves as a visual cue that your cursor is graphically linked to something; in this case, it's a parcel segment.

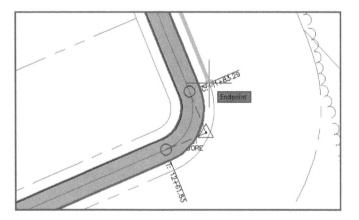

FIGURE 12.10   Selecting the endpoint of the frontage

7. When you're prompted to specify the angle, type **90** at the command line, and press Enter.

   A preview of the new parcel appears near the start point of the frontage.

> Because 90° is the default, you could simply press Enter when prompted for the angle.

8. Press Enter to accept the current sizing parameters and create the parcel. Press Esc to exit the current command but keep the Parcel Layout Tools toolbar open.

9. Click Swing Line – Create, and click the label that reads Property : 2 near the southeastern corner of the project.

10. When you're prompted for the start point of the frontage, snap to the northern endpoint of the Property : 2 parcel, as shown in Figure 12.11.

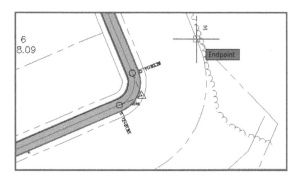

FIGURE 1 2 . 1 1   Selecting the beginning point of the frontage

11. When you're prompted for the endpoint of the frontage, move your cursor in a westerly direction along the property line and snap to the western endpoint of the same parcel (see Figure 12.12).

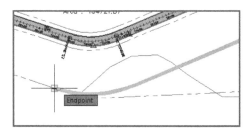

FIGURE 1 2 . 1 2   Selecting the ending point of the frontage

12. When you're prompted for the swing point, use an Endpoint object snap to select the property corner just south of the Property : 2 label.
    A preview of the parcel is displayed using the current Minimum Area setting of 10890 Sq. Ft. (1500 sq.m.).

13. If the chevron at the right end of the Parcel Layout Tools toolbar is pointing downward, click it. If not, skip to the next step.

To use an Endpoint object snap, hold down the Shift key and right-click; then select Endpoint.

14. In the expanded area beneath the Parcel Layout Tools toolbar, type **1acre (0.4hectare)** for the Minimum Area value, and press Enter. The preview is updated to reflect the new area.

15. Press Enter to create the parcel.

    One scenario where this type of parcel might be used would be if an environmental agency requested a 1-acre (0.4-hectare) preservation area to mitigate environmental impacts elsewhere on the site.

16. Press Esc to clear the current command. On the Parcel Layout Tools toolbar, click Free Form Create. Move your cursor along the property line to the east of the Property : 25 label.

    Note how the line preview attaches itself to the parcel segment and extends outward until it intersects another parcel segment.

17. With your cursor on the west side of the line, snap to the midpoint of the parcel segment. When you're prompted for a direction, press Enter to specify perpendicular.

18. Press Esc twice to clear the current command and close the Parcel Layout Tools toolbar.

19. Save and close the drawing.

You can view the results of successfully completing this exercise by opening `Using the Parcel Sizing Tools - Complete.dwg`.

Using Parcel Sizing and Layout Parameters

The Parcel Layout Tools toolbar includes commands for creating new parcel geometry as well as editing it. The toolbar expands downward to reveal parameters that determine the dimensions of the lots that are created. This enables you to include size requirements in your parcel design that may have been requested by the developer or dictated by zoning laws.

The layout parameters available to you are listed here. The image next to each parameter matches the schematic preview shown in the bottom of the Parcel Layout Tools toolbar as you click each parameter:

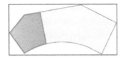

Minimum Area   This is the minimum area occupied by the lot. Minimum area is a common requirement that designers must meet to satisfy zoning requirements.

Minimum Frontage   This is the minimum length of the lines or arcs that make up the side of the lot that is coincident with a road right-of-way. This is also a common parameter that designers must meet to satisfy zoning requirements.

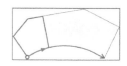

Use Minimum Frontage At Offset   Some zoning regulations allow the frontage to be measured at the building setback line rather than at the frontage line itself. This would enable you to create a larger number of smaller lots, especially when creating lots along the outside of a curve.

Frontage Offset   This parameter is typically used to define the building setback line.

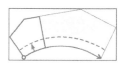

Minimum Width   This is the minimum width allowed for the resulting parcel.

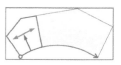

Minimum Depth   This is the minimum depth allowed for the parcel, measured perpendicular to the frontage at its midpoint.

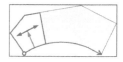

Use Maximum Depth   This parameter prevents the development of exceedingly deep lots, potentially enabling the area to be subdivided more efficiently.

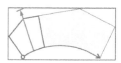

Maximum Depth   This is the maximum depth allowed for the parcel, measured perpendicular to the frontage at its midpoint.

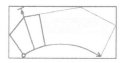

Multiple Solution Preference – Use Shortest Frontage   When multiple solutions are possible, the one that produces the shortest frontage is selected.

Multiple Solution Preference – Use Smallest Area   When multiple solutions are possible, the one that produces the smallest area is selected.

In addition to the parcel-sizing parameters, there are parcel-layout parameters that affect the creation of multiple parcels. The first is Automatic Mode, which determines whether parcels are created individually or all at once, as follows:

Automatic Mode – On   Multiple parcels are created within the selected area based on the parameters that have been specified.

Automatic Mode – Off   Parcels are created one at a time, and you're prompted for information for each parcel.

The second parcel-layout parameter is Remainder Distribution, which determines what is done with the "leftover" area after all parcels that meet the size requirements have been created. The Remainder Distribution options are as follows:

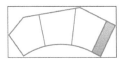

Create Parcel From Remainder   A new parcel is created that is smaller than the specified sizing parameters.

Place Remainder In Last Parcel   The last parcel is oversized by adding the remainder to it.

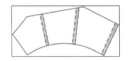

Redistribute Remainder   All parcels are oversized by a small amount so that the leftover area is spread across all parcels.

Exercise 12.4: Create Multiple Parcels

In this exercise, you'll create multiple parcels by using the Slide Line Create command with Automatic Mode turned on.

1. Open the drawing named Using Parcel Sizing Parameters.dwg located in the Chapter 12 class data folder.

2. On the Home tab of the ribbon, click Parcel ➤ Parcel Creation Tools. On the Parcel Layout Tools toolbar, change Automatic Mode to On.

3. Click Slide Line – Create, and then click OK to dismiss the Create Parcels – Layout dialog box. When you're prompted to select a parcel, click the label that reads Property : 30.

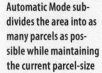

If you haven't already done so, download and install the files for Chapter 12 according to the instructions in this book's Introduction.

Automatic Mode subdivides the area into as many parcels as possible while maintaining the current parcel-size requirements.

4. When you're prompted for the start point of the frontage, snap to the endpoint of the right-of-way line at the entrance of Jordan Court, as shown in Figure 12.13.

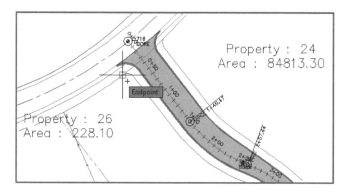

FIGURE 12.13   Selecting the beginning point of the frontage

5. When you're prompted for the endpoint of the frontage, move your cursor along the west right-of-way line of Jordan Court and then along the north right-of-way line of Madison Lane. Move your cursor around the Madison Lane cul-de-sac, and snap to the endpoint of the right-of-way line at the intersection of Madison Lane and Logan Court, as shown in Figure 12.14.

How you move your cursor controls the path taken by the orange jig line. If the jig line takes a wrong turn, move your cursor back to the frontage start point and start over.

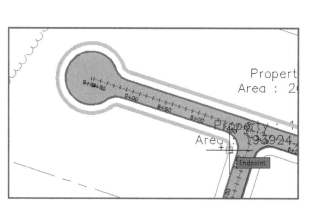

FIGURE 12.14   Selecting the ending point of the frontage

6. When you're prompted to specify an angle, press Enter.

7. On the Parcel Layout Tools toolbar, type 0.333acres (or 0.135hectares) for Minimum Area, and press Enter. The preview updates.

A preview of the parcels is shown.

8. Change the following settings (noting how the preview updates after each):

   ▶ Minimum Frontage: 100 (35)

   ▶ Frontage Offset: 25 (8)

   ▶ Remainder Distribution: Redistribute Remainder

   ▶ Multiple Solution Preference: Use Smallest Area

9. Press Enter to create the parcels. Press Esc twice to end the command.

10. Save and close the drawing.

You can view the results of successfully completing this exercise by opening Using Parcel Sizing Parameters - Complete.dwg.

Editing Parcels

As you have seen with other design elements, the ability to edit parcels is even more important than their initial layout. Civil 3D provides you with three fundamental tools to edit your parcel geometry: grips, Edit Geometry commands, and Parcel Layout Tools.

Editing Parcels Using Grips

Graphically editing parcels is fairly simple when compared to editing alignments or profiles. There are only two types of grips to learn: the square grip and the diamond-shaped grip. The square grip is simply the standard grip that allows movement in any direction with no restriction. The diamond-shaped grip is displayed on parcel lines that have been created using the Parcel Layout Tools. These grips slide one parcel line along another parcel line or curve while maintaining the angle (usually perpendicular) between the two lines.

Exercise 12.5: Edit Parcels with Grips

If you haven't already done so, download and install the files for Chapter 12 according to the instructions in this book's Introduction.

In this exercise, you'll experiment with grip-editing parcel lines and observing their behavior.

1. Open the drawing named Editing Parcels Using Grips.dwg located in the Chapter 12 class data folder.

2. Zoom in to the parcel labeled Property : 28. Click the northern side of this parcel, and notice the square grips that appear on either end of the line.

3. Click the eastern square grip to select it. Move your cursor around the screen, and notice the behavior of this grip.

You can move it in any direction.

4. Hold down the Shift key, and right-click to reveal the object snap context menu. Select Nearest.

5. Pick a point somewhere along the property line that forms the eastern side of the lot.

Notice that the value for the area of this parcel changes.

6. Press Esc to clear your selection. Click the line that forms the southern boundary of this parcel.
   Notice that a single diamond-shaped grip appears.

7. Click the diamond-shaped grip, and slide it along the parcel line it's attached to. Slide it north to the curved areas, and notice how it stays perpendicular to the parcel segments it's attached to (see Figure 12.15).

If the line isn't sliding along smoothly, it might be because you have running object snaps turned on. Try pressing F3 to turn them off.

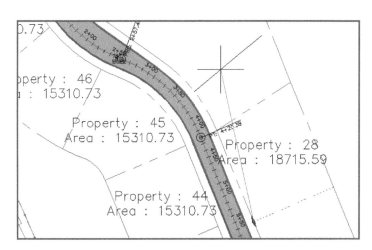

FIGURE 12.15 As it's moved with the diamond-shaped grip, the parcel line stays perpendicular to the parcel segments it's associated with.

8. Pick a new location for the line, and note the change to the parcel label.

9. Save and close the drawing.

You can view the results of successfully completing this exercise by opening Editing Parcels Using Grips - Complete.dwg.

Editing Parcels Using the Edit Geometry Commands

When you need to modify the parcel lines and curves themselves, you can use the commands found on the Edit Geometry panel of the Parcel ribbon tab. The commands included on this panel are as follows:

 Insert PI   Inserts an angle point into a parcel line segment.

 Delete PI   Removes an angle point from a parcel line segment.

 Break   Creates a gap in a parcel segment.

 Trim   Shortens a parcel segment using some other entity as a cutting edge.

 Join   Joins two parcel segments together.

 Reverse Direction   Changes the direction of the parcel segment.

 Edit Curve   Allows you to change the radius of a parcel curve segment.

 Fillet   Replaces an angle point with a parcel curve segment that is tangent at either end.

 Fit Curve   Replaces a series of parcel line segments with a parcel curve segment.

 Stepped Offset   Similar to the AutoCAD offset command, except that it prompts you for an elevation; the resulting entity is a polyline, not a parcel segment.

Exercise 12.6: Edit Parcels with the Edit Geometry Commands

If you haven't already done so, download and install the files for Chapter 12 according to the instructions in this book's Introduction.

In this exercise, you'll improve the geometry of several parcels using the Edit Geometry commands on the ribbon.

1. Open the drawing named Editing Parcels Using Edit Commands .dwg located in the Chapter 12 class data folder.

2. Zoom in to the area of the farm buildings, and notice the small triangular parcel labeled Property : 26.

 3. Click the Property : 26 label. If the Edit Geometry panel isn't visible on the ribbon, click Edit Geometry.

This parcel was created when the new parcel segments were added along the fence line.

4. Click Trim on the Edit Geometry panel of the contextual ribbon. When you're prompted for the cutting edge, select the parcel segment that is drawn along the fence. Press Enter.

5. When you're prompted for the objects to trim, click the west side of the small triangular parcel. The Property : 26 parcel disappears (see Figure 12.16), and the area of Property : 27 is updated.

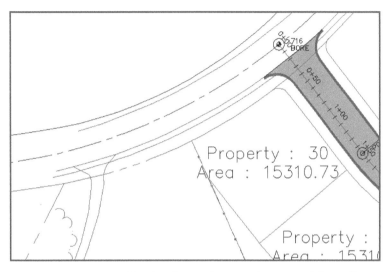

F I G U R E   1 2 . 1 6   Trimming the parcel segment has removed the small triangular parcel.

6. Press Esc to clear the current command. Pan southward, and click the Property : 7 parcel label. Click Edit Curve on the ribbon.

7. Click the curve just north of the Property : 7 label. In the Edit Feature Line Curve dialog box, enter **250 (85)** for the radius value and click OK. The parcel is updated.

FEATURE LINE OR PARCEL?

You may have noticed that the dialog box that appears when you're editing the curve refers to the entity as a *feature line*. Parcel segments are close relatives of feature lines, and many of the feature-line commands can be used on them. In fact, all the Edit Geometry commands in this section work for feature lines too.

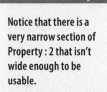

Notice that there is a very narrow section of Property : 2 that isn't wide enough to be usable.

8. Press Esc twice to clear the current command and the current selection. Zoom in to the western end of the Property : 2 parcel.

9. Click the north boundary of the Property : 2 parcel, and then click Delete PI on the ribbon. Click the triangle marker at the western end of the parcel line to delete the PI at that location.

10. Press Esc twice to end the previous command, and then click the parcel line again to reveal its grips. Click the westernmost grip, and snap it to the center of the red circle.

    The parcel geometry has been improved (see Figure 12.17).

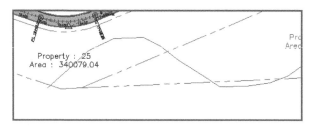

FIGURE 12.17   The western end of the parcel has been simplified.

11. Save and close the drawing.

You can view the results of successfully completing this exercise by opening `Editing Parcels Using Edit Commands - Complete.dwg`.

Editing Parcels Using the Parcel Layout Tools

For the most advanced parcel editing, you can look to the Parcel Layout Tools toolbar. This toolbar includes some of the same tools the Edit Geometry panel of the Parcel ribbon tab includes, such as Insert PI and Delete PI. You'll also find editing versions of the parcel-sizing commands that you used earlier to create parcels. The Slide Line – Edit and Swing Line – Edit commands work much like their Create counterparts, but instead of creating new parcel lines, they slide or rotate existing parcel lines to meet new size requirements. In addition, you can create a parcel union that combines multiple parcels into a single identity. There is also a command that will dissolve this union, returning the component parcels to their individual status.

Exercise 12.7: Edit Parcels with the Parcel Layout Tools

In this exercise, you'll use a few of the tools on the Parcel Layout Tools toolbar to edit parcels.

If you haven't already done so, download and install the files for Chapter 12 according to the instructions in this book's Introduction.

1. Open the drawing named Editing Parcels Using the Layout Tools.dwg located in the Chapter 12 class data folder.

2. Click the Property : 28 parcel label, and then click Parcel Layout Tools on the ribbon.

3. On the Parcel Layout Tools toolbar, type **0.5acres** (or **0.20hectares**) for the minimum area, and press Enter.

4. Expand the parcel sizing tools, and click Slide Line – Edit. Click OK to dismiss the Create Parcels – Layout dialog box.

5. When you're prompted to select a lot line, click the southern boundary line of Property : 28.

6. When you're prompted to select a parcel to adjust, click somewhere in the Property : 28 parcel.

7. When you're prompted for the start point of the frontage, snap to the northwest corner of the Property : 28 parcel.

8. Move your cursor southward along the right-of-way line, and click somewhere near station 7+00 (0+210), as shown in Figure 12.18.

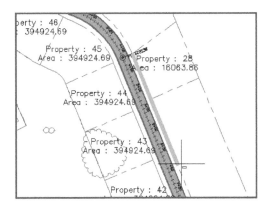

FIGURE 12.18   Defining the frontage for the parcel-editing command

9. When you're prompted to specify the angle, press Enter. A preview of the resized parcel is shown.

10. Press Enter to complete the command and resize the parcel.

11. Press Esc three times to clear the current command and clear the current selection. Click the Property : 27 label, and then click Parcel Layout Tools on the ribbon.

12. On the Parcel Layout Tools toolbar, click Parcel Union.

13. When you're prompted for the destination parcel, click the Property : 3 label. The Property : 27 label disappears, and the area of Property : 3 is updated.

14. Expand the Parcel Union icon, and select Dissolve Parcel Union.

15. Click the Property : 3 label. Two new parcels are created to replace the original parcels 3 and 27.

16. Save and close the drawing.

You can view the results of successfully completing this exercise by opening Editing Parcels Using the Layout Tools - Complete.dwg.

Now You Know

Now that you have completed this chapter, you're able to create parcels by converting objects in the drawing and by drawing your own parcel geometry from scratch. You can create parcels that automatically meet area, frontage, and other requirements, and you can do this for individual parcels or large numbers of them. You can edit parcels using grips, commands on the ribbon, and commands on the Parcel Layout Tools toolbar.

You're ready to begin creating and modifying parcels in a production environment.

CHAPTER 13

Displaying and Annotating Parcels

In the previous chapter, you used AutoCAD® Civil 3D® software to design a layout for subdividing the original project parcel into many smaller parcels. The reason for this was to create pieces of land that were the right size and shape for selling to prospective homeowners. However, before any sales can take place, that subdivision plan typically has to be reviewed and approved by an agency that oversees planning for that region. In many places, it must also be presented as an official legal document to be recorded at the local courthouse. Because of the need to create documentation of your layout, you must now address the appearance of the layout as well as the annotation needed to convey important information about it. In this chapter, you'll study the use of parcel styles, parcel labels, and tables to effectively display and annotate your parcel layout.

In this chapter, you'll learn to:

▶ **Apply parcel styles**

▶ **Apply parcel area labels**

▶ **Create parcel segment labels**

▶ **Edit parcel segment labels**

▶ **Create parcel tables**

Applying Parcel Styles

If you haven't already done so, download and install the files for Chapter 13 according to the instructions in this book's Introduction. Because working with parcels is done in 2D, the drawings in this chapter aren't set up with multiple viewports as in other chapters.

Parcels can represent individually owned lots, public areas, road rights-of-way, easements, and so on. When different types of parcels are shown on the same plan, there must be some way of visually differentiating them. When using Civil 3D, this is best handled through parcel styles.

Using Parcel Styles to Control Appearance

Using a parcel style, you can control the appearance of the edges of a parcel as well as any hatching that is applied to the area. The hatching can be applied through the entire area or as a strip along the edges. Using these capabilities, you can graphically differentiate one type of parcel from another.

Exercise 13.1: Apply Parcel Styles

In this exercise, you'll apply different styles to differentiate types of legal parcels. These include adjoiner parcels, rights-of-way, individual lots, open space lots, and easements.

One way to select a parcel is to click its label. You can't select a parcel by clicking one of its segments.

1. Open the drawing named Applying Parcel Styles.dwg located in the Chapter 13 class data folder.

   The drawing contains a complete parcel layout, and all the parcels have been assigned a style of Standard.

2. Click the Standard : 3 label located near the center of the area containing the farm buildings. On the ribbon, click Parcel Properties.

3. On the Information tab of the Parcel Properties dialog box, change Object Style to Adjoiner. Click OK.

   The linetype of the parcel segments changes to a double-dashed pattern. Also, the label changes and now reads Adjoiner : 3.

This parcel is renamed automatically because of a setting in the style that combines its style name with a number.

4. Press Esc to clear the previous selection. Click the Standard : 6 label located in the cul-de-sac of Madison Lane. Right-click, and select Properties.

5. Using the Properties window, change Style to ROW. Press Esc to clear your selection.

    The right-of-way area is now outlined by a dashed line and has been hatched with a dot pattern.

6. Use either the Parcel Properties command or the Properties window to change the large parcels at the northeast and southeast corners of the site (Standard : 7 and Standard : 4) to a style of Open Space.

    These parcels are now outlined in green and hatched with a green crossing pattern.

7. Zoom in to the 90° bend on Jordan Court, and note the narrow Standard : 1 parcel located there.

8. Change the style of the Standard : 1 parcel to Easement.

    The area is hatched with a diagonal stripe pattern.

9. Click one of the remaining parcels that is still labeled Standard, and change its style to Lot.

10. Go to Prospector, and expand Sites ➤ Lot Layout. Click Parcels to display all the parcels in the item view at the bottom of Prospector.

11. In the bottom section of Prospector, scroll to the right until you can see the Style column. Click the Style column heading to sort the parcels by style.

12. Click the first parcel with a style of Standard. Then press and hold the Shift key, scroll down, and select the last parcel with a style of Standard.

13. Right-click the Style column heading, and select Edit. In the Select Style dialog box, select Lot and click OK.

    Now, all the parcels you selected in Prospector have been assigned the Lot style (see Figure 13.1).

Using the Properties window is faster because you can change both parcels at once.

This is a drainage easement for installing a storm pipe that leads to the creek.

The color of the parcel outline changes to blue and appears with a smaller dashed pattern.

This selects all parcels that have a style of Standard assigned to them.

In the Prospector item view area, you can make multiple edits by selecting multiple rows, right-clicking a column heading, and selecting Edit. There is a pause as all the parcels in the drawing are updated.

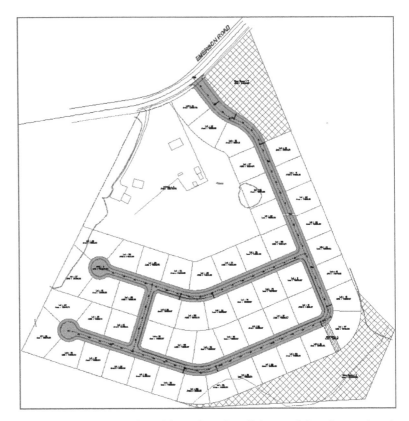

FIGURE 13.1   **A view of the project after all the parcels have been assigned the appropriate styles**

14. Save and close the drawing.

You can view the results of successfully completing this exercise by opening Applying Parcel Styles - Complete.dwg.

Applying Parcel Style Display Order

It's quite common for adjacent parcels to share one or more segments. If the adjacent parcels have different styles assigned to them, you can control which style is used for the shared segments via the Site Parcel Properties dialog box. To access this dialog box, right-click Parcels in Prospector and select Properties. The Parcel Style Display Order list is displayed on the Composition tab, as shown in Figure 13.2. When two different styles are used for adjacent parcels, the style that is higher in this list is assigned to the shared segments. You can control the result for the shared segments by using the arrow keys or by dragging and dropping the style names to change the order of the list.

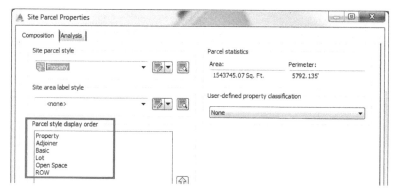

FIGURE 13.2   Parcel Style Display Order shown in the Site Parcel Properties dialog box

Typically you'll want certain types of parcel line styles to always override others. For example, right-of-way lines are considered one of the most important boundaries in the drawing, so their style is often placed at the top of the list. As a result, the color and linetype of the right-of-way lines are uninterrupted throughout the drawing. On the other hand, the lot lines are considered one of the least important, so their styles are typically placed at the bottom of the list.

> If you haven't already done so, download and install the files for Chapter 13 according to the instructions in this book's Introduction.

Exercise 13.2: Control Parcel Style Display Order

In this exercise, you'll apply the Parcel Style Display Order function to control the display behavior when parcels of different styles share common segments.

1. Open the drawing named Applying Parcel Style Display Order.dwg located in the Chapter 13 class data folder.

2. In Prospector, expand Sites ➤ Lot Layout.

3. Right-click Parcels, and select Properties.

4. On the Composition tab of the Site Parcel Properties dialog box, click ROW under Parcel Style Display Order.

5. Click the upward-pointing arrow icon multiple times until ROW is at the top of the list. Click OK.

> The drawing is zoomed in to Lot : 23, where the entire lot is outlined in blue.

   Lot : 23 is now bounded by a purple dashed line on the south and east sides and a blue dashed line on the north and west sides. The ROW parcel style is being displayed "on top of" the Lot style, as dictated by Parcel Style Display Order (see Figure 13.3).

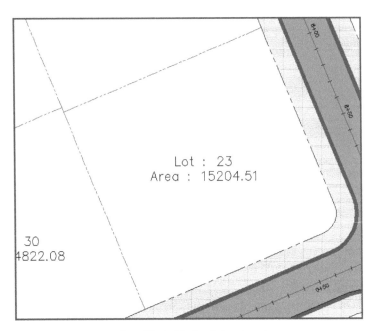

FIGURE 13.3   Parcel Style Display Order at work

6. In Prospector, right-click Parcels and select Properties.

7. Arrange the styles under Parcel Style Display Order as follows: ROW, Adjoiner, Open Space, Lot, Property, and Basic. Click OK.

8. Zoom in to the drawing, and study the different areas where parcels of different styles are adjacent to one another.

9. Save and close the drawing.

The back line of lots 48 through 50 is green because the Open Space style has been placed above the Lot style in Parcel Style Display Order.

You can view the results of successfully completing this exercise by opening Applying Parcel Style Display Order - Complete.dwg.

Applying Parcel Area Labels

The labels you have seen at the center of each parcel are known as *parcel area labels*. They don't have to contain information about the area of the parcel; however, they often do. You can create parcel area labels by using the Add Labels command as you have done before to create other labels. One unique capability of parcel area labels is that they can also be assigned through the Parcel Properties command. As with all other labels you have learned about, the appearance and content of parcel area labels are controlled by styles.

Exercise 13.3: Apply Parcel Area Labels

In this exercise, you'll apply parcel area label styles in a number of ways. For adjoiner parcels, you'll use them to display ownership information. For the ROW parcel, you'll remove the area label because it isn't needed. Finally, for individual lots, you'll apply a style that shows only the lot number.

If you haven't already done so, download and install the files for Chapter 13 according to the instructions in this book's Introduction.

1. Open the drawing named Applying Parcel Area Labels.dwg located in the Chapter 13 class data folder.

2. Click the Adjoiner : 3 label, and then click Parcel Properties on the ribbon.

3. Click the Composition tab of the Parcel Properties dialog box. For Area Selection Label Style, select Existing Description And Area.

4. Click the Information tab. In the Description box, enter **JOHN SMITH** on the first line and **DBV 1234, PG 567** on the second line, as shown in Figure 13.4. Click OK, and press Esc to clear the selection.

FIGURE 13.4 Entering a description for the Adjoiner : 3 parcel

The appearance and content of the label changes dramatically. This is a possible format for labeling a parcel that isn't part of the main project but is adjacent or nearby. It includes the owner's name plus the deed book and page where the official documentation of the parcel is recorded. Notice how this label style combines the hand-entered Description value along with the calculated area value.

5. Click the ROW : 6 label located in the cul-de-sac at the end of Madison Lane, and then click Parcel Properties on the ribbon.

This removes the label from the parcel. Now that there is no parcel area label, the only way to select this parcel is by right-clicking it in Prospector and then clicking Select.

The descriptions of COMMON AREA and RESOURCE PROTECTION AREA were already entered for you.

This selection process is much like a fence selection in AutoCAD.

This applies your choice to all the parcels you've selected. A dialog box opens, asking if you would like to apply the change to the number of parcels you've selected.

6. On the Composition tab of the Parcel Properties dialog box, change Area Selection Label Style to <None>. Click OK. Press Esc to clear your selection.

7. Click the parcel area labels for both open space parcels hatched in green. Right-click, and select Properties.

8. Use the Properties window to change the Parcel Area Label Style value to Proposed Description And Area.

   The labels now display the lot description and area using a different text style and color.

9. Press Esc to clear the selection from the previous command. On the Annotate tab of the ribbon, click Add Labels.

10. In the Add Labels dialog box, do the following:

    a. For Feature, select Parcel.

    b. For Label Type, select Replace Area.

    c. For Area Label Style, select Lot Number.

    d. Click Add.

11. Click several parcels labeled Lot, and press Enter.

    The labels are updated and appear simply as a number within a circle.

12. Click one of the parcels, and then click Multiple Parcel Properties on the ribbon.

13. When prompted for a start point, pick a point in one of the parcels with the original Lot label style. Then click several more points to create a line through several parcels with the same label style. Press Enter when you have finished selecting points.

14. Press Enter again when prompted for a start point.

15. In the Edit Parcel Properties dialog box, set Area Selection Label Style to Lot Number.

16. Click the disk icon to the right of Lot Number.

17. Click Yes to apply the change. You should see the area label styles immediately change for the parcels you selected.

18. Click OK to dismiss the Edit Parcel Properties dialog box. Repeat steps 12–17 until all the Lot parcels have the Lot Number area label style.

19. Save and close the drawing.

You can view the results of successfully completing this exercise by opening `Applying Parcel Area Labels - Complete.dwg`.

Creating Parcel Segment Labels

The most common use of parcel segment labels is to provide numerical information that defines the geometry of property boundaries. This numerical information appears as bearings and distances for line segments and curve data for curve segments. When an adequate numerical description of a parcel is provided, the parcel can be re-created either on paper or in the field.

To add labels to parcel segments, you use the Add Labels command. You can label the segments one by one, or you can provide labels for all the segments that make up a parcel.

Exercise 13.4: Label Parcel Segments

In this exercise, you'll use parcel segment labels to provide bearings, distances, and curve data in your drawing.

If you haven't already done so, download and install the files for Chapter 13 according to the instructions in this book's Introduction.

1. Open the drawing named `Creating Parcel Segment Labels.dwg` located in the `Chapter 13` class data folder.

2. Zoom in to lots 32 and 33 near the center of the project.

3. On the Annotate tab of the ribbon, click Add Labels.

4. In the Add Labels dialog box, select Parcel as the feature. Click Add.

5. Click the north side of lot 33.
   A new bearing and distance label is added.

6. Click the east and west sides of lot 33.
   Two more bearing and distance labels are created. The labels will be created at the location you click, so you should click near the midpoint of the line.

7. Pan south to lot 69, and click the curve that makes up the south boundary of the lot.

   A curve label is created that displays the delta, length, and radius.

8. In the Add Labels dialog box, select Multiple Segment as the label type, and then click Add.

LABELING LINES AND CURVES

Thus far in this chapter, you've learned how to label parcel segments, but what about plain old lines, arcs, and polylines? Do these entities have to be converted to parcel segments in order to be labeled? The answer is no. Civil 3D enables you to label basic AutoCAD entities using the same Add Labels command you used for labeling parcel segments. Just remember that you need to choose Line And Curve as the feature in the Add Labels dialog box, as shown here.

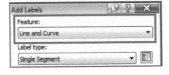

9. Click the parcel area label for lot 32. When you're prompted to select a direction, press Enter to accept the default direction of clockwise.

   All segments for lot 32 are labeled simultaneously.

10. Save and close the drawing.

You can view the results of successfully completing this exercise by opening `Creating Parcel Segment Labels - Complete.dwg`.

CURVE DATA

Many geometric properties can be used to define a curve. The most common properties are shown in the following drawing and then described:

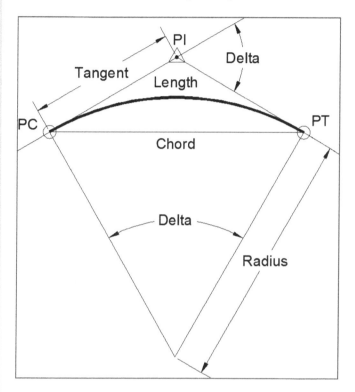

▶ *Length*: The length of the curve, measured along its arc.

▶ *Radius*: The distance from the center point of the curve to a point on the curve.

▶ *Chord*: The straight line from the beginning point of the curve to the ending point of the curve. The bearing and distance of this line can be labeled.

▶ *Delta*: The change in direction between a line tangent to the curve at its beginning point and a line tangent to the curve at its ending point.

▶ *Tangent*: The distance between the point of curvature (PC) and the point of intersection (PI) or between the point of tangency (PT) and the PI.

Depending on the requirements, you may need to include different combinations of these curve dimensions. Typically, you must create multiple curve-dimension labels in order to provide enough information to reconstruct a curve.

Editing Parcel Segment Labels

Once you have placed parcel segment labels in the drawing, you usually need to do some work to change their position, style, orientation, and whatever else is necessary to create a readable, professional-looking legal document. Fortunately, Civil 3D provides a number of ways for you to do this.

Applying Segment Label Styles

You can use parcel segment label styles to change the appearance, content, and behavior of the segment labels. For example, when labeling an existing property line, you could assign a different style that displays the bearing and distance text slanted—a common practice for differentiating text that refers to existing features. In another part of the drawing, you might assign a different style to a curve label so that the appropriate combination of dimensions is shown according to local requirements.

Exercise 13.5: Apply Parcel Segment Label Styles

In this exercise, you'll apply different parcel segment label styles to differentiate between different types of labels and to control the content that is shown for each label.

1. Open the drawing named Applying Parcel Segment Label Styles.dwg located in the Chapter 13 class data folder.

2. Zoom in to the bearing and distance labels along the west side of the project.
   Currently, these labels are all shown in a proposed style with both bearing and distance.

3. Click the label for the west side of the John Smith property, and then click Label Properties on the ribbon.

4. In the Properties window, change Line Label Style to (Span) Bearing And Distance With Crows Feet [Existing].
   The color and text style of the label are changed, and the label now reflects the full length of the line.

5. On the Annotate tab of the ribbon, click Add Labels.

6. In the Add Labels dialog box, do the following:

   a. For Feature, select Parcel.

   b. For Label Type, select Single Segment.

If you haven't already done so, download and install the files for Chapter 13 according to the instructions in this book's Introduction.

▶

This side of the project is actually a mixture of existing and proposed geometry, and displaying the same bearing multiple times is redundant.

▶

▶

Label styles can be set up to *span* across the outside of multiple end-to-end segments and display the overall length. *Crow's-feet* are the curved tick marks at either end of the line that indicate the extents of the distance that is being labeled.

     c. For Line Label Style, select Distance [Existing].

     d. Click Add.

7. Click the west side of the John Smith property. A new label is created that reflects the distance associated with just the John Smith property, not the overall distance.

8. Close the Add Labels dialog box, and press Esc to end the command. Pan to the south to view the labels for lots 36, 37, 60, and 59.

9. Click these four labels, and then click Label Properties on the ribbon.

10. In the Properties window, change Line Label Style to Distance. The text of each label changes to include only the inside distance of the associated parcel.

11. Save and close the drawing.

You can view the results of successfully completing this exercise by opening `Applying Parcel Segment Label Styles - Complete.dwg`.

The bearing for the individual segments can be omitted because the bearing on the opposite side of the line provides that information.

Editing Parcel Segment Labels Graphically

You can use a number of methods to graphically edit parcel segment labels. The labels are equipped with special grips that enable you to move them easily. You can also capitalize on their built-in dragged state in areas where there isn't enough room for the label to be placed right on the line or curve. In addition, you can flip labels to change which side of a line or curve they are placed on, and you can reverse labels to change a NE bearing to SW and vice versa.

Exercise 13.6: Edit Parcel Segment Labels Graphically

If you haven't already done so, download and install the files for Chapter 13 according to the instructions in this book's Introduction.

In this exercise, you'll employ several graphical editing techniques on parcel segment labels in your drawing. These include grip-editing, flipping, and reversing labels as well as moving them to initiate their dragged state.

1. Open the drawing named `Editing Labels Graphically.dwg` located in the `Chapter 13` class data folder. The drawing is zoomed in to lot 68. Notice the bearing and distance labels for the west sides of lots 68 and 62. The bearing is listed twice, which is redundant.

2. Click the label on the west side of lot 68, and then click Label Properties on the ribbon.

3. In the Properties window, change Line Label Style to Bearing. Close the Properties window.

4. With the label still selected, click Flip Label on the ribbon.
   The label is now displayed on the west side of the line.

5. Click the diamond-shaped grip of the label, and slide it south to the line that is shared between lots 68 and 62.
   This bearing now serves both lots. Notice that this is a NE bearing, whereas those to the east are SW bearings.

6. With the label still selected, click Reverse Label on the ribbon. The bearing now reflects a SW orientation.

7. Press Esc to clear your current selection. Then repeat steps 2 through 4 for the label on the west side of lot 62 using a label style of Distance.
   The label should now show only the distance, and it should be located on the east side of the line.

8. Use the Add Labels command to add a new distance label to the west side of lot 68. Don't forget to flip the label so that it's shown on the inside of the lot.

9. Click the curve label at the northwest corner of lot 68. Click the square grip, and drag it to the south and east. Place it in the open space between the lot 68 area label and the northwest corner of the lot.
   The label is reoriented, and a leader appears that points back to the curve (see Figure 13.5).

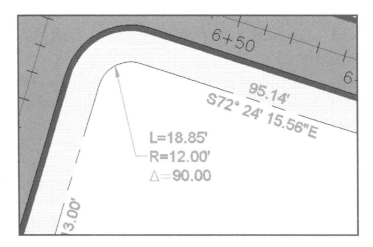

FIGURE 13.5 A curve label that has been dragged away from the curve to reveal its dragged state

10. Continue moving, flipping, and reversing labels to improve the readability of the drawing and remove redundant bearings. Assign new styles where applicable.

11. Save and close the drawing.

You can view the results of successfully completing this exercise by opening Editing Labels Graphically - Complete.dwg.

Creating Parcel Tables

As you can guess, property drawings can become cluttered with many labels for areas, bearings, distances, and curve dimensions. As the drawing becomes more complex, it might make sense to put all that information in a table instead of trying to place it directly on the lines and curves. Line labels can be replaced with tags such as L1, L2, and so on, and the same can be done for curves. These abbreviated labels take up much less space than the full bearing and distance labels, making the drawing appear less cluttered and easier to read. Of course, the trade-off is that now the person viewing the drawing will have to scan back and forth between the drawing and the table to obtain all the information that pertains to a given parcel. This is why not all drawings use tables to store parcel information. A drawing can be read more easily, and information obtained from it more efficiently, if the labels are placed directly on the lines and curves. However, for some drawings you simply can't show the information directly on the lines and curves, and you must use a table.

Creating Area Tables

You can use area tables to display information about each parcel in the drawing. Depending on the table style you use, you can vary the amount of information as well as the formatting.

One thing you'll probably need to do prior to creating an area table is renumber the lots. You do this by using the Renumber/Rename command on the ribbon.

Exercise 13.7: Create an Area Table

In this exercise, you'll first renumber the lots in the drawing. Then you'll create an area table that shows the lot number and corresponding area for each lot parcel.

1. Open the drawing named Creating An Area Table.dwg located in the Chapter 13 class data folder.

If you haven't already done so, download and install the files for Chapter 13 according to the instructions in this book's Introduction.

2. Click one of the lot number labels, and then click Renumber/Rename on the ribbon.

3. In the Renumber/Rename Parcels dialog box, check the box next to Use Name Template In Parcel Style. Click OK.

4. When you're prompted to specify a start point, click near the center of lot 24. Then, to select the parcels in the correct order, draw the line segments indicated by the red arrows in Figure 13.6.

This setting will cause the parcels to be automatically renamed to reflect their new numbers.

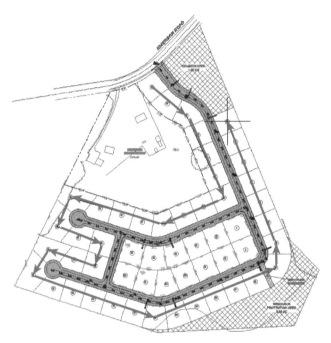

FIGURE 13.6   Selecting parcels in the order they are to be renumbered

5. Press Enter twice to end the command and update the numbers. The numbers should now start at 1 and end at 40 along the same path you selected.

6. Press Esc to clear the previous selection. Zoom to the lots in the center of the project. Select one of the lot labels, and then click Renumber/Rename on the ribbon.

Notice that the starting number is 41. The command remembered that you stopped at 40 during the previous renumbering process.

7. In the Renumber/Rename Parcels dialog box, check the box next to Use Name Template In Parcel Style. Click OK.

8. Draw lines through the parcels as you did before, beginning at lot 68, drawing in a clockwise fashion and ending at lot 62. Press Enter twice to end the command.

These lots should now be numbered from 41 to 53.

9. Press Esc to clear the previous selection. Click one of the lot labels, and then click Add Tables ➢ Add Area on the ribbon.

10. In the Table Creation dialog box, do the following:

    a. For Table Style, select Area Only.

    b. Under Select By Label Or Style, check the box in the Apply column that is across from Lot Number.

    c. Click OK.

You may need to resize the dialog box or scroll to the right to see the Apply column where the box can be checked.

11. Click a point in an open area of the drawing to insert the tables. A new set of tables is inserted.

12. Save and close the drawing.

You can view the results of successfully completing this exercise by opening Creating an Area Table - Complete.dwg.

Creating Parcel Segment Tables

The process of creating parcel segment tables is similar to the way you create area tables. You can select the segments that are listed in the table based on their label style or select each segment individually. When a segment is listed in the table, its label is transformed into a tag that simply assigns a number to the segment. Usually, you'll want to renumber these tags to follow a sequential order that matches how they are laid out in the drawing. You can do this using the Renumber Tags command on the ribbon.

You can create three types of segment tables: line, curve, and segment. The last type (segment) is simply a combination of line and curve data in the same table.

If you haven't already done so, download and install the files for Chapter 13 according to the instructions in this book's Introduction.

Exercise 13.8: Create a Parcel Segment Table

In this exercise, you'll create a parcel segment table that will contain curve tag numbers and corresponding curve geometry information. This will improve the appearance and clarity of the drawing by taking crowded curve labels and moving their information to a neat, organized table.

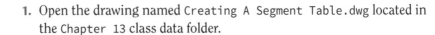

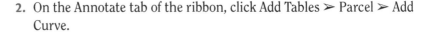

The drawing is zoomed in to the central portion of the project where the interior lots have been labeled. There are many short curves in this layout, and in many cases, the labels don't fit on the curves. To improve the clarity of the drawing, you're going to put all curve data in a table.

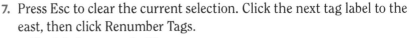

You can click each label and press Enter to repeat the Renumber Tags command. This makes the process go a little quicker.

1. Open the drawing named Creating A Segment Table.dwg located in the Chapter 13 class data folder.

2. On the Annotate tab of the ribbon, click Add Tables ➢ Parcel ➢ Add Curve.

3. In the Table Creation dialog box, do the following:

   a. For Table Style, verify that Length Radius & Delta is selected.

   b. Under Label Style Name, scroll down and check the box in the Apply column across from Parcel Curve: Delta Over Length And Radius.

   c. Click OK.

4. Pick a point in an open area of the drawing to insert the table.

5. Click the curve label at the northwest corner of lot 41, and click the circular grip to reset the label and place it back on the curve.

6. With the label still selected, click Renumber Tags on the ribbon. The label now reads C1.

7. Press Esc to clear the current selection. Click the next tag label to the east, then click Renumber Tags. The label now reads C2.

8. Continue working in a clockwise direction, clicking curve labels and then clicking Renumber Tags until all the tags have been renumbered. Remember to press Esc to clear the selection of the last label before clicking the next one.

9. On the Annotate tab of the ribbon, click Add Labels.

10. In the Add Labels dialog box, select Parcel as the feature and select Multiple Segment as the label type. Click Add.

11. Click the lot 17 label, and press Enter to accept the default direction of clockwise. Do the same for the lot 18 label. New line and curve labels are placed in the drawing.

12. Renumber the new curve tags so they continue the numbering sequence.

13. Click the curve table, and then click Add Items on the ribbon. In the Add Selection dialog box, check the box across from Parcel Curve: Delta Over Length And Radius. Click OK.

14. Pan over to the table, and note that the information was automatically added (see Figure 13.7).

				Curve Table		
Curve #	Length	Radius	Delta	Chord Direction	Chord Length	
C1	18.85	12.00	90.00	N62° 35' 44"E	16.97	
C2	10.75	225.00	2.74	S73° 46' 23"E	10.75	
C3	97.34	225.00	24.79	S87° 32' 06"E	96.58	
C4	49.56	225.00	12.62	N73° 45' 41"E	49.46	
C5	18.85	12.00	90.00	S67° 32' 57"E	16.97	
C6	39.27	25.00	90.00	S22° 27' 03"W	35.36	
C7	96.39	175.00	31.56	S83° 13' 45"W	95.17	
C8	26.23	175.00	8.59	N76° 41' 54"W	26.21	
C9	18.85	12.00	90.00	N27° 24' 16"W	16.97	
C10	12.79	350.00	2.09	N73° 27' 03"W	12.79	
C11	3.94	350.00	0.64	N74° 49' 11"W	3.94	
C12	99.69	350.00	16.32	N83° 18' 05"W	99.35	
C13	51.72	350.00	8.47	S84° 18' 20"W	51.68	
C14	17.24	350.00	2.82	S78° 39' 40"W	17.23	
C15	59.86	350.00	9.80	S72° 21' 02"W	59.79	
C16	18.85	12.00	90.00	S27° 24' 16"E	16.97	
C17	18.85	12.00	90.00	S62° 35' 44"W	16.97	

FIGURE 13.7 New lines added to a curve table

15. Save and close the drawing.

You can view the results of successfully completing this exercise by opening Creating a Segment Table - Complete.dwg.

Now You Know

Now that you have completed this exercise, you're ready to work with parcel styles and annotations. You know how to make parcels appear differently by applying styles, and you can use the Parcel Style Display Order feature to control what happens when adjacent parcels with different styles share common segments. You can apply area labels and segment labels, and you can modify them to suit your needs. You're able to renumber parcels and segment label tags and create tables showing their information.

You're ready to begin working with the display and annotation of parcels in a production environment.

Designing Gravity Pipe Networks

With the completion of parcel design, you're ready to move on to another major area of design: pipe design. One type of pipe design that you must address as a designer is the safe and efficient collection and conveyance of water that falls on a site during a rainstorm. This type of pipe design is part of a larger design process called *stormwater management*. Because the development of land often involves turning absorbent surfaces (soft grassy soil, trees, and forest floors) into impervious surfaces (pavement, concrete, and asphalt rooftops), rain that falls on a developed site will travel farther and much faster when compared to rain that fell on the site before it was developed. This water on the move can cause erosion or flooding, so it must be safely collected and placed in surface channels or underground pipes. The pipes and channels then carry the water to a safe place where it can be discharged without doing harm.

In this chapter, you'll learn to:

▶ **Understand gravity pipe networks**

▶ **Create gravity pipe networks**

▶ **Edit gravity pipe networks**

Understanding Gravity Pipe Networks

Pipe network design in the AutoCAD® Civil 3D® software is divided into two types: gravity networks and pressure networks. Because the performance requirements for these two types of systems are so different, the approach to designing and constructing them is also quite different. In this chapter, we'll cover gravity pipe network design.

For a gravity pipe network design to be a success, it must meet the following basic requirements:

▶ The pipes must be sloped enough for water to flow through them.

▶ The pipes must be large enough to allow the expected amount of water to pass.

▶ The pipes must be far enough underground to avoid being damaged by freezing or by activities on the site.

▶ The pipes must not be so far underground that it's cost prohibitive to install them.

▶ Structures must be provided that allow people to access the pipes to perform maintenance.

▶ In the case of stormwater management, structures must be provided that allow surface water to enter the pipes.

These requirements relate to two basic types of gravity pipe design components: structures and pipes. This chapter describes these components as well as their relationship to each other when represented in a Civil 3D pipe network.

Understanding Structures

Structures provide access to the pipes underground. This access can be for people, or it can be for rainwater that is flowing across the surface of the ground, also known as *runoff*. In the case of stormwater management design, structures called *inlets* or *catch basins* are placed on the site at locations that are best for collecting runoff. Typically, the runoff falls through a grate into a concrete chamber and then out through a pipe toward its final destination. For other types of pipelines, manholes and cleanouts are placed at predetermined increments so that workers can access the pipes to perform maintenance. Manholes are also used to create a bend in a pipeline when one pipe enters in one direction and a second pipe exits in another. Whatever the case, the placement of these structures is part of the pipe network design process, and it isn't done arbitrarily.

Understanding Pipes

Pipes are used to safely convey water to a predetermined destination. In the case of stormwater pipes, collected runoff commonly passes through one or more forms of onsite treatment and then empties into a nearby stream or ditch. In the case of a sanitary sewer, the journey can be much longer—connecting to a local sewer main, and then merging with any number of larger and larger mains until the water reaches a treatment plant. In some cases, the length of that journey can be quite a few miles.

In these systems, the flow of water depends on gravity. This means part of your job as the designer is to ensure that all the pipes are pointing downhill. That may sound like an easy task by itself, but when you introduce other design requirements, it can become quite challenging. For example, you also need to ensure that the pipes are at a depth that is neither too shallow nor too deep. Another part of the design is to ensure that the pipes are large enough to convey the amount of water that is expected. This part is usually handled by a licensed engineer or trained designer and is beyond the scope of this book.

Exploring the Pipe Network

Civil 3D enables you to create objects that represent structures and pipes. It also establishes relationships between the structures and pipes as well as other important design elements such as surfaces, alignments, profiles, and profile views. The pipes, the structures, and their associated relationships are referred to as a Civil 3D *pipe network*. In Figure 14.1, a plan view of a few pipes and structures is shown on the left, and the same pipes and structures are shown in profile view on the top right and 3D view on the bottom right.

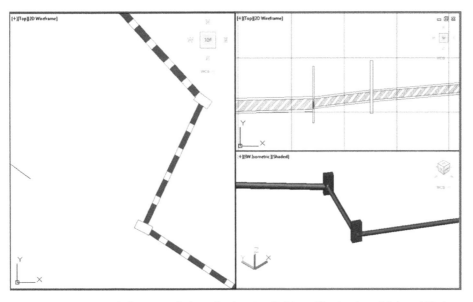

FIGURE 14.1   A pipe network shown in plan view (left), profile view (top right), and 3D view (bottom right)

In Prospector, gravity systems are listed under Pipe Networks, and pressure systems (covered in Chapter 15, "Designing Pressure Pipe Networks") are listed under Pressure Networks.

Each component of a pipe network is shown in Prospector. From here, you can right-click each component to access various context commands for it. You can also use the item view at the bottom of Prospector to edit information about each component. Figure 14.2 shows the contents of a pipe network in Prospector.

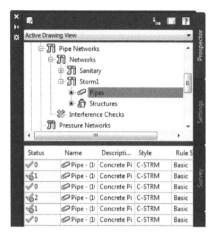

F I G U R E   1 4 . 2   A pipe network shown in Prospector

The shape, dimensions, and behavior of a pipe network component are determined by the *part* that represents it. Parts are stored in a *parts list*, which is a kind of library from which you can select parts for the different components in your pipe network. Most companies have several parts lists, each one containing parts for a certain type of system such as storm, sanitary, or water. Parts lists can be stored in a template file so they are available in each new drawing that is created from that template. Figure 14.3 shows an example of a very basic parts list that would be used for storm sewer design.

Name	Style	Rules	Render Material	Pay Item
Storm Sewer				
Null Structure				
Null Structure	Null	Basic	ByLayer	[none]
Cylindrical Junction Structure NF				
Storm Manhole	C-STRM - MH	Basic	ByLayer	[none]
Rectangular Junction Structure NF				
Yard Drain	C-STRM	Basic	ByLayer	[none]
Curb Inlet	C-STRM	Basic	ByLayer	[none]
Concrete Rectangular Winged Headwall				
Winged Headwall for 15" Pipe	C-STRM	Basic	ByLayer	[none]
Winged Headwall for 24" Pipe	C-STRM	Basic	ByLayer	[none]
Winged Headwall for 36" Pipe	C-STRM	Basic	ByLayer	[none]
Winged Headwall for 48" Pipe	C-STRM	Basic	ByLayer	[none]

F I G U R E   1 4 . 3   A parts list configured for storm sewer design

Creating Gravity Pipe Networks

Gravity pipe networks can be created in two basic ways. The first is to create a pipe network from one or more objects that have been drawn beforehand, such as lines, arcs, or a polyline. With this approach, all the pipes and structures are created at once. The other approach is to create the pipes and structures one by one. This is referred to as creating a pipe network by layout.

Certification
Objective

Creating a Pipe Network from Objects

At times, you'll find it easier to start with AutoCAD® commands to sketch your pipe network using basic entities. This approach works well because Civil 3D provides a command that converts these basic entities to pipe networks: the Create Pipe Network From Object command. This command creates pipe networks from Civil 3D alignments and feature lines as well. One disadvantage to this method is that the same parts are used for pipes and structures throughout the entire network.

If you haven't already done so, download and install the files for Chapter 14 according to the instructions in this book's Introduction.

Exercise 14.1: Create a Pipe Network from Objects

In this exercise, you'll use the Create Pipe Network From Object command to create several sanitary sewer networks from polylines provided in the drawing.

Make sure your screen background color is set to white before continuing this exercise.

1. Open the drawing named Creating Pipe Networks From Objects.dwg located in the Chapter 14 class data folder.

2. In the left viewport, zoom in to the beginning of the Jordan Court alignment at the north end of the project.
   Note the heavy green polyline marked SAN that has been sketched in to represent the location of a new sanitary sewer pipeline.

Some black arrows appear that point toward the south. These arrows indicate the assumed flow direction of the pipes.

3. On the Home tab of the ribbon, click Pipe Network ➤ Create Pipe Network From Object.

4. Click the green polyline with the SAN label on it. Press Enter to accept the current flow direction.

5. In the Create Pipe Network From Object dialog box, do the following:

   a. For Network Name, enter **Sanitary**.

   b. For Network Parts List, select Sanitary Sewer.

   c. For Surface Name, select Road FG.

This surface will be used to automatically set the top elevations of the structures.

By referencing an alignment, you'll be able to express the locations of pipes and structures using station and offset values.

Note the green polyline that starts near Madison Lane station 2+50 (0+080) and ends near Jordan Court station 21+50 (0+660).

Some black arrows should appear that point toward the south. These arrows indicate the assumed flow direction of the pipes.

d. For Alignment Name, select Jordan Court.

e. Check the box next to Erase Existing Entity.

f. Click OK.

A new pipe network is created in place of the polyline.

6. In the bottom-right viewport, zoom in to one of the manholes.

In plan view, the entities look simple, but in this view you see that they are actually 3D pipe and structure objects (see Figure 14.4).

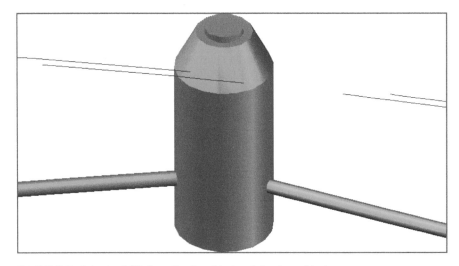

FIGURE 14.4   A 3D view of a pipe object and structure object

7. In the left viewport, pan southward until you can see Madison Lane.

8. On the Home tab of the ribbon, click Pipe Network ➢ Create Pipe Network From Object.

9. Click the green polyline somewhere along Madison Lane.

10. Press Enter to accept the flow direction indicated by the black arrows.

11. In the Create Pipe Network From Object dialog box, do the following:

a. For Network Name, enter **Sanitary-2**.

b. For Network Parts List, select Sanitary Sewer.

c. For Surface Name, select Road FG.

d. For Alignment Name, select Madison Lane.

e. Check the box next to Erase Existing Entity.

f. Click OK.

12. Repeat steps 8–11 with the remaining polyline that begins at the Madison Lane cul-de-sac. This time, use a Network Name of Sanitary-3.

13. Pan and zoom in the lower-right viewport to inspect the pipes and structures in 3D.

14. Save and close the drawing.

You can view the results of successfully completing this exercise by opening Creating Pipe Networks from Objects - Complete.dwg.

Now all the sketch polylines have been converted to sanitary sewer pipes and structures.

Notice that one of the pipes along Madison Lane is located at a much lower elevation than the others. This will be addressed later in this chapter.

Creating a Pipe Network by Layout

If you haven't sketched the pipe design, or when you want more control of the design as you go, the best choice is to create a pipe network by layout. This is done by using the Pipe Network Creation Tools command. After you launch this command and enter some information about the pipe network, you're presented with the Network Layout Tools toolbar (see Figure 14.5). This is similar to the toolbars you have used for other layout designs, such as creating alignments by layout or profiles by layout.

FIGURE 14.5 The Network Layout Tools toolbar

From the Network Layout Tools toolbar, you can choose pipes and structures from a parts list and then use commands on the toolbar to insert those parts into the drawing. You can change parts at any time and apply different types and sizes as you go. As you draw pipes and structures, special icons next to the cursor inform you when you're connecting parts to one another. For example, Figure 14.6 shows a pipe being drawn between two inlets. The yellow icon indicates that the pipe will be connected to the inlet when the user clicks the mouse.

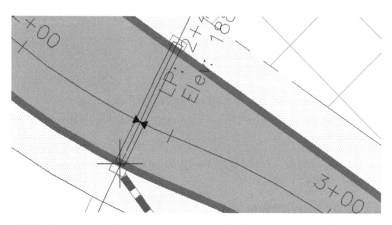

FIGURE 14.6   Icon indicating a connection between a pipe and a structure

Exercise 14.2: Create a Pipe Network by Layout

If you haven't already done so, download and install the files for Chapter 14 according to the instructions in this book's Introduction.

In this exercise, you'll create part of the storm system using the Pipe Network Creation Tools command.

1. Open the drawing named Creating Pipe Networks By Layout.dwg located in the Chapter 14 class data folder.

    In this drawing, red circles have been provided that indicate the locations of inlets. If you study the placement of these inlets, you'll notice that some of them have been placed at low points, as indicated by the alignment labels. To prevent the inlets at the low points from being overloaded, additional inlets have been placed between low points and high points to collect some of the runoff. Figure 14.7 further illustrates inlet placement in the drawing.

2. On the Home tab of the ribbon, click Pipe Network ➤ Pipe Network Creation Tools.

3. In the Create Pipe Network dialog box, do the following:

    a. For Network Name, enter **Storm1**.

    b. For Network Parts List, select Storm Sewer.

    c. For Surface Name, select Road FG.

    d. For Alignment Name, select Jordan Court.

    e. Click OK.

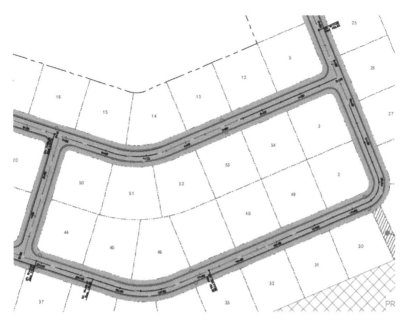

FIGURE 14.7   Inlet placement

4. You're prompted to specify a structure insertion point. In the left viewport, zoom in to the red circles at Jordan Court station 5+50 (0+170). On the Network Layout Tools toolbar, do the following:

   ▶ To choose a structure, select Rectangular Junction Structure NF (SI) ➤ Curb Inlet from the first drop-down list.

   ▶ To choose a pipe, select Concrete Pipe (SI) ➤ 15 Inch (400mm) Concrete Pipe from the second drop-down list.
      The Network Layout Tools toolbar should appear as shown in Figure 14.8.

FIGURE 14.8   The Network Layout Tools toolbar after selecting the structure and pipe

5. Right-click the Osnap icon at the bottom of the screen, and then click Object Snap Settings.

If the Osnap icon isn't visible, turn it on using the status bar customization menu, accessed by clicking the icon in the bottom-right corner of your screen.

These settings will cause the Center object snap to be used each time you click a point in the drawing. This will help you do the next few steps a bit more quickly.

6. On the Object Snap tab of the Drafting Settings dialog box, do the following:

    a. Check the box next to Object Snap On (F3).

    b. Click Clear All.

    c. Check the box next to Center.

    d. Click OK.

7. Click the center of the red circle to the east of station 5+50 (0+170).

8. Click the center of the red circle to the west of station 5+50 (0+170).

9. Pan northward until you can see the two red circles at the low point of station 2+40.42 (0+073.28). Click the circle to the south of the road.

10. On the Network Layout Tools toolbar, choose the pipe Concrete Pipe (SI) ➢ 18 Inch (450mm) Concrete Pipe.

11. Click the center of the red circle located north of station 2+40.42 (0+073.28).

As you create each pipe and structure, you can click over to the bottom-right viewport at any time to see the system being constructed in 3D. Then you can click back to plan view to continue with the actual steps.

12. On the Network Layout Tools toolbar, do the following:

    a. Choose the structure Cylindrical Junction Structure NF (SI) ➢ Storm Manhole.

    b. Choose the pipe Concrete Pipe (SI) ➢ 24 Inch (600mm) Concrete Pipe.

13. Click the red circle located at the western corner of the common area.

14. On the Network Layout Tools toolbar, choose a structure of Concrete Rectangular Winged Headwall (SI) ➢ Winged Headwall for 24" (600mm) Pipe.

15. Click the red circle on the opposite side of Emerson Road.

16. Press Esc to end the command.

    You have created a storm sewer network, which discharges at a location across Emerson Road (see Figure 14.9).

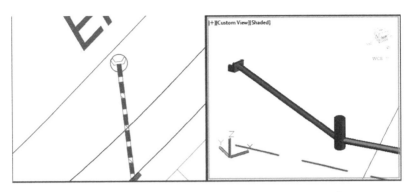

FIGURE 14.9 A portion of the newly created storm pipe network

17. Save and close the drawing.

You can view the results of successfully completing this exercise by opening
Creating Pipe Networks By Layout - Complete.dwg.

Drawing a Pipe Network in a Profile View

Viewing a pipe network in a profile view is critical to performing an accurate
design. The depths, slopes, and elevations of an underground pipe system are
every bit as important as the horizontal location of each component on the plan.
Civil 3D enables you to represent a pipe network in profile view, which is the ideal
way to visualize and modify the vertical aspect of a pipe network design.

You can use the Draw Parts In Profile command to draw an entire network in
profile view or to draw select parts. When this is done, the pipes and structures
shown in plan view are the same pipes and structures shown in profile view. Any
change or addition to the pipe network will be visible in both views.

Exercise 14.3: Draw a Pipe Network in Profile View

In this exercise, you'll use the Draw Parts In Profile command to show the
storm network in a profile view.

1. Open the drawing named Drawing Pipe Networks in Profile
   View.dwg located in the Chapter 14 class data folder.

2. In the left viewport, select the new storm manhole near the western
   corner of the Common Area, and then click Draw Parts In Profile on
   the ribbon.

If you haven't already
done so, download
and install the files for
Chapter 14 according to
the instructions in this
book's Introduction.

3. In the top-right viewport, click one of the grid lines of the Jordan Court profile view. The manhole is drawn in the profile view. Press Esc to clear the selection.

4. Click the pipe that connects to the manhole from the southeast.

5. Click Draw Parts In Profile on the ribbon, and again click the grid of the Jordan Court profile view.

6. Repeat steps 2 and 3 for the inlet located north of station 2+40.42 (0+073.28).

7. Repeat steps 2 and 3 for the pipe that begins at station 2+40.42 (0+073.28) and ends at station 5+50 (0+170).

8. Repeat steps 2 and 3 for the inlet located to the west of station 5+50 (0+170).

   Now there are two pipes and three structures drawn in the profile view (see Figure 14.10).

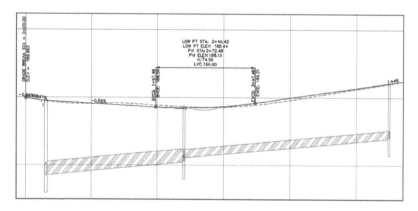

FIGURE 14.10   Two pipes and three structures drawn in a profile view

9. Save and close the drawing.

You can view the results of successfully completing this exercise by opening Drawing Pipe Networks in Profile View - Complete.dwg.

Editing Gravity Pipe Networks

As you might guess, the tools for editing pipe networks are even more extensive than the tools used to create them. This is one reason the recommended way to approach pipe design is to perform a rough layout and then use the editing tools to perfect the design. As you're about to learn, Civil 3D provides many ways to edit pipe networks. In the following sections, the ways to edit pipe networks are presented in four groups: grips, editing tools, properties, and the Pipe Network Vistas.

Editing Pipe Networks Using Grips

Grips are a great tool for making quick and simple graphical edits. Civil 3D provides the following specialized grips for pipes and structures:

Structure – Square Grip – Plan View   This grip changes the location of the structure without changing its rotation. As a structure is moved, the ends of any pipes that connect to it move with it.

Structure – Circular Grip – Plan View   This grip changes the rotation of the structure without changing its location.

Structure – Top Triangular Grip – Profile View   This grip changes the elevation of the top of the structure. Use caution when editing the top of a structure because, depending on its properties, the software may automatically reset it to match a surface.

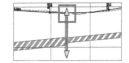

Structure – Bottom Triangular Grip – Profile View   This grip changes the elevation of the sump (inside floor) of the structure. This elevation can't be placed above the invert (bottom of the inside wall) of the lowest incoming pipe.

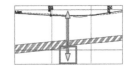

Pipe Midpoint – Triangle Grip – Plan View   This grip is used to change the diameter of a pipe. Dragging it away from the pipe increases the diameter, and dragging it toward the pipe decreases the diameter. This grip can be used in conjunction with the AutoCAD Dynamic Input feature to view the diameter or even type it in.

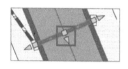

Pipe Midpoint – Square Grip – Plan View   This grip moves the pipe to a new location without changing its angle or its slope.

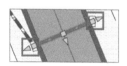

Pipe Endpoint – Square Grip – Plan View   This grip moves the location of one end of the pipe while keeping the other end fixed. In profile view, it maintains the current elevation of that end of the pipe.

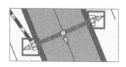

Pipe Endpoint – Triangular Grip – Plan View   This grip changes the length of the pipe while maintaining the angle of the pipe and the location of the opposite end.

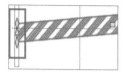

Pipe Endpoint Grips – Profile View   These grips change the elevation of a pipe at its endpoint. The diamond-shaped grip at the top sets the crown (top of the inside wall) elevation. The diamond-shaped grip at the bottom sets the invert (bottom of the inside wall) elevation. The triangular grip sets the centerline elevation. These grips can be used in conjunction with the AutoCAD Dynamic Input feature to view the elevation or even type it in. They don't change the horizontal location of the pipe's endpoint.

Pipe Midpoint – Square Grip – Profile View   This grip changes the elevation of the pipe without changing its slope. It doesn't affect the location of the pipe in plan view.

You should note that when you change the location of the endpoint of a pipe in plan view, the structure connected to it doesn't move with it. To place the structure at the end of the pipe, you must move the structure as a separate action. If you don't update the location of the structure, the pipe may reset to match the structure at some point in the future.

Exercise 14.4: Edit a Pipe Network Using Grips

If you haven't already done so, download and install the files for Chapter 14 according to the instructions in this book's Introduction.

In this exercise, you'll use grips to make some adjustments to the storm network.

1. Open the drawing named `Editing Pipe Networks Using Grips.dwg` located in the `Chapter 14` class data folder.

2. In the plan view on the left, zoom in to the inlets located at station 5+50 (0+170).

3. Click both inlets to select them, and then click the circular grip on the inlet to the east.

4. Click the square grip of the west inlet.
   This rotates the east inlet to align it with the west inlet, which also aligns the east inlet with the curb.

5. If it isn't already turned on, click the Dynamic Input icon at the bottom of your screen to turn it on.

6. Zoom in to the pipe at station 5+50 (0+170), and select it. Click the triangular grip at the midpoint of the pipe.

7. Drag the grip away from the pipe, and click when the dynamic input text box reads 1.5 (0.450). Or you can just type 1.5 (0.450) in the box, as shown in Figure 14.11.
   This changes the diameter of the pipe to 18 inches (450mm).

Step 4 will be easier if you press F3 to turn off running object snaps.

If the Dynamic Input icon isn't visible, turn it on using the status bar customization menu, accessed by clicking the icon in the bottom-right corner of your screen.

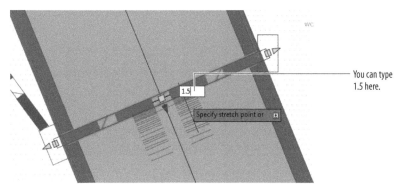

You can type 1.5 here.

FIGURE 14.11   Using Dynamic Input to enter a pipe diameter value

8. In the bottom-right viewport, zoom in to the manhole located near the west corner of the Common Area. Click the manhole, and then click the square grip at its center.

9. If your Osnap icon is turned off, click it to turn it on.

10. Click the center of the red circle west of the manhole.

11. Click in the top-right viewport, and then click the pipe in the Jordan Court profile view that is farthest to the left.

12. Click the bottom diamond-shaped grip on the left end of the pipe, and then zoom out until you can see the dynamic input dimension and text box. Type 180 (54.864) in the text box, and press Enter.

If you watch carefully, you'll see the position of the manhole change slightly in the profile view.

The next steps will be easier if you turn off your running Osnaps. You can use the F3 key to do so.

13. Press Esc to clear any selections. Click the Dynamic Input icon to turn off that feature, and then click the structure farthest to the left in the Jordan Court profile view.

14. Click the triangle grip at the bottom of the structure, and drag it upward until a red dashed line appears (see Figure 14.12). Click while this symbol is visible.

    The sump elevation of the structure is raised slightly, but Civil 3D won't allow the sump to be placed above the lowest connecting pipe.

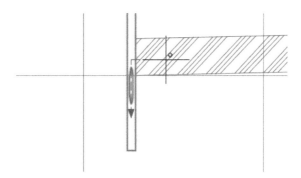

FIGURE 14.12 Editing the sump elevation of a structure using grips

15. Save and close the drawing.

You can view the results of successfully completing this exercise by opening `Editing Pipe Networks Using Grips - Complete.dwg`.

Editing Pipe Networks Using Editing Tools

Another way to edit a pipe network is to use the Network Layout Tools toolbar, which is the same toolbar you used initially to create the pipe network. To launch the toolbar in editing mode instead of creation mode, you use the Edit Pipe Network command.

In addition to the Network Layout Tools toolbar, there are several commands located on the ribbon and in a context menu that give you even more functionality:

Swap Part This command calls up the current parts list, and it enables you to select a part and replace it with any part in the parts list.

Disconnect Part This command disconnects a pipe from a structure, enabling you to connect it to a different part or move it independently of other parts.

Connect Part   This command connects a pipe to a structure to reestablish the dynamic behavior of connected parts.

Split Network   This command divides a network into two separate networks.

Merge Networks   This command combines two or more networks into a single network.

Exercise 14.5: Edit Pipe Networks Using Editing Tools

In this exercise, you'll use the ribbon commands and Network Layout Tools toolbar to edit the storm and sanitary networks in your drawing.

If you haven't already done so, download and install the files for Chapter 14 according to the instructions in this book's Introduction.

1. Open the drawing named `Editing Pipe Networks Using Editing Tools.dwg` located in the `Chapter 14` class data folder.

2. Click any storm pipe or structure in the drawing, and then click Edit Pipe Network on the ribbon.
   This opens the Network Layout Tools toolbar.

3. On the Network Layout Tools toolbar, do the following:

   a. Choose the structure Cylindrical Junction Structure NF (SI) ➢ Storm Manhole.

   b. Click the small black triangle to expand the button to the right of the pipe drop-down list. Select Structures Only.

4. If your Osnap icon is turned on, click it to turn it off.

5. In either the plan viewport or the 3D viewport, click near the midpoint of the pipe that begins at station 2+40.42 (0+073.280) and ends at station 5+50 (0+170).
   A new manhole is inserted along the pipe.

6. Press Esc to clear the current command. Click the newly created structure, and then click the square grip at its center.

7. Snap to the center of the red circle located near Jordan Court station 3+50 (0+110).

8. Press Esc to clear the previous selection. In the left viewport, click the pipe that enters the new manhole from the south. Click Swap Part on the ribbon.

9. In the Swap Part Size dialog box, click Concrete Pipe (SI) ➤ 18 Inch (450mm) Concrete Pipe and then click OK.

10. Repeat steps 8 and 9 for the pipe that exits the new manhole to the north.

   You have now inserted a new manhole and resized the pipes that connect to it (see Figure 14.13).

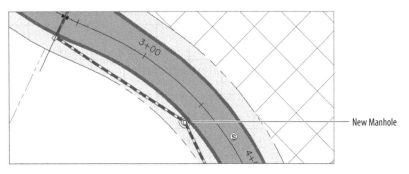

New Manhole

FIGURE 14.13   **Newly created manhole and resized connecting pipes**

11. Close the Network Layout Tools toolbar, and press Esc to clear the previous selection. Click one of the sanitary sewer pipes in the drawing, and then click Merge Networks on the ribbon.

12. In the first dialog box, click Sanitary-2 and then click OK.

   Here, you're selecting a network that will be merged into another. When the process is complete, a network of this name will no longer exist.

13. In the second dialog box, click Sanitary and then click OK.

   Here, you're selecting the network that is having Sanitary-2 merged into it.

14. In Prospector, expand Pipe Networks ➤ Networks. Note that the Sanitary-2 network is no longer listed.

15. Repeat steps 11–13, this time selecting Sanitary-3 in the first dialog box.

   All sanitary sewer networks have been merged into one; therefore, only one sanitary sewer network is listed in Prospector.

16. Save and close the drawing.

You can view the results of successfully completing this exercise by opening `Editing Pipe Networks Using Editing Tools - Complete.dwg`.

Editing Pipe Networks Using Properties

Many of the values you need to change when editing pipes and structures can be found in their *properties*. There are two ways to access the properties of a pipe or structure: the Civil 3D method and the AutoCAD method. To use the Civil 3D method, you select a pipe or structure and then click Pipe Properties or Structure Properties on the ribbon. This method provides extensive information about the pipe or structure, much of which can be edited to change the design. The one disadvantage of this method is that you must launch the Pipe Properties or Structure Properties command separately for each pipe or structure you want to edit.

With the AutoCAD method, you select the pipe or structure and then use the Properties command from the ribbon or the context menu. Here you're given access to a limited number of properties, but the advantage is that you can modify multiple pipes or structures simultaneously.

Exercise 14.6: Edit a Pipe Network Using Properties

In this exercise, you'll fix the issue with the sanitary pipe that is located far below the others. You'll use properties to complete this task. The problem with the incorrect pipe elevation was brought to your attention during the first exercise in this chapter, when the sanitary sewer pipe networks were first created.

If you haven't already done so, download and install the files for Chapter 14 according to the instructions in this book's Introduction.

1. Open the drawing named Editing Pipe Networks Using Properties.dwg located in the Chapter 14 class data folder.

   In this exercise, you'll focus on the sanitary sewer pipes that lie in Madison Lane. In the profile view on the top right, notice that the pipe beginning at the intersection with Logan Court and ending at the Madison Lane cul-de-sac has been incorrectly placed at a very low elevation.

2. In the upper-right viewport, zoom in to the Madison Lane profile and note the label at the right end that reads ELEV = 180.972 (55.160).

   This elevation corresponds with the center point of the cul-de-sac, which is also the location of the manhole.

3. Click in the left viewport, and then zoom in and click the manhole located at the center of the Madison Lane cul-de-sac. Click Structure Properties on the ribbon.

4. On the Part Properties tab of the Structure Properties dialog box, do the following:

   a. For Automatic Surface Adjustment, select False.

   b. For Insertion Rim Elevation, enter **180.972** (55.160).

   c. Click OK.

   In the 3D viewport, you'll see the manhole become very tall, like the one just down the road from it.

   This corrects the top elevation of the structure, but the pipe still requires some editing.

5. Press Esc to clear the selection of the manhole. Then, in the left viewport, select the pipe that begins at the Madison Lane cul-de-sac. Right-click, and select Properties.

6. In the Properties window, change Start Invert Elevation to **176.972** (53.941).

7. With the pipe still selected, click Pipe Properties on the ribbon.

8. On the Part Properties tab of the Pipe Properties dialog box, enter **-1.5** for Pipe Slope (Hold Start). Click OK.

   The effects of these pipe edits are much more obvious in the 3D viewport. The pipe is corrected, but the sump of the manhole at the cul-de-sac is still incorrect.

9. Press Esc to clear the selection of the pipe. Click the manhole at the center of the Madison Lane cul-de-sac, right-click, and select Structure Properties.

10. Although it's already set to 2.000 (0.600), type **2** (0.6) for Sump Depth, and press Enter. Click OK.

    The manhole depth is updated because the apparent change to the sump depth triggered a recalculation of the manhole dimensions. If you're zoomed in closely to the profile view in the top-right viewport, it may seem as though it has disappeared.

11. Click the top-right viewport, and zoom out until you can see the Madison Lane profile view.

The profile view has become much shorter because it no longer needs to accommodate the excessively tall manhole (see Figure 14.14).

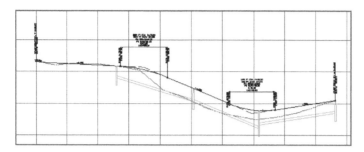

FIGURE 14.14   The sanitary pipe network in profile view after several elevations were corrected

12. Save and close the drawing.

You can view the results of successfully completing this exercise by opening Editing Pipe Networks Using Properties - Complete.dwg.

Editing Pipe Networks Using the Pipe Network Vistas

The pipe network editing methods you've learned about thus far in this chapter are great for working with individual pipes and structures, but what if you want to see the entire network or make edits to multiple parts simultaneously? Luckily, you can do these things with the Pipe Network Vistas command, which opens Panorama and displays two tabs: Structures and Pipes. Each of these tabs displays all the pipes or structures in the entire network in a spreadsheet format, enabling you to view and edit the properties of multiple components at once.

The Pipe Network Vistas button is located near the right end of the Network Layout Tools toolbar (see Figure 14.15).

FIGURE 14.15   The Pipe Network Vistas button highlighted on the Network Layout Tools toolbar

Exercise 14.7: Edit a Pipe Network Using the Pipe Network Vistas

In this exercise, you'll use the Pipe Network Vistas to change the names of some of the structures and change the style of some of the pipes.

1. Open the drawing named Editing Pipe Networks Using the Pipe Network Vistas.dwg located in the Chapter 14 class data folder.

2. Click any storm pipe or structure in the drawing, and then click Edit Pipe Network on the ribbon.

3. On the Network Layout Tools toolbar, click Pipe Network Vistas. Panorama opens, displaying the Pipes and Structures tabs.

4. Click the Structures tab. While holding down the Ctrl key, click the four rows that currently have Rectangular Junction Structure NF (SI) as the description (see Figure 14.16).

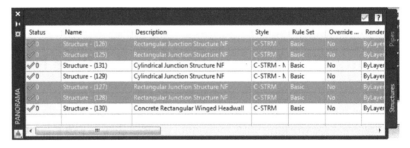

Status	Name	Description	Style	Rule Set	Override ...	Render
0	Structure - (126)	Rectangular Junction Structure NF	C-STRM	Basic	No	ByLayer
0	Structure - (125)	Rectangular Junction Structure NF	C-STRM	Basic	No	ByLayer
0	Structure - (131)	Cylindrical Junction Structure NF	C-STRM - N	Basic	No	ByLayer
0	Structure - (129)	Cylindrical Junction Structure NF	C-STRM - N	Basic	No	ByLayer
0	Structure - (127)	Rectangular Junction Structure NF	C-STRM	Basic	No	ByLayer
0	Structure - (128)	Rectangular Junction Structure NF	C-STRM	Basic	No	ByLayer
0	Structure - (130)	Concrete Rectangular Winged Headwall	C-STRM	Basic	No	ByLayer

FIGURE 14.16 Selecting multiple rows in the Structures tab of Panorama

5. Right-click the Description column heading, and select Edit.

6. Type **INLET**, and press Enter.
   All four Description values change to INLET.

7. In the Description column, change any instances of Cylindrical Junction Structure NF (SI) to **MANHOLE**.

8. Change the description for the last structure to **ENDWALL**.

9. Click the Pipes tab. While holding down the Shift key, click the first and last rows. All rows should now be selected.

10. Right-click the Style column, and select Edit. In the Select Pipe Style dialog box, select C-STRM – Walls In Profile. Click OK.

The appearance of the pipes in profile view changes so that the inside and outside pipe walls are shown (see Figure 14.17).

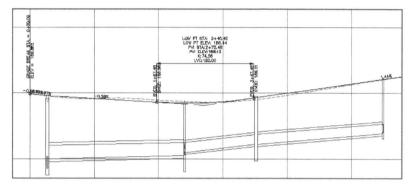

FIGURE 14.17   Pipes in profile view shown with inside and outside walls

11. Save and close the drawing.

You can view the results of successfully completing this exercise by opening `Editing Pipe Networks Using the Pipe Network Vistas - Complete.dwg`.

Now You Know

Now that you have completed this chapter, you're ready to begin creating and modifying gravity pipe networks. You can create these networks from objects in the drawing or by drawing them yourself using the Network Layout Tools toolbar. Once you have created a network, you can display it in profile view and edit it using grips, editing tools, properties, and the Pipe Network Vistas.

You're ready to begin working with gravity pipe networks in a production environment.

CHAPTER 15

Designing Pressure Pipe Networks

Now that you have studied gravity pipe networks, it's time to move on to a different type of pipe design: one that involves pipes under pressure. If you're unfamiliar with pipe design, you may be surprised to discover that the design process for gravity and pressure systems is quite different. For this reason, the AutoCAD® Civil 3D® software provides two unique tool sets: one for gravity pipe design and one for pressure pipe design.

Pressure pipe design most commonly refers to water supply lines but it can also apply to natural gas and sanitary sewer lines. These pipelines provide valuable utility services to the new residents of the land you're developing and must undergo extensive design to ensure that they function as intended and integrate well with surrounding features, whether new or existing.

In this chapter, you'll learn to:

▶ **Understand pressure pipe networks**

▶ **Create pressure pipe networks**

▶ **Edit pressure pipe networks**

Understanding Pressure Pipe Networks

Gravity system designs and pressure system designs are quite different and must be addressed using different tools. For a pressure pipe network design to be a success, it must meet the following basic requirements:

▶ The bends and curves must be constructed according to industry-standard fittings and allowable joint deflections.

▶ The pipes must be sized according to specific flows and pressures.

▶ The pipes must be far enough underground to avoid being damaged by freezing or by activities on the site.

▶ The pipes must not be so far underground that it is cost prohibitive to install them.

▶ Appurtenances such as valves and hydrants must be included in the design to allow the lines to be controlled, accessed, and maintained.

These requirements relate to three basic types of pressure pipe design components: fittings, pipes, and appurtenances. This chapter describes these components as well as their relationship to each other when represented in a Civil 3D pressure network.

Understanding Fittings, Angles, and Appurtenances

Pressure pipe fittings serve two purposes. The first, like structures in gravity systems, is to enable two or more pipes to connect. For example, a tee or wye fitting provides a connection for three pipes, and a crossing fitting provides a connection for four. The second purpose of a fitting is to create a bend in the direction of the pipeline, the angle of which is typically dictated by manufacturing standards. For example, elbows are commonly available in 90°, 45°, 22.5°, and 11.25° versions. For this reason, bend angles are a big part of pressure pipe design.

In addition to bend angles, a slight amount of deflection is allowed within connections. This deflection angle is part of the design and varies depending on how the pipes or fittings have been manufactured. This allowable deflection also enables a series of pipes to form a curve by providing a little deflection at each joint but without bending the pipes. Therefore, pressure pipes can be laid out on a curve, with the radius determined by the allowable deflection.

Another factor that can be incorporated into the design is the allowable bending radius of the pipes. Bending the pipes is another way a system can be laid out along a curve. The allowable bending radius is a function of the size, material, and manufacturer specifications of the pipe.

Because of available fittings, allowable deflection angles, and allowable bend radius, each bend in a pressure pipe is a design in itself. As a designer, you'll be required to choose the right combination of fitting, deflection angle, and bend radius to make each bend in the pipeline.

Appurtenances are another component of pressure pipe designs. The challenge with appurtenances is that they usually require consideration for human access. For example, a fire hydrant must be properly located at ground level so that firefighters or maintenance personnel can access it.

Understanding Pressure Pipes

Like gravity pipes, pressure pipes are used to convey a substance, but the main difference, of course, is that the substance is moved by pressure rather than gravity. For this reason, elevations aren't nearly as important to ensure adequate flow. They are important, however, to ensure that the pipeline has adequate cover to prevent freezing or physical damage and that it avoids underground obstacles, including other pipes. In the event of a conflict, because pressure pipe flow isn't dependent on elevation, a designer will typically bend a pressure pipe to avoid a gravity pipe rather than the other way around. As discussed previously, the required bends are a design challenge because of the limitations of available fittings and deflection angles.

Exploring the Pressure Network

Civil 3D enables you to create objects that represent fittings, pipes, and appurtenances. It also establishes relationships between these components as well as relationships with other important design elements such as surfaces, alignments, profiles, and profile views. The pipes, fittings, and appurtenances and their associated relationships are referred to as a Civil 3D *pressure network*. In Figure 15.1, a few pipes and fittings are shown in plan view on the left, profile view in the center, and 3D view on the right.

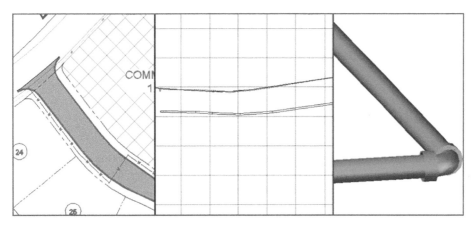

FIGURE 15.1 A pressure network shown in plan view (left), profile view (center), and 3D view (right)

Each component of a pressure network is shown in Prospector beneath the Pressure Networks node. From here, you can right-click each component to access various context commands for it. You can also use the item view at the bottom of Prospector to edit information about each component. Figure 15.2 shows the contents of a pressure network in Prospector.

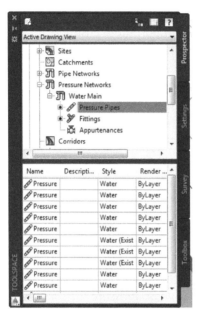

FIGURE 15.2 A pressure network shown in Prospector

Just as in gravity networks, the shape, dimensions, and behavior of a pressure network component are determined by the *part* that represents it. Pressure networks have their own parts lists, separate from gravity networks. Most companies have several parts lists, each one containing parts for a certain type of system such as water, sanitary, or natural gas.

Creating Pressure Pipe Networks

Certification Objective

As with gravity networks, pressure networks can be created in one of two ways. The first is to lay out the pressure network using basic AutoCAD® entities such as lines or polylines and then convert those objects to a pressure network. Another is to create the pressure network using layout tools. One difference with pressure networks is that the layout tools are housed in the ribbon rather than on a toolbar. The specialized ribbon tab (see Figure 15.3) is launched by using the Pressure Network Creation Tools command.

FIGURE 15.3   The specialized ribbon tab for pressure network layout

Creating a Pressure Network from Objects

At times, you'll find it easier to start with AutoCAD commands to sketch your pressure network using basic entities. This approach works quite well because Civil 3D provides a command that converts these basic entities to pressure networks: the Create Pressure Network From Object command. This command creates pipe networks from Civil 3D alignments and feature lines as well. One disadvantage of this method is that the same parts are used for pipes and fittings throughout the entire network.

Exercise 15.1: Create a Pressure Network from Objects

In this exercise, you'll create a waterline pressure network along Madison Lane by converting objects in the drawing. You'll also draw that pressure network in profile view.

1. Open the drawing named Creating Pressure Networks from Objects.dwg located in the Chapter 15 class data folder.

2. In the left viewport, note the heavy blue polyline along Madison Lane labeled with W, indicating a schematic location for a proposed waterline.

3. On the Home tab of the ribbon, click Pipe Network ➤ Create Pressure Network From Object.

4. Click the heavy blue polyline, and press Enter to accept the default direction assumed by the command.

5. In the Create Pressure Pipe Network From Object dialog box, do the following:

   a. For Network Name, enter **Madison Lane Water**.

   b. For Network Parts List, select Water Supply.

   c. For Size And Material, select 4 INCH (100mm) DUCTILE IRON.

> If you haven't already done so, download and install the files for Chapter 15 according to the instructions in this book's Introduction.

> You may notice that the storm system has been changed to red in the example drawings for this chapter. This is to make it easier to differentiate the storm pipes from the water pipes you'll be creating.

    d. For Surface Name, select Road FG.

    e. For Alignment Name, select Madison Lane.

    f. For Depth Of Cover, verify that 3.000' (1.000m) is the value currently applied.

    g. Check the box next to Erase Existing Entity.

    h. Click OK.

It may not appear that much has happened, but the polyline has been converted to a 3D model of a waterline, complete with pipes and bends. You can zoom in to the newly created waterline model in the 3D view to examine the result.

6. Click the Modify tab of the ribbon. Then expand the Design panel, and select Pressure Pipe Network.

7. Click Draw Parts In Profile on the ribbon. Click one of the new waterline parts, and press Enter to indicate that you would like to draw the entire network.

8. Click one of the grid lines of the Madison Lane profile view in the top-right viewport. The waterline parts are displayed in the profile view, as shown in Figure 15.4.

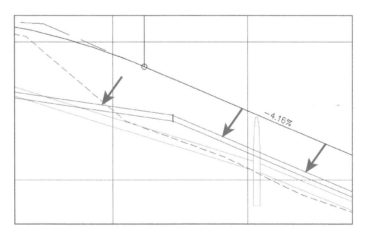

FIGURE 15.4 Pressure network parts (indicated with red arrows) shown in profile view along with other profile information

9. Save and close the drawing.

You can view the results of successfully completing this exercise by opening Creating Pressure Networks from Objects - Complete.dwg.

PRESSURE NETWORKS FROM FEATURE LINES

You may have noticed the Use Vertex Elevations option in the Create Pressure Pipe Network From Object dialog box. If you create a pressure network from a feature line, you can use this option to set the elevations of the pipes and fittings based on the elevations of the feature line. You can also choose the reference point that is used when assigning elevations such as Outside, Top, Crown, Centerline, and so on. This is an effective way to convert a rough 3D sketch of a pressure pipe design into a full-fledged 3D pressure network model.

Creating a Pressure Network by Layout

Another way to create pressure networks is using the Pressure Network Creation Tools command. When you launch this command, you will see a specialized ribbon tab (as shown previously in Figure 15.3) that contains tools for pressure network layout. From this specialized ribbon tab, you can choose the pipes, fittings, and appurtenances from the parts list and use the commands on the ribbon to insert those parts into the drawing. You can change parts at any time and apply different types and sizes as you go.

To guide your design, Civil 3D provides a *compass* (see Figure 15.5), which displays the bend angles and deflections available at a given point, based on information stored in the parts list. The compass automatically "snaps" your cursor to an available bend angle to prevent you from laying out a nonstandard bend in the pipeline.

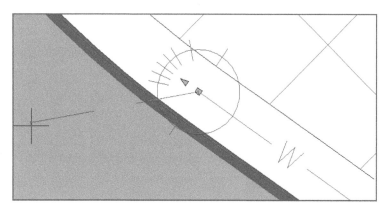

F I G U R E   1 5 . 5   The compass (the red circle) shows the available bend angles and deflections.

Another fundamental difference with pressure network layout is that you provide a value for *cover*, and Civil 3D automatically sets the elevation at each end of a pipe according to that value. You can change the cover value as you design.

Exercise 15.2: Create a Pressure Network by Layout

In this exercise, you'll use layout tools to begin designing the waterline pressure network along Jordan Court.

1. Open the drawing named Creating Pressure Networks by Layout .dwg located in the Chapter 15 class data folder.

2. On the Home tab of the ribbon, click Pipe Network ➤ Pressure Network Creation Tools.

3. In the Create Pressure Pipe Network dialog box, do the following:

   a. For Network Name, enter **Water Main**.

   b. For Parts List, select Water Supply.

   c. For Surface Name, select Road FG.

   d. For Alignment Name, select Jordan Court.

   e. Click OK.

4. The Pressure Network Plan Layout ribbon tab opens. Do the following:

   a. In the Network Settings panel, enter 4.5 (**1.5**) for Cover.

   b. Under Select A Size And Material, select 6 INCH (150mm) DUCTILE IRON.

5. Click Pipes Only. Snap to the center of the circle marked A; then snap to the center of the circle marked B.

6. At the command line, click Curve to apply the Curve option. Snap to the center of the circle marked C.

7. At the command line, click Straight to apply the Straight option. Snap to the center of the circle marked D.

8. On the ribbon, to the right of Add Fitting, select 6 INCH (150mm) ELBOW 90 DEG. Click Add Fitting. Snap to the end of the last pipe you drew.

Cover refers to the distance from the top of the pipe to the surface of the ground.

If you haven't already done so, download and install the files for Chapter 15 according to the instructions in this book's Introduction.

In this drawing, red circles have been provided to indicate the locations of bends.

Notice the compass that appears at point B, which shows the allowable deflection at the pipe joint and restricts the ability to draw the next pipe, to stay in that allowable deflection.

A new 90° fitting should be placed at the end of the pipe, but it curves in the wrong direction.

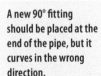

9. Press Esc to end the current command. In the lower-right viewport, zoom in to the area where you inserted the fitting so you can observe the development of the design in 3D.

10. In the left viewport, click the new fitting, and then click the northward-pointing arrow grip to flip the fitting so it curves toward the southwest. Press Esc to clear the selection of the fitting.

11. Click Pipes & Bends on the ribbon. In the left viewport, click the 90° elbow, and then snap to the center of the circle marked E.

12. On the command line, click Curve to apply the Curve option. Click a point somewhere between circles E and F; then snap to the center of circle F. Press Esc to end the command.

    A new 90° elbow has been inserted, and a curved section of pipe has been drawn from circle E to circle F (see Figure 15.6).

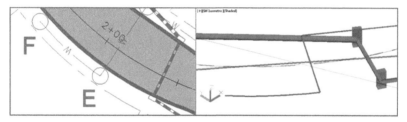

F I G U R E 1 5 . 6   **The newly drawn waterline, including the 90° elbow at circle E and the curved section of pipe between circles E and F**

13. Save and close the drawing.

You can view the results of successfully completing this exercise by opening `Creating Pressure Networks by Layout - Complete.dwg`.

Editing Pressure Pipe Networks

Before editing a pressure network, it's best to display it in profile view so that you can analyze your design from more than one perspective. This is done using the Draw Parts In Profile View command, much as you did with gravity networks. And just like gravity networks, pressure networks can be edited using four basic approaches: grips, layout tools, properties, and Pipe Network Vistas. Of these four approaches, the grips and layout tools approaches differ

---

Notice the difference in the compass, which now shows available bend angles rather than deflections. The available angles are based on the fittings listed in the parts list.

considerably from how they are applied in gravity systems. The sections entitled, "Editing Pressure Networks Using Grips" and "Editing Pressure Networks Using the Plan Layout Tools" explain the details of how these two approaches are applied to pressure networks.

Editing Pressure Networks Using Grips

Grips are a great tool for making quick and simple graphical edits. Civil 3D provides the following specialized grips for pressure pipes and fittings:

 **Fitting – Square Grip – Plan View**   This grip changes the location of the fitting without changing its rotation. As the fitting is moved, the ends of any pipes that connect to it will move with it.

 **Fitting – Arrow Grip – Plan View**   This grip changes the direction of the fitting by flipping it around the axis of the connecting pipe.

 **Fitting – Diamond Grip – Plan View**   This grip slides the fitting along the pipe it's connected to without changing the rotation angle of the fitting.

 **Fitting – Plus Grip – Plan View**   This grip creates a new pipe projecting from the end of the fitting, with the angle restricted to the allowable deflection at the joint. This grip doesn't appear in a location where a pipe is already connected.

 Fitting – Diamond Grip – Profile View   This grip changes the elevation of the fitting.

 **Pipe Endpoint – Square Grip – Plan View**   This grip changes the location of one end of the pipe without changing the location of the other. It's available only if neither end of the pipe is connected to a fitting.

 **Pipe Endpoint – Diamond Grip – Plan View**   This grip swings the pipe around a fitting at the opposite end. A graphic displays the allowable deflection but doesn't restrict movement to stay within it. This grip doesn't change the length of the pipe.

Pipe Endpoint – Plus Grip – Plan View   This grip creates a new fitting and pipe projecting from the end of the pipe you've selected. The angle of the new pipe is restricted to the allowable angles as per the fittings in the parts list. This grip doesn't appear in a location where a fitting is already connected.

Pipe Endpoint – Triangular Grip – Plan View   This grip changes the length of the pipe while maintaining the angle of the pipe and the location of the opposite end. If the pipe is curved, it maintains the radius of the pipe while extending it along its own curvature.

Pipe Midpoint Grip – Plan View   For a straight pipe, this grip changes the location of the pipe without changing its rotation. It disconnects the pipe from any fittings it's attached to. For a curved pipe with a connection at both ends, this grip changes the radius of the curve without changing the location of either endpoint. If one or both of the ends aren't connected, it works the same as if it's a straight pipe.

Pipe Endpoint Grips – Profile View   These grips change the elevation of a pipe at its endpoint. The diamond-shaped grip at the top sets the crown (top of the inside wall) elevation. The diamond-shaped grip at the bottom sets the invert (bottom of the inside wall) elevation. The triangular grip sets the centerline elevation. These grips can be used in conjunction with the AutoCAD Dynamic Input feature to view the elevation or even type it in. They don't change the horizontal location of the pipe's endpoint.

Pipe Endpoint – Triangle Grip – Profile View   This grip changes the length of the pipe while holding its slope.

Pipe Midpoint – Square Grip – Profile View   This grip changes the elevation of the pipe without changing its slope. It doesn't affect the location of the pipe in plan view. It disconnects the pipe from any fittings or appurtenances it's connected to.

Pipe Midpoint – Circular Grip – Profile View   This grip curves the pipe by holding the endpoints and forcing it to pass through the new location that you select for the grip. Movement isn't restricted based on allowable deflections.

Exercise 15.3: Edit a Pressure Network Using Grips

If you haven't already done so, download and install the files for Chapter 15 according to the instructions in this book's Introduction.

In this exercise, you'll make some adjustments to the layout of the waterline pressure network along Jordan Court. You'll use some of the specialized grips to make these adjustments in plan and profile.

1. Open the drawing named `Editing Pressure Networks Using Grips.dwg` located in the `Chapter 15` class data folder.

2. In the left viewport, zoom in to the circle marked D1, and click the 90° elbow fitting near its center. Click the fitting, and then click the square grip.

The location of the next fitting will be outside the area covered by the Road FG surface, and it will therefore be based on EG surface elevations.

3. Snap to the center of the circle marked D2. The fitting moves to the new location along with the ends of the two pipes that are connected to it.

   The geometry of the fitting looks a bit odd at the moment because the fitting should be changed to a 45° elbow. This will be addressed in a later exercise.

4. In the lower-right viewport, click the curved pipe between E and F1; then click the triangular grip at circle F1. Snap to the center of circle F2.

Notice how the end of the pipe isn't located at the elevation of the center of circle G, even though that's where you snapped. Civil 3D calculated the elevation based on the surface and the Cover value you specified.

5. Click the plus-sign grip at circle F2. On the ribbon, select EG as the surface, and change the Cover value to 4.5 (1.5). Select 6 INCH (150mm) DUCTILE IRON as the pipe size, and snap to the center of circle G.

6. Press Esc to end the current command and clear any selections in the drawing. Click the pipe between E and F2, and then click Draw Parts In Profile on the Pipe Networks: Water Main ribbon tab.

7. Click one of the grid lines of the Jordan Court profile view.
   The water pipe should appear in the profile view.

8. Press Esc to clear the current selection. Select all pipes and fittings from circle E to circle A; then use the Draw Parts In Profile command to add them to the profile view.

   The waterline should now appear in the profile view, as shown in Figure 15.7.

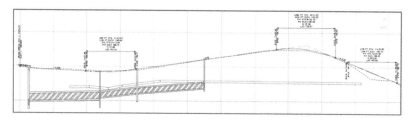

FIGURE 15.7   The water main pressure pipes and fittings shown in profile view

9. In the profile view, click the second fitting from the left, located near station 2+75 (0+080). Click the diamond-shaped grip. If Dynamic Input is turned off, turn it on by clicking the icon at the bottom of your screen.

10. Zoom out until you can see the Dynamic Input elevation value for the grip. Type 184 (55.45), and press Enter.

11. Pan to the right, and click the long pipe at the right end of the water main. Click the circular grip; then click a point slightly above the pipe.

The pipe curves upward so that it passes through the point you selected.

12. Save and close the drawing.

You can view the results of successfully completing this exercise by opening Editing Pressure Networks Using Grips - Complete.dwg.

Checking Design and Depth

Before performing any edits on a pressure network, you may find it helpful to use the Design Check and Depth Check commands to identify necessary edits. Both these commands are found on the Pressure Networks ribbon tab. The Design Check command checks for issues with deflection, mismatched pipe diameters, open connections, and radius of curvature. Depth Check finds issues with minimum and maximum cover.

If you haven't already done so, download and install the files for Chapter 15 according to the instructions in this book's Introduction.

Exercise 15.4: Check Design and Depth

In this exercise, you'll check the waterline along Jordan Court for deflection and depth issues.

1. Open the drawing named Checking Design and Depth.dwg located in the Chapter 15 class data folder.

2. Click the pipe that runs from circle D2 to circle E. Then click Design Check on the ribbon.

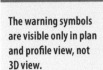

The warning symbols are visible only in plan and profile view, not 3D view.

3. In the Run Design Check dialog box, uncheck all boxes except Deflection, and then click OK.
   Two warning symbols appear, one at each end of the pipe.

4. Zoom in to one of the warning symbols, and hover your cursor over it. The tooltip should indicate that deflection has been exceeded.

5. Press Esc to clear the current selection. Then, in the Jordan Court profile view, select the long water pipe that extends under the hill. Click Depth Check on the ribbon.

6. Select the same pipe again, and press Enter. In the Run Depth Check dialog box, check the box next to Maximum Depth Of Cover. Enter 4.5 (1.5) for Minimum Depth Of Cover and 10 (3) for Maximum Depth Of Cover. Click OK.

If you're having trouble getting the tooltips to appear, try zooming in and then running the REGEN command.

7. In the top-right viewport, notice the warning symbol that appears on the pipe directly below the high point of the hill. Hover over the warning symbol to reveal the tooltip, which states that maximum depth of cover has been exceeded.

8. Save and close the drawing.

You can view the results of successfully completing this exercise by opening Checking Design and Depth - Complete.dwg.

Editing Pressure Networks Using the Plan Layout Tools

One way to edit a pressure network is to use the Pressure Network Plan Layout ribbon tab, which is the same one you used initially to create the pressure network. To launch the ribbon in editing mode instead of creation mode, you select a component of the pressure network and then click Edit Network ➤ Plan Layout Tools (see Figure 15.8).

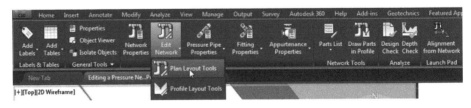

FIGURE 15.8   Launching the Pressure Network Plan Layout ribbon tab by clicking the Plan Layout Tools command

Exercise 15.5: Use the Plan Layout Tools

In this exercise, you'll use the Plan Layout Tools to change out several fittings and add a pipe to the end of the waterline network along Jordan Court.

If you haven't already done so, download and install the files for Chapter 15 according to the instructions in this book's Introduction.

1. Open the drawing named Editing a Pressure Network Using Plan Layout Tools.dwg located in the Chapter 15 class data folder.

2. In the left viewport and the lower-right viewport, zoom in to circle D2. Click the elbow located near the center of the red circle at D2, and press the Delete key to delete it.

3. Click one of the pipes to display the Pressure Networks ribbon tab. Then click Edit Network ➤ Plan Layout Tools.

4. On the Pressure Network Plan Layout ribbon tab, do the following:

    a. Verify that Road FG is the selected surface.

    b. For Cover, enter 4.5 (1.5).

    c. Select 6 INCH (150mm) DUCTILE IRON as the pipe size.

    d. Select 6 INCH (150mm) ELBOW 45 DEG as the fitting.

5. Click Add Fitting; then, in the left viewport, click the end of either pipe in the D2 circle. Press Esc twice to end the command and clear the selection. If the fitting is turned the wrong way, click it and use the arrow grip to flip it in the right direction.

6. Click the pipe that isn't connected, to display its grips. Click the diamond-shaped grip; then click the new fitting to connect the pipe to the fitting. Press Esc to clear the selection of the pipe.

7. Delete the 90° fitting at circle E, and repeat steps 5 and 6 to replace it with a 45° fitting.

8. On the ribbon, select 6 INCH (150mm) TEE as the current fitting.

9. Delete the 90° fitting at circle F2, and repeat steps 5 and 6 to replace it with a 6 INCH (150mm) TEE.

10. In the plan view on the left, click the newly created tee; then click the northern plus-sign grip. Snap to the center of circle H to create a new pipe. Press Esc twice to end the command and clear the selection.

11. Save and close the drawing.

You can view the results of successfully completing this exercise by opening Editing a Pressure Network Using Plan Layout Tools - Complete.dwg

Editing Pressure Networks Using the Profile Layout Tools

As you may have noticed in Figure 15.8, there is also a *Profile Layout Tools* command. The editing tools available for pressure networks in profile view are a bit more numerous when compared to gravity networks. For example, with pressure networks, you can add new pipes, add fittings, extend pipes, and perform several other functions that aren't possible with gravity pipes. When you click the Profile Layout Tools command, the Pressure Network Profile Layout ribbon tab opens (see Figure 15.9); it provides many useful editing commands that are carried out in profile view.

FIGURE 15.9   The specialized ribbon tab for pressure pipe layout in profile view

Exercise 15.6: Use the Profile Layout Tools

If you haven't already done so, download and install the files for Chapter 15 according to the instructions in this book's Introduction.

In this exercise, you'll use the Profile Layout Tools to design the portion of the Jordan Court waterline that connects to the existing water main. You'll add vertical bends as well as a valve.

1. Open the drawing named Editing a Pressure Network Using Profile Layout Tools.dwg located in the Chapter 15 class data folder.

2. Click the new pipe that runs from circle H to circle F2 and the tee fitting at Circle F2. Click Draw Parts In Profile on the ribbon, and click one of the grid lines in the Jordan Court profile view.

    The new pipe and fitting are drawn in the profile view. Notice the tee connection and the short pipe stub located down from and to the left of the new pipe. This is the location where the new waterline will connect to the existing waterline.

3. With one of the pipes or fittings selected, select Edit Network ➤ Profile Layout Tools on the ribbon.

4. Next to Add Bend, select 6 INCH (150mm) ELBOW 45 DEG. Then click Add Bend.

5. In the upper-right viewport, place your cursor near the right end of the short pipe segment located just below the red circle. When the glyph appears, as shown in Figure 15.10, click the pipe. Click Counterclockwise on the command line.

A new 45° bend should appear. It may look odd in profile view because of the vertical exaggeration. If you zoom in to the new fitting in the 3D view, it will look more like you would expect.

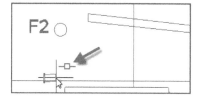

F I G U R E   1 5 . 1 0   A glyph indicating the proper connection of a pipe to a fitting

6. Verify that 6 INCH (150mm) DUCTILE IRON is selected as the current pipe size, and click Add Pressure Pipe. When prompted for the part at the start of the range, click the newly created elbow.

7. When prompted for the part at the end of the range, click the pipe to the right of the red circle. Click Yes when asked if you want to continue.

8. Click the newly created elbow, and then snap to the center of the red circle located above the new bend.

9. Click Add Bend; then click the end of the newly created pipe, making sure the proper glyph is displayed, as previously shown in Figure 15.10. Click Clockwise on the command line to invoke the Clockwise option. Another 45° bend is created.

10. Click the pipe just to the right of the newly created bend. Click the upright triangle grip at the left end of the pipe, and drag it toward the new bend. Click the newly created bend to connect the pipe to it.

You could have also done this step using the 3D view or the plan view.

In the 3D view, you can now see the complete design of the connection between the existing and proposed water mains (see Figure 15.11).

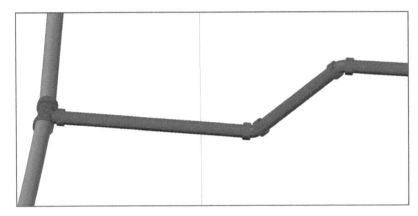

F I G U R E 1 5 . 1 1   The connection of the proposed waterline to the existing waterline, shown in a 3D perspective

11. On the ribbon, click Break Pipe. Locate the two vertical red lines on the first pipe segment, and click where the red line on the left crosses the top of the pipe.

12. Repeat the previous step for the red line on the right.

13. On the ribbon, click Delete Part. Click the pipe segment between the red lines.

14. Click Add Appurtenance, and then click the left side of the gap created by deleting the pipe segment in the previous step.

A valve symbol should appear in the profile view.

15. Click the pipe on the right side of the gap to display its grips. Click the upright triangle grip, and drag it toward the new valve. Click when the glyph appears, indicating that a connection is going to be made. View the tee and valve assembly in the lower-right viewport (see Figure 15.12).

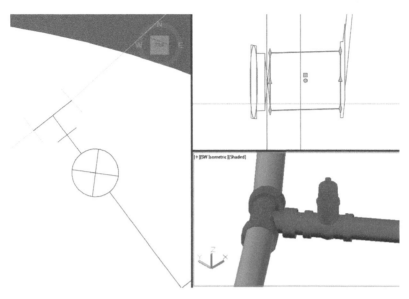

FIGURE 15.12   The connection of the proposed waterline to the existing waterline, shown in plan, profile, and 3D perspective

16. Press Esc to clear all the selections in the drawing. In profile view, pan to the right and select the long pipe. Click Follow Surface on the Pressure Network Profile Layout tab of the ribbon.

17. Press Enter; then type **4.5 (1.5)** at the command line when prompted for the depth below the surface. Press Enter to complete the command.

The pipe has been broken into segments so that it can maintain a constant depth below the surface.

18. Save and close the drawing.

You can view the results of successfully completing this exercise by opening Editing a Pressure Network Using Profile Layout Tools - Complete.dwg.

Now You Know

Now that you have completed this chapter, you understand pressure networks and how they differ from gravity networks. You're able to create pressure networks by converting objects already in the drawing or by creating them from scratch using the layout tools. You know several methods for editing pressure networks, including the use of grips, Plan Layout Tools, and Profile Layout Tools.

You're ready to begin creating and editing pressure networks in a production environment.

CHAPTER 16

Displaying and Annotating Pipe Networks

As you have learned with other types of design that I have discussed to this point, simply designing an object or a system isn't the end of the story. Your ability to share important information about the design is as important as the design itself. After all, without the effective sharing of information, the design can't be properly reviewed or constructed. Pipe network design is no different, and it relies heavily on graphical appearance and annotation to convey design information.

In this chapter, you'll study the use of pipe, structure, fitting, and appurtenance styles to control the appearance of pipe networks in plan and profile view. You'll also learn about annotating pipe networks using labels and tables. In a more general sense, you'll learn how to combine all these features to effectively communicate the intent of your design to others.

In the previous two chapters, gravity and pressure networks were presented separately because they each require a unique approach for layout and design. The stylization and annotation of gravity and pressure networks are virtually the same, however, with the only exception being the difference between fitting styles and structure styles. For this reason, most of the information in this chapter doesn't need to be duplicated for both types of networks as it was in the previous chapters.

In this chapter, you'll learn to:

▶ **Display pipe networks using styles**

▶ **Annotate pipe networks in plan view**

▶ **Annotate pipe networks in profile view**

▶ **Create pipe network tables**

Displaying Pipe Networks Using Styles

Pipe and structure styles are two of the most sophisticated styles in the AutoCAD® Civil 3D® software. They provide many options for displaying the components of your pipe network design in plan, profile, model (3D), and even section view. It's important to have many options for displaying pipe networks because often you have different types of systems in the same drawing that need to be differentiated graphically.

Applying Structure, Fitting, and Appurtenance Styles

Civil 3D styles provide a number of fundamental ways to display structures, fittings, and appurtenances. In plan view, you can display a structure as an outline of its 3D form, or you can use an AutoCAD® block as a symbol representing the structure. When you use a block, you can determine its size according to the drawing scale, a fixed scale, or the actual dimensions of the part. Figure 16.1 shows a structure represented using an AutoCAD block on the left and as an outline of its 3D shape on the right.

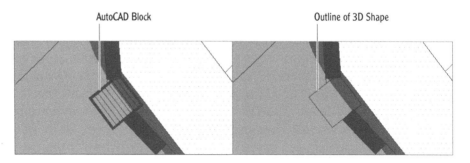

FIGURE 16.1   A structure shown as a block (left) and as an outline of a 3D shape (right)

There are three ways to display a structure in profile view (Figure 16.2).

Solid   The structure is shown as a slice through the 3D model of the part, which means the size, shape, and dimensions are an accurate representation (see Figure 16.2, left). Any detail within the interior of the part is visible with this option.

Boundary   An outline of the 3D model of the part is shown (see Figure 16.2, center). This is also an accurate representation of the part but without the interior detail.

Block   A block (see Figure 16.2, right) is inserted and sized based on one of several options. The most common option is to scale the block vertically to match the height of the part and horizontally to match the width of the part. A block can provide the desired appearance of the part, but because of the horizontal and vertical scaling, it may not be an exact dimensional match to the actual part.

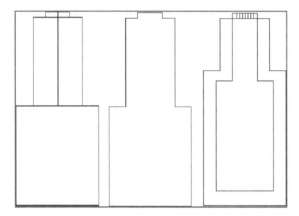

FIGURE   16.2   A structure shown as a solid (left), boundary (center), and block (right)

There are three ways to display fittings and appurtenances (Figure 16.3).

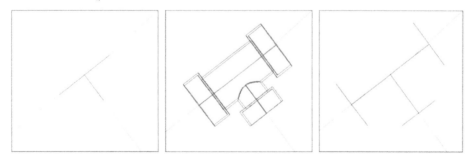

FIGURE   16.3   A tee fitting shown as a centerline (left), catalog defined block (center), and user-defined block (right)

Centerline   The Centerline option (see Figure 16.3, left) is the simplest choice and represents the fitting or appurtenance as a single line.

Catalog Defined Block   The Catalog Defined Block option (see Figure 16.3, center) is the true 3D form of the fitting or appurtenance shown in plan view.

User Defined Block   The User Defined Block (see Figure 16.3, right) option allows you to use any AutoCAD block to represent the fitting or appurtenance.

In profile view, there are no options for the display of fittings and appurtenances; fittings are simply represented as an outline, and appurtenances are represented by a symbol that resembles their type.

As a designer, it isn't likely that you'll be responsible for configuring styles or having to choose which display configuration to use—these things are typically taken care of by a CAD manager. However, knowing the ways in which structures, fittings, and appurtenances can be displayed will be helpful when you're asking your CAD manager to build some styles for you.

Exercise 16.1: Control the Display of Structures

In this exercise, you'll assign different styles to gravity and pressure structures to change their appearance. You'll observe the changes made to the appearance of those structures and see how they can potentially affect your design.

If you haven't already done so, download and install the files for Chapter 16 according to the instructions in this book's Introduction.

1. Open the drawing named `Applying Structure and Fitting Styles.dwg` located in the `Chapter 16` class data folder.

2. In the left viewport, click the sanitary manhole (the one with the *S* inside the circle), and then click Structure Properties on the ribbon.
   This opens the Structure Properties dialog box.

3. Click the Information tab, and then select C-SSWR – Outline as the style. Click OK.
   This style shows the outline of the actual 3D part, which reveals that the manhole is actually much larger than the symbol suggests.

In the left view, the drawing is zoomed in to two manholes that are in close proximity to one another but don't appear to be conflicting. In the lower-right view, it appears there could be a conflict, but at the current view angle, it isn't absolutely certain.

4. Press Esc to clear the selection of the sanitary manhole. Click the storm manhole (the one with the *D* inside the circle), and then select Structure Properties on the ribbon.

D is for *drainage*, a term that is often considered interchangeable with *stormwater*.

5. Change the style of this manhole to C-STRM – Outline. Click OK to dismiss the Structure Properties dialog. Press Esc to clear the selection.
   With both manholes shown at their actual size, there is an obvious conflict (see Figure 16.4). Next you'll use styles to change the appearance of some pressure network structures.

6. In the left viewport, pan northward to the beginning of Jordan Court where the new water line ties to the existing water line. Click the tee fitting and the two elbow fittings near the connection point.

In plan view, the fittings now appear in their true 3D form as a result of the style change.

7. Right-click, and select Properties. Change the Style property to Water 3D.

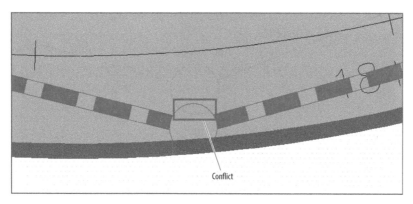

FIGURE 16.4   A conflict between two manholes is evident when the style reflects their true size.

8. Press Esc to clear the previous selection but keep the Properties window open. Pan northeast to the other corner of the Jordan Court – Emerson Road intersection, and select the storm manhole there.

IT'S NOT CALLED 3D FOR NOTHING

The true form of a Civil 3D pipe or structure is a 3D object. For example, a manhole structure is typically some form of cylinder and is often somewhat complex, including tapers, eccentric cylinders, and so on. Some of the ways in which structures can be displayed involve slicing through this shape or showing an outline of it. In the following image, the same structure is shown from a 3D perspective (left), in plan view as an outline (center), and in profile view as a slice through the part (right). By using 3D representations of structures in your drawings, you can design more accurately and ensure that your structures aren't conflicting with other underground objects.

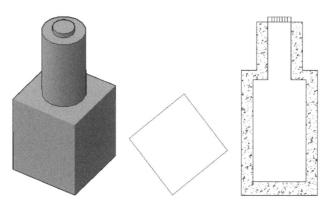

This may be acceptable for some instances, but when you need to see the exact dimensions of a manhole, you would use a different style.

9. In the Properties window, change the style to C-STRM – MH Symbol Plan & Profile.

    As you select the new style, watch the manhole in the profile view in the top-right viewport to see its shape change slightly. This is because the block isn't an accurate dimensional representation of the manhole.

10. Save and close the drawing.

You can view the results of successfully completing this exercise by opening Applying Structure and Fitting Styles - Complete.dwg.

Applying Pipe Styles

A pipe object is a bit simpler than a structure object in that it's essentially the extrusion of a circle, an ellipse, or a rectangle. Even so, the graphical representation of a pipe is broken down into numerous parts, each of which can be stylized differently. Figure 16.5 shows a pipe and its components in profile view.

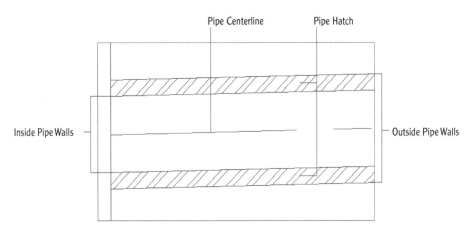

FIGURE 16.5   A pipe in profile view

You can use pipe styles to control the various pipe components as follows:

Pipe Centerline   In addition to controlling the visibility and graphical properties of the pipe centerline, such as layer, color, and linetype, you can also control the width of the centerline in several ways, including setting it to match the diameter of the pipe. The striped appearance of the storm pipes you have seen in the example drawings was achieved by setting the centerline width to the inside pipe diameter and using a dashed linetype.

Inside and Outside Pipe Walls   You can use styles to control the visibility and graphical properties of the inner and outer walls.

Pipe End Line   This is a line drawn across either end of the pipe. The style can determine whether this line is drawn to the outer pipe wall or inner pipe wall.

Pipe Hatch   You can use a pipe style to hatch a pipe across its inside or outside diameter or in the area between the inner and outer walls. The pattern, scale, and rotation of the hatch can be specified as part of the style.

Crossing Pipe   You can use a pipe style to show a pipe as though it's crossing through the profile view rather than oriented parallel to it. This typically takes the form of an ellipse, either because of vertical exaggeration or because the pipe crosses through at an angle. This is extremely useful for ensuring that crossing pipes don't conflict with one another. In profile view, you can control the visibility and graphical properties of the crossing pipe components such as inside walls, outside walls, and hatching.

   Again, you aren't likely to be responsible for creating the styles that configure these different display options. However, if you have a basic understanding of what is possible, you can more accurately request the specific styles you need from your CAD manager.

> If you haven't already done so, download and install the files for Chapter 16 according to the instructions in this book's Introduction.

Exercise 16.2: Control the Display of Pipes

In this exercise, you'll alter the appearance of two pipes by changing their style assignment. In one case, this change will be apparent in plan view, and in the other it will be shown in profile view.

1. Open the drawing named Applying Pipe Styles.dwg located in the Chapter 16 class data folder.
    In this drawing, the left view is zoomed in to Logan Court where a sanitary pipe crosses a storm pipe, and the same pipes are shown in profile view on the top right and 3D view on the bottom right.

> The appearance of the pipe changes in the plan view. The SAN label has been turned off, and the pipe is now shown as a double line representing the inside diameter.

2. In the left view, click the green pipe labeled SAN. Click Pipe Properties on the ribbon.

3. In the Pipe Properties dialog box, click the Information tab. Change the style to C-SSWR – Double Line, and click OK.

4. Press Esc to clear the previous selection, and then click the profile view grid in the top-right viewport. Click Profile View Properties on the ribbon.

5. In the Profile View Properties dialog box, click the Pipe Networks tab. Scroll, and locate the pipes listed beneath the Storm2 network. One of the pipes is set to Yes in the Draw column. Check the box in the Style Override column for this pipe.

6. In the Pick Pipe Style dialog box, select C-PROF-STRM – Crossing and click OK. Click OK once more to dismiss the Profile View Properties dialog box.

    You're returned to the drawing, and the storm pipe is now represented as an ellipse. The ellipse is placed at the location where the storm pipe crosses the alignment (see Figure 16.6).

When you view the storm and sanitary pipes this way, you can clearly see that there is a conflict and that you need to change the design.

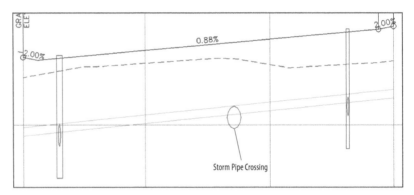

FIGURE 16.6　A storm pipe crossing shown as an ellipse indicates a conflict with a sanitary pipe.

7. Save and close the drawing.

You can view the results of successfully completing this exercise by opening `Applying Pipe Styles - Complete.dwg`.

PROFILE VIEW OVERRIDES

The Profile View Properties dialog box has a special Pipe Networks tab that lists all the pipes and structures in the drawing. You can display any of them in a given profile view by simply checking a box in the Draw column. You can even perform a style override so that a pipe or structure can be displayed in a given profile view using a different style than the one assigned to it in the Pipe Properties dialog box. This is especially handy when you need to show a pipe using a crossing style in one profile view and using a "normal" style in another. The following image shows the Pipe Networks tab of the Profile View Properties dialog box.

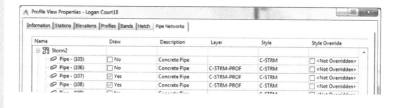

Annotating Pipe Networks in Plan View

For a pipe system to function properly, it must be installed with a considerable amount of accuracy. And for this to take place, detailed information must be conveyed to the contractor installing the pipes and structures in the field. The most common way to do this is to add text to your drawing. With stations and offsets, you provide the horizontal location of each structure, and with slopes and elevations, you dictate the depth of each pipe and the slope needed for water to flow through it properly. These values are typically expressed to the nearest hundredth of a foot or thousandth of a meter. It's amazing to think that a trench can be excavated and a heavy concrete pipe laid in it with such accuracy, but it happens every day.

So far, you have worked with functions that create pipes and structures, edit their design, and control their graphical appearance in the drawing. In the following sections, you'll learn how to annotate your design, which is arguably even more important than the design itself. The lines and symbols provide a useful picture of the design, but the stations, offsets, elevations, slopes, and so on provided by your annotations are used to make precise measurements that locate and orient each pipe and structure in the field.

Renaming Pipes and Structures

Many pipe network designs involve a large number of pipes and structures. For this reason, it's good design practice to have a naming and/or numbering system that helps you keep track of these many components. Before labeling pipes and structures, you should spend some time renaming them according to the system you'll use.

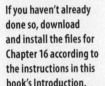

Exercise 16.3: Rename Pipes and Structures

If you haven't already done so, download and install the files for Chapter 16 according to the instructions in this book's Introduction.

In this exercise, you'll do some "bookkeeping" to rename the pipes and structures in the Storm1 network according to a numerical sequence.

1. Open the drawing named Renaming Pipes and Structures.dwg located in the Chapter 16 class data folder.

2. In the viewport on the left, click the inlet at station 5+50 (0+170) that is on the east side of Jordan Court. Right-click, and select Properties.

3. In the Properties window, change the name to **INLET-01**. Press Esc to clear the selection, and then click the inlet across the street from INLET-01.

4. In the Properties window, change the name to **INLET-02**. Press Esc to clear the selection.

5. Click the pipe between INLET-01 and INLET-02, and change its name to **STM-01**.

6. Change the name of the pipe exiting INLET-02 to the north to **STM-02**.

7. Change the name of the manhole near station 3+50 (0+110) to **STMH-01**.

8. Continue working along the pipe network, renaming the inlets, pipes, and manholes according to this sequence. When you get to the final structure, the endwall, name it **ENDWALL-01**.

9. In Prospector, expand Pipe Networks ➤ Networks ➤ Storm1. Under Storm1, click Pipes.

In the item view at the bottom of Prospector, the pipe names should all be updated as shown in Figure 16.7, but they may appear in a different order.

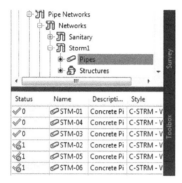

FIGURE 16.7   Revised pipe names shown in the item view of Prospector

10. Under Storm1, click Structures.

In the item view at the bottom of Prospector, the values listed in the Name column should match Figure 16.8.

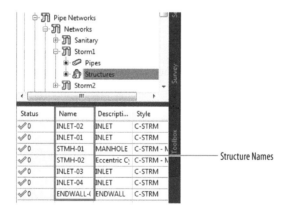

FIGURE 16.8   Revised structure names shown in the item view of Prospector

11. Save and close the drawing.

You can view the results of successfully completing this exercise by opening Renaming Pipes and Structures - Complete.dwg.

Creating Labels in Plan View

To create labels in plan view, you use the Add Labels command. You can create labels one by one or for all the parts of the network at once. After the labels are in place, you may have to drag them to clear areas in the drawing so that they can be read more easily.

Exercise 16.4: Create Plan View Labels

If you haven't already done so, download and install the files for Chapter 16 according to the instructions in this book's Introduction.

In this exercise, you'll create all the plan view labels at once for the Storm1 network. The labels will be cluttered, but you'll address that in the next exercise.

1. Open the drawing named Creating Labels in Plan View.dwg located in the Chapter 16 class data folder.

2. On the Annotate tab of the ribbon, click Add Labels.

3. In the Add Labels dialog box, do the following:

   a. For Feature, select Pipe Network.

   b. For Label Type, select Entire Network Plan.

   c. For Pipe Label Style, select C-STRM – Pipe Data (One Line).

   d. For Structure Label Style, select C-STRM – Structure Data.

   e. Click Add.

4. Click any pipe or structure in the storm network near the entrance to Jordan Court.

   Labels are added on every pipe and structure in the network, which makes the drawing look cluttered (see Figure 16.9).

This will be addressed in the next exercise.

5. Save and close the drawing.

You can view the results of successfully completing this exercise by opening Creating Labels in Plan View - Complete.dwg.

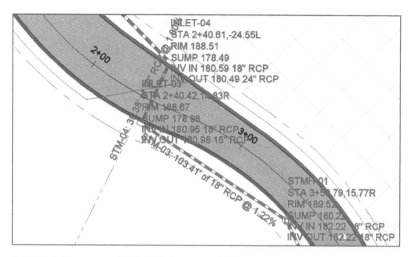

FIGURE 16.9 The initial placement of labels in the drawing is rather cluttered and will require modification.

Editing Labels in Plan View

After creating pipe network labels in your drawing, you may need to do a fair amount of editing to improve their appearance and readability. This can involve assigning different styles and/or moving the labels using their grips.

Certification Objective

Exercise 16.5: Edit Plan View Labels

In this exercise, you'll address the cluttered labeling created in Exercise 16.4. You'll do this through a combination of grip-editing and assigning different styles.

1. Open the drawing named `Editing Labels in Plan View.dwg` located in the `Chapter 16` class data folder.

2. In the left viewport, zoom in to INLET-01, which is on the east side of Jordan Court near station 5+50 (0+170). Click the label, and then click the square grip. Drag the label to an open area in the drawing where it isn't conflicting with any other text or linework.

3. Repeat step 2 for INLET-02, which is across the road from INLET-01.

If you haven't already done so, download and install the files for Chapter 16 according to the instructions in this book's Introduction.

4. Press Esc to clear the previous selection. Click the pipe label for STM-01 (the pipe that connects INLET-01 to INLET-02). Right-click, and select Properties.

5. In the Properties window, change the value for Pipe Label Style to C-STRM – Pipe Data (Stacked).

6. With the label still selected, click the square grip and drag it to a clear location in the drawing.

7. Use the square label grip to move the STMH-01, INLET-03, and INLET-04 labels to a clear location in the drawing.

8. Change the style for the STM-04 label to C-STRM – Pipe Data (Stacked) as you did in steps 4 and 5 for the STM-01 label. Drag it to a clear location in the drawing as you did the STM-01 label in step 6.

This places the label on the east side of the pipe, where it's much more readable.

9. Press Esc to clear any label selections. Click the STM-05 label, and then click Flip Label on the ribbon.

10. With the STM-05 label still selected, click its diamond-shaped grip, and drag the label along the pipe to demonstrate the behavior of this grip.

11. Drag the remaining structure labels to clear areas in the drawing, and change the label style for STM-06 to C-STRM – Pipe Data (Stacked).

   With all the edits to the labels complete, the annotation of the design is much clearer and more readable, as you can see if you compare Figure 16.10 to Figure 16.9.

12. Save and close the drawing.

You can view the results of successfully completing this exercise by opening `Editing Labels in Plan View - Complete.dwg`.

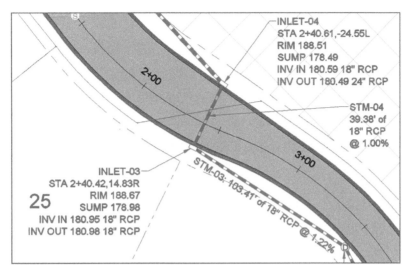

F I G U R E 1 6 . 1 0   The same area shown in Figure 16.9 after edits have been
made to the labels

Annotating Pipe Networks in Profile View

Profile view is just as important as plan view for illustrating the design and
providing important textual and numerical information about it. For this reason, you'll frequently have to provide profile labels in addition to plan labels.
Often, you'll duplicate the information shown in plan view, enabling the contractor or the reviewer of the drawing to have the information they need in
both places, without having to flip back and forth between drawings.

   You don't need to rename the pipes and structures for the profile view if you
have already done so in plan view. This is because the plan and profile versions
of the pipe network are the same objects viewed from different perspectives. In
other words, renaming a pipe in plan view automatically renames it in profile
view because the two versions of the pipe represent a single object.

Creating Labels in Profile View

Once again, creating pipe network labels in profile view is done using the Add
Labels dialog box. You can use either the Entire Network Profile option to label
all the pipes and structures at once or the Single Part Profile option to label
them one by one.

If you haven't already done so, download and install the files for Chapter 16 according to the instructions in this book's Introduction.

Exercise 16.6: Create Profile View Labels

In this exercise, you'll create pipe and structure labels in profile view.

1. Open the drawing named Creating Labels in Profile View.dwg located in the Chapter 16 class data folder.

2. On the Annotate tab, click Add Labels.

3. In the Add Labels dialog box, do the following:

   a. For Feature, select Pipe Network.

   b. For Label Type, select Single Part Profile.

   c. For Pipe Label Style, select C-PROF-STRM – Pipe Data.

   d. For Structure Label Style, select C-PROF-STRM – Structure Data (Above).

   e. Click Add.

   Figure 16.11 shows the Add Labels dialog box with these settings.

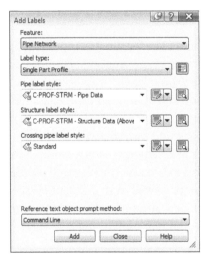

FIGURE 16.11   The Add Labels dialog box showing the styles selected for labeling pipes and structures in profile view

This creates labels that are oriented above these two structures. For the remaining two structures, the road profile label is in the way, so the structure labels will be placed below the structures.

4. Click the first and last structures in the upper-right profile view.

5. In the Add Labels dialog box, select C-PROF-STRM – Structure Data (Below) as the structure label style. Click Add.

6. Click the second and third structures.

   The labels are still placed above the structure, but notice that the formatting is a bit different. You'll reposition these structure labels in the next exercise.

7. Click the three pipes in the profile view to place a label above each one. The drawing should now look like Figure 16.12.

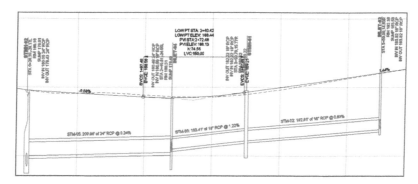

F I G U R E   1 6 . 1 2   The initial placement of pipe network labels in profile view

8. Save and close the drawing.

You can view the results of successfully completing this exercise by opening `Creating Labels in Profile View - Complete.dwg`.

Editing Labels in Profile View

Just as in plan view, you'll most likely have to change the initial placement and styles of your profile view labels in order to make them easier to read. As you did before, you can assign different styles to change formatting, and you can use grips to move the labels. For some label styles, you have an extra grip located at the *dimension anchor*. The dimension anchor is a floating point that can only be moved vertically. This can be useful because you often need to move a label up or down to improve readability while maintaining its horizontal position on the profile view. Additional dimension anchor settings enable you to position a label based on the location of a part or the profile view grid. Simply put, the dimension anchor gives you more options and more flexibility for label placement in profile view.

Certification
Objective

Exercise 16.7: Edit Profile View Labels

If you haven't already done so, download and install the files for Chapter 16 according to the instructions in this book's Introduction.

In this exercise, you'll edit the labels that were created in the previous exercise to improve their appearance and readability.

1. Open the drawing named Editing Labels in Profile View.dwg located in the Chapter 16 class data folder.

2. In the upper-right viewport, click the first structure label (STMH-02), and then click the square grip at the top of the label and drag it upward to a clear area in the drawing.

Note that this grip is constrained to up and down movements. This is because the grip is located at the *dimension anchor*.

3. Press Esc to clear the previous selection. Click the second structure label (INLET-04), and then click Label Properties on the ribbon.

4. In the Properties window, change Dimension Anchor Option to Below. The label flips to a downward position but is still overlapping the structure.

Ortho mode restricts the movement of your cursor to up, down, left, and right. This will help you keep the label aligned with the structure as you move it down.

5. Click the square grip at the top of the label. Then click the Ortho Mode button at the bottom of your screen, and move the label downward until the end of the line is at the bottom of the structure.

6. Repeat steps 3–5 for the third structure label (INLET-05).

   With the label edits you have made, the annotation of the pipe network in profile view has been greatly improved. Compare the result in Figure 16.13 with the initial placement of the labels in Figure 16.12.

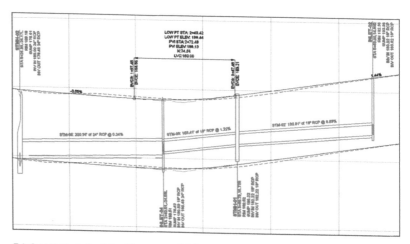

FIGURE 16.13   Pipe network labels in profile view that have been edited to improve readability

7. Save and close the drawing.

You can view the results of successfully completing this exercise by opening Editing Labels in Profile View - Complete.dwg.

Creating Pipe Network Tables

As you have learned in previous chapters, tables are an effective way to convey information about a design. The main advantage of tables is that they organize the information in an orderly fashion, making it easy to read. The disadvantage is that the reader has two places to look for information: the main drawing for the graphical representation of the design and the table for the numerical and textual information. For this reason, tables are typically used if the main drawing would be too cluttered or difficult to read if the textual and numerical information were included in it.

In previous chapters, you created tables for parcels and alignments. One fundamental difference when working with pipe network tables is that they don't need to reference labels in the drawing. For parcels and alignments, you had to create tag labels and then create the tables by selecting those labels. For a pipe network, the table references the pipes and structures directly, so no tag labels are required. However, it's good practice to provide labels in the drawing that identify each pipe and structure so the reader of the drawing can see how they relate to the table.

> If you haven't already done so, download and install the files for Chapter 16 according to the instructions in this book's Introduction.
>
> ◀

Exercise 16.8: Create a Pipe Network Table

In this exercise, you'll create a pipe network table and then create a series of labels in the drawing that will correlate the drawing objects with the table. You'll edit these labels so that they are clear and legible.

1. Open the drawing named Creating Pipe Network Tables.dwg located in the Chapter 16 class data folder.

2. On the Annotate tab of the ribbon, click Add Tables ➢ Pipe Network ➢ Add Structure. This opens the Structure Table Creation dialog box.

3. For Table Style, select C-SSWR – Structure & Pipe Data.

4. Verify that By Network is selected and that Sanitary is chosen under Select Network. Click OK.

> With these settings, all the pipes and structures in the sanitary pipe network will be included in the table. There is also a Multiple Selection option, which enables you to handpick the items you want represented in the table.
>
> ◀

5. Pick a point in the left viewport in some open space.

 The table is inserted into the drawing. Zoom in, and study the information shown in the table (see Figure 16.14).

STRUCTURE TABLE			
STRUCTURE NAME:	DETAILS:	PIPE(S) IN:	PIPE(S) OUT
SSMH-01	JORDAN COURT STA 1+44.11, 0.00' RIM = 186.87 SUMP = 183.2		SAN-01, 8" PVC, INV OUT =185.18
SSMH-02	JORDAN COURT STA 3+79.77, 4.19'L RIM = 189.59 SUMP = 178.5	SAN-01, 8" PVC, INV IN =180.61	SAN-02, 8" PVC, INV OUT =180.61
SSMH-03	JORDAN COURT STA 6+79.31, 0.12'L RIM = 193.66 SUMP = 175.6	SAN-02, 8" PVC, INV IN =177.57	SAN-03, 8" PVC, INV OUT =177.57
SSMH-04	JORDAN COURT STA 9+39.29, 0.00' RIM = 193.22 SUMP = 173.0	SAN-03, 8" PVC, INV IN =174.97	SAN-04, 8" PVC, INV OUT =174.97
SSMH-05	JORDAN COURT STA 12+22.00, 9.72'L RIM = 182.07 SUMP = 170.0	SAN-04, 8" PVC, INV IN =172.05	SAN-05, 8" PVC, INV OUT =172.05
SSMH-06	JORDAN COURT STA 15+25.31, 0.00' RIM = 171.23 SUMP = 163.9	SAN-05, 8" PVC, INV IN =166.92	SAN-06, 8" PVC, INV OUT =166.92

FIGURE 16.14   **A portion of a structure table created for a sanitary sewer pipe network**

6. On the Annotate tab of the ribbon, click Add Labels.

7. In the Add Labels dialog box, do the following:

 a. For Feature, select Pipe Network.

 b. For Label Type, select Entire Network Plan.

 c. For Pipe Label Style, select C-SSWR – Name Only.

 d. For Structure Label Style, select C-SSWR – Name Only.

 e. Click Add.

8. Click any sanitary pipe or structure in the drawing.

9. For each sanitary sewer manhole, click the label and then use the square grip to drag the label into a clear location of the drawing.

The entire network is labeled with the name of each pipe and structure.

10. For each sanitary sewer pipe label, click the label and use its diamond-shaped grip to slide it to a location that is clear of other text or linework. If that isn't possible, use the square grip to drag it to a clear area in the drawing.

11. Save and close the drawing.

You can view the results of successfully completing this exercise by opening `Creating Pipe Network Tables - Complete.dwg`.

With the labels you have added, a person reading the drawing can match the name of a pipe or structure with information in the table.

Now You Know

Now that you have completed this chapter, you're able to change the appearance of structures and pipes by assigning different styles to them. You have learned the importance of good bookkeeping when working with pipe networks, and you know how to rename pipes and structures according to a logical labeling system. You can also create annotations for pipes and structures and edit them to create clear labeling in a drawing. You can do this in plan view as well as profile view. Finally, you're able to create tables that show pipe network information and create labels in the drawing that show the correlation between the information in the table and the items it represents.

You're ready to begin displaying and annotating pipes in a production environment.

CHAPTER 17

Designing New Terrain

With the completion of the pipe networks, the design of the road is nearly finished. It's now time to move on to the next area of the design: the shaping of the land, or *grading*, of the adjacent areas. In Chapter 9, "Designing in 3D Using Corridors," you designed a 3D model of the road in the form of a corridor. This model will serve as a basis for much of the adjacent design that will take place, such as the shaping of individual lots and grading in the stormwater management area.

Each of these areas has unique design objectives. The individual lots will be shaped so that homes can be built on them without requiring significant earthmoving. The stormwater management area will require a pond to serve as a means of collecting and treating the stormwater runoff. These designs will serve as opportunities for you to study the two primary grading tools contained in the AutoCAD® Civil 3D® software: feature lines and grading objects.

In this chapter, you'll learn to:

▶ **Understand grading**

▶ **Understand feature lines**

▶ **Create feature lines**

▶ **Edit feature lines**

▶ **Understand grading objects**

▶ **Create grading objects**

▶ **Edit grading objects**

Understanding Grading

Grading is the term that is most often used to describe the shaping of the land as a construction or design activity. From a design perspective, it's usually considered different than corridor design, which is also a form of terrain shaping but most often used for long, uniform, linear designs such as roads, channels, and so on. The term *grading* is typically used to describe shaping the land in small areas or modeling features that aren't long and uniform.

The final product of a grading design is a surface—the same type of object you used to model the existing terrain in Chapter 4, "Modeling the Existing Terrain Using Surfaces." As you may recall, to create a surface representing existing ground (EG) elevations, you use breaklines drawn along linear terrain features such as curb lines, ditch lines, and so on. You can use the Civil 3D tools to make these breaklines from data collected in the field by surveyors. To create a design surface, you draw breaklines along curbs and ditch lines that are *going* to be built in the field. The process is fundamentally the same as creating an EG surface except that, in this case, the linear features are part of your design. For example, in Figure 17.1, you see the grading design for a pond represented by the red and blue contours. Civil 3D tools were used to draw the edges of this pond according to the required design specifications such as size, shape, depth, and so on. The objects representing the edges were then used to build a pond surface.

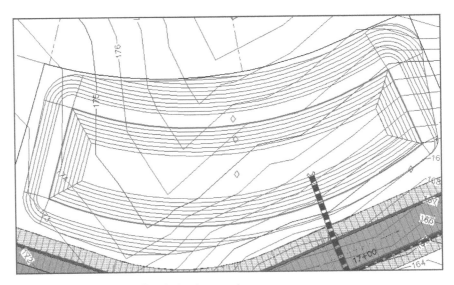

FIGURE 17.1 A grading design for a pond

Understanding Feature Lines

In Chapter 4, you used survey figures to serve as breaklines in the EG surface. For a design surface, you'll use *feature lines* for most of your breaklines. Survey figures and feature lines are fundamentally similar: They are three-dimensional linear objects that can be named, stylized, and shown in Prospector. The primary difference is that you design feature lines, whereas survey figures are driven by data collected in the field.

Understanding Sites

When working with feature lines, you have to consider the use of *sites*. Feature lines in the same site are "aware" of one another and will try to interact if the opportunity presents itself. For example, if one feature line crosses over another feature line in the same site, one of the feature lines will bend so the two share the same elevation at the intersection point. The point where they intersect is called a *split point*. In cases where this interaction needs to be prevented, you can simply place each feature line in its own site. Figure 17.2 shows two crossing feature lines in plan view (left) and 3D view (right). Because these two feature lines are in the same site, a split point is created, causing the red feature line to bend so that it can match the green feature line.

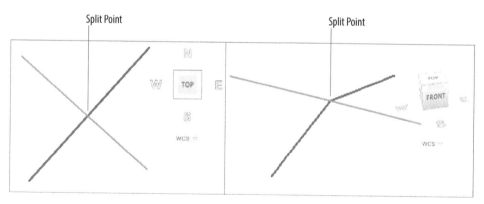

FIGURE 17.2 Two crossing feature lines that occupy the same site

Understanding Feature-Line Geometry

Feature lines have two types of points that define their geometry: *PIs* and *elevation points*. A PI is represented by a square grip and can be modified in all three dimensions. An elevation point is represented by a circle grip and has more constrained editing behavior. Figure 17.3 shows both types of grips on the same feature line. The elevation of an elevation point can be edited, but its location in plan view must slide along the feature-line geometry determined by the PIs. This constrained behavior is actually quite handy because you can create many elevation points on a simple plan view shape such as a rectangle.

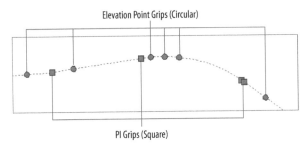

Elevation Point Grips (Circular)

PI Grips (Square)

FIGURE 17.3   A plan view of PI and elevation point grips on a feature line

Creating Feature Lines

Certification
Objective

Civil 3D provides a comprehensive set of tools for creating feature lines. They can be drawn from scratch, by converting an AutoCAD® polyline, or by extracting them from more complex Civil 3D objects such as corridors or profiles. When drawing a feature line from scratch, you must provide the elevation of each PI. For all other methods, the elevations are obtained from the object you have selected.

Exercise 17.1: Create Feature Lines

If you haven't already done so, download and install the files for Chapter 17 according to the instructions in this book's Introduction.

In this exercise, you'll create feature lines representing elevations along a lot boundary as well as elevations for a building pad within the interior of the lot. You'll create one feature line from a corridor, another from scratch by drawing it, and a third by selecting objects in the drawing.

1. Open the drawing named Creating Feature Lines.dwg located in the Chapter 17 class data folder.

   This drawing is zoomed in to lot 25 in the top-right and bottom-right viewports. Also notice that the corridor layer has been thawed to reveal the road corridor.

2. On the Home tab of the ribbon, click Feature Line ➤ Create Feature Line From Corridor.

3. When prompted on the command line to select a corridor feature line, in either the top-right or bottom-right viewport, click the edge of the corridor that aligns with the front of lot 25.
   The Create Feature Line From Corridor dialog box opens.

4. Verify that Site is set to Lot Grading. For Style, select Lot Grading – ROW, and then click OK.
   The new feature line is displayed as a thick red line.

Note the Create Dynamic Link To Corridor option. If the corridor is modified, this feature line will respond to match the new design.

5. Press Esc to end the previous command. On the Home tab of the ribbon, click Feature Line ➢ Create Feature Line.

6. On the Create Feature Lines dialog, for Style, select Lot Grading, and then click OK. When prompted to specify the start point, in the top-right viewport, use the Center object snap to select the center of the red circle at the north corner of lot 25.

7. When you're prompted to specify an elevation, press Enter. When prompted to specify the next point, in the top-right viewport, use the Endpoint object snap to pick the west corner of lot 25.

8. When prompted to specify an elevation on the command line, click Surface to invoke the Surface option.
   The Select Surface dialog box opens.

Although 0.000 is listed as the elevation, feature-line interaction will match this feature line to the corridor feature line at this location.

9. Verify that EG is selected, and click OK.
   The default elevation on the command line becomes 190.059 (57.930), which is the elevation of the EG surface at the corner of the lot.

10. Press Enter to accept the elevation.

11. When prompted to specify the next point, on the command line, click Arc to invoke the Arc option. When prompted to specify the arc endpoint on the command line, click Secondpnt to invoke the Secondpnt option.

12. When prompted to specify the second point, in the top-right viewport, use the Nearest object snap to select a point along the back line of lot 25.

13. When prompted to specify the endpoint of the arc, in the top-right viewport, use the Endpoint object snap to select the south corner of lot 25.

14. When prompted to specify the elevation, at the command line, click SUrface and press Enter to accept the default elevation of 190.456 (58.027).

15. When prompted to specify an arc endpoint, at the command line, click Line. When prompted to specify the next point, in the top-right viewport, use the Center object snap to pick the circle at the east corner of lot 25.

16. When prompted to specify the elevation, press Enter. Press Esc to end the command.

    You have drawn a feature line that matches the edge of the corridor at the front of the lot and EG elevations at the back lot corners.

17. On the Home tab of the ribbon, click Feature Line ➤ Create Feature Lines From Objects. When prompted to select an object, click the rectangle at the center of lot 25, and press Enter.

18. On the Create Feature Lines dialog, check the box next to Style, and select Lot Grading. Click OK.

    The feature line is created, but it's located at elevation zero. If you zoom out in the lower-right viewport, you'll see the blue rectangle at the location of the lot label and parcel lines.

19. Save and close the drawing.

You can view the results of successfully completing this exercise by opening Creating Feature Lines - Complete.dwg.

Editing Feature Lines

Civil 3D provides an extensive set of tools for editing feature lines. The tools are divided into two categories represented by two panels on the Feature Line ribbon tab: Edit Geometry and Edit Elevations (see Figure 17.4).

F I G U R E 1 7 . 4   **The Edit Geometry and Edit Elevations panels of the Feature Line ribbon tab**

Using Edit Geometry Commands

The feature-line geometry-editing commands provided by Civil 3D are as follows:

Insert PI   Use this command to insert a new PI at a point you specify. A PI can be edited in all three dimensions.

Delete PI   Use this command to remove PIs from the feature line.

Break   Use this command to break one feature line into two feature lines. You can do this by creating a gap between the two feature lines, or you can have them meet end to end.

Trim   Use this command to shorten a feature line by making it end precisely at another object.

Join   Use this command to join two or more feature lines to make one feature line. If there is a gap between the two feature lines, it must lie within a certain tolerance or they won't be joined.

Reverse   Use this command to change the direction of the feature line. This swaps the beginning and ending points as well as reverses the direction of stationing. This can affect editing and labeling.

Edit Curve   Use this command to change the radius of a feature-line curve.

Fillet   Use this command to add a feature-line curve where there is currently a PI. The command includes options to set the radius of the curve and to create multiple fillets at once.

Fit Curve   Use this command to replace a series of line segments with an arc. This helps to simplify the feature line by replacing multiple points with an arc. This command differs from the Smooth command in that you can control where curves are created. Also, the curves it creates are static, meaning they don't change when adjacent geometry changes.

Smooth   Use this command to replace PIs with curves. This command is different from the Fit Curve command in that it creates curves for the entire feature line and the curves are dynamic, meaning they remain tangent as the feature line is modified.

Weed   Use this command to simplify a feature line by reducing the number of vertices. The command includes several options for determining which vertices to remove.

 Stepped Offset   This command creates a new feature line that is parallel to another. The command includes several options for determining the elevations of the new feature line.

Exercise 17.2: Edit Feature Lines with Geometry Commands

If you haven't already done so, download and install the files for Chapter 17 according to the instructions in this book's Introduction.

In this drawing, two more feature lines have been added for lot 26. You'll begin by adding more PIs and a curve to the back of lot 26.

In this exercise, you'll edit the feature line you created in the previous exercise and then join it to another feature line.

1. Open the drawing named Editing Feature Line Geometry.dwg located in the Chapter 17 class data folder.

 2. Click the green feature line. If the Edit Geometry panel isn't visible, click Edit Geometry on the ribbon.

 3. Click Insert PI. When you're prompted to specify a point, use the Center object snap to select the center of the blue circle.

4. When prompted to specify an elevation, on the command line, click Surface to invoke the Surface option.
   The Select Surface dialog box opens.

5. Verify that EG is selected, and click OK. Press Enter to accept the elevation shown on the command line.

6. When prompted to specify the next point, use the Center object snap to select the center of the red circle.

7. When prompted to specify an elevation on the command line, click Surface to invoke the Surface option. Press Enter again to accept the surface elevation.
   Additional PIs have been added, but you still need to address the missing curve.

 8. Press Esc twice to clear the previous command. Click the green feature line, and then click Fit Curve on the ribbon.

9. When prompted to specify a point on the command line, click Points to invoke the Points option.

10. When prompted to specify a start point, use the Center object snap to select the center of the blue circle.

11. Use the Center object snap to select the center of the red circle. Press Esc twice to end the command and clear the selection.

    A curve is added to match the geometry of the back lot line. Next, you'll break the feature line for lot 25 and join it to the feature line for lot 26.

12. Click any feature line in the drawing, and then click Break on the ribbon.

13. When prompted to select an object to break, click the blue perimeter feature line for lot 25.

14. When prompted to specify a second break point, on the command line, click First point to invoke the First point option.

15. Use the Endpoint object snap to select the back corner where lots 25 and 26 meet.

16. When prompted to select the second break point, repeat the previous step to select the same point again. Press Esc twice to end the command and clear the selection.

    By choosing the same location for the first and second points, you break the feature line without creating a gap. The drawing doesn't appear different, but the blue feature line has been broken into two feature lines.

17. Click the blue feature line at the back of lot 25, and then click Join on the ribbon.

18. Click the green feature line, and then press Esc twice to end the command and clear the selection.

    The green changes to blue, indicating that the feature lines are joined to create a single feature line (see Figure 17.5).

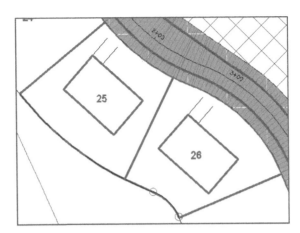

FIGURE 17.5   **The result of editing the feature lines in this exercise**

19. Save and close the drawing.

You can view the results of successfully completing this exercise by opening `Editing Feature Line Geometry - Complete.dwg`.

Using Edit Elevation Commands

The feature-line elevation-editing commands provided by Civil 3D are as follows:

 Elevation Editor   Use this command to open the Grading Elevation Editor tab in Panorama. From here, you can perform a number of edits while viewing all the feature-line data at once.

 Insert Elevation Point   Use this command to create one or more elevation points on a feature line.

 Delete Elevation Point   Use this command to simplify a feature line by removing elevation points from it.

 Quick Elevation Edit   Use this command to interactively edit the elevations and slopes of a feature line. The command uses tooltips to show you elevations, slopes, and slope directions.

 Edit Elevations   Use this command to edit individual points and segments on the command line.

 Set Grade/Slope Between Points   Use this command to set a constant grade through multiple points. You do this by specifying a start point and an endpoint, and the command calculates the elevations of any points in between.

Insert High/Low Elevation Point   Use this command to have Civil 3D calculate a high or low point on a feature line. You do this by selecting two points and specifying the slope that should be projected from each point. Civil 3D then calculates the intersection of the two slopes and creates a point at the correct location and elevation. This command is especially useful for setting high and low points along curb lines to control drainage.

Raise/Lower By Reference   Use this command to adjust all the elevations of a feature line simultaneously by specifying a reference point and an elevation difference.

Set Elevation By Reference   Use this command to calculate the elevations of individual points on a feature line by specifying a reference point and an elevation difference for each point.

Adjacent Elevations By Reference   Use this command to project the elevations from one feature line to another while providing an elevation difference, if desired. This command is especially useful for parallel feature lines such as curb lines or wall lines.

Grade Extension By Reference   Use this command to calculate the elevation of a point on a feature line by extending the grade of another feature line.

Elevations From Surface   Use this command to project a feature line onto a surface. This command has the option to create elevation points at locations where the feature line crosses triangle edges in the surface. When this option is used, the feature line becomes an exact match to the terrain represented by the surface.

Raise/Lower   Use this command to edit all the elevations of a feature line simultaneously by providing an elevation difference.

Exercise 17.3: Edit Feature Lines with Elevation Commands

In this exercise, you'll use the feature-line elevation-editing commands to place the lot 25 building pad at the correct elevation and to make the back-lot lines for lots 25 and 26 match existing ground elevations more closely.

> If you haven't already done so, download and install the files for Chapter 17 according to the instructions in this book's Introduction.

1. Open the drawing named Editing Feature Line Elevations.dwg located in the Chapter 17 class data folder.

2. Click any feature line in the drawing. If the Edit Elevations panel isn't visible, click Edit Elevations on the ribbon.

3. Click Quick Elevation Edit. Place your cursor over the north corner of lot 25.

   The elevation on the tooltip should read 189.297′ (57.695m).

4. Place your cursor at each corner of lot 25, and take note of the elevations.

   The highest elevation is the south corner, which is at 190.456′ (58.027m). The goal is to make sure water flows away from the building pad (the blue rectangle). To do this, you'll place the building pad at an elevation slightly higher than the highest lot corner.

YOUR PAD OR MINE?

For land-development projects that involve buildings, it's common for the contractor to prepare a flat area where the building will be placed. This is often referred to as the *building pad*. In a residential development such as the example in this book, a building pad is often prepared for each lot to accommodate the home that will be built.

5. Press Esc twice to end the current command and clear the feature-line selection. Click the building pad feature line of lot 25.

6. On the ribbon, click Raise/Lower By Reference.

7. When prompted to specify a reference point, invoke the Endpoint object snap, and place your cursor on the south corner of lot 25, but don't click the mouse.

8. Look at the coordinate readout at the bottom center of your screen. If the third value in the coordinate readout is 0.0000, press the Tab key. Keep pressing the Tab key until the value reads 190.4564 (58.027), as shown in Figure 17.6.

   The Tab key allows you to toggle between the parcel geometry, which is at elevation zero, and the feature lines, which are at true design elevations.

If you don't see coordinates at all, click the customization menu at the bottom-right corner of your screen, and click Coordinates at the top of the menu.

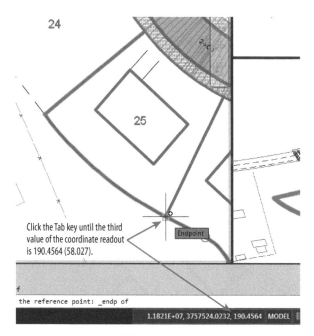

24

25

Click the Tab key until the third
value of the coordinate readout
is 190.4564 (58.027).

Endpoint

the reference point: _endp of

1.1821E+07, 3757524.0232, 190.4564   MODEL

FIGURE 17.6   Using the Tab key and coordinate readout to select the correct
elevation

9. With the proper value shown in the coordinate readout, click the
   point to snap to it.

10. When prompted to specify a point on the building pad feature line,
    click the south corner of the building pad feature line. When you're
    prompted to specify the grade, type 2 and press Enter.

    If you watch the lower-right viewport carefully, you'll see the fea-
    ture line move upward to join the perimeter feature line. This places
    the building pad at an elevation that creates a 2 percent downward
    slope from the south corner of the building pad to the south corner
    of the lot. All the other slopes will be steeper because the other lot
    corners are lower than the south corner.

11. Press Esc to clear the previous selection. Click the feature line
    that represents the rear of the lots, and then click Elevations
    From Surface on the ribbon.

> Notice that there are
> only five square grips
> along the rear lot line.
> We'll look at this again
> after the next few steps.

12. On the Set Elevations From Surface dialog, verify that EG is selected
    and that the box next to Insert Intermediate Grade Break Points is
    checked. Click OK.

13. At the command line, click `Partial` to invoke the Partial option. Select the feature line representing the rear of the lots.

14. When prompted to specify the start point, click the west corner of lot 25, and then click the south corner of lot 26 to specify the endpoint. A series of green circle markers appears on the feature line.

15. Press Enter to complete the command.

    A number of circular grips are now visible on the feature line (see Figure 17.7). These represent additional elevation points that were required for the feature line to match the surface precisely.

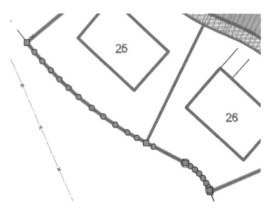

FIGURE 17.7 Circular grips mark elevation points added to match the feature line to the surface.

16. Save and close the drawing.

You can view the results of successfully completing this exercise by opening `Editing Feature Line Elevations - Complete.dwg`.

Understanding Grading Objects

At times, you'll want Civil 3D to calculate the location, shape, and elevations of feature lines rather than designing them yourself. Examples of this situation would be projecting a slope through a certain distance or elevation or finding the intersection of a slope with a surface. For these cases, Civil 3D provides the *grading object*. Figure 17.8 shows a pond design composed of several grading objects, each one using a different set of parameters to calculate an edge that defines the shape of the pond.

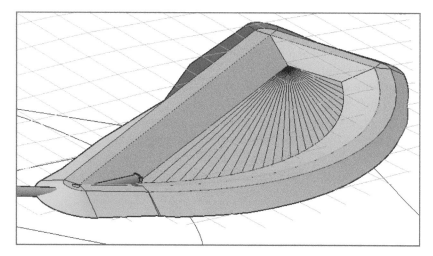

FIGURE 17.8 **A pond design composed of grading objects**

A *grading object* is a collection of feature lines whose geometry, location, and elevation are calculated by Civil 3D based on design parameters that you have applied to a feature line. That's quite a daunting definition, so here's a look at it broken down into several parts:

▶ A grading object is a *collection* of feature lines (and other things not important to name at this time), so it behaves as one object. The feature lines in this collection have many of the same characteristics as individual feature lines as well as some unique characteristics that relate to being part of a grading object.

▶ Everything about a grading object is calculated by Civil 3D. Very similar to the way Civil 3D calculates a corridor, grading objects can't be edited directly, but they respond automatically when their design parameters are edited. This is a little different from an individual feature line, which you can grip-edit at will.

▶ You assign the design parameters to a feature line. To create a grading object, you start by picking a feature line in the drawing. The design parameters you provide, such as slope, distance, elevation, and so on, are projected from this feature line to create the resulting grading object. A feature line that serves as the basis for a grading object is called a *baseline*.

Understanding Grading Criteria

The design parameters you apply to a grading object can require multiple pieces of information. For this reason, Civil 3D utilizes a system of *grading criteria*, which enables you to refer to a set of instructions by name rather than having to re-specify them for each grading design. For example, you might have criteria with the name Curb, which instruct Civil 3D to project upward at a very steep slope for a very short distance. Similar criteria with names like Pond Embankment, Ditch Slope, and so on might be created alongside your Curb criteria. You can organize your named grading criteria even further by grouping them into *grading criteria sets*. For example, you might have one criteria set for pond grading, another for parking lots, another for athletic fields, and so on. Figure 17.9 shows grading criteria that would be used to create the inside slope of a pond.

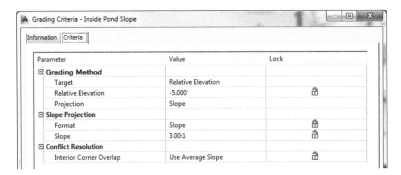

FIGURE 17.9 An example of grading criteria typically used for the inside slope of a pond

Understanding Grading Groups

A *grading group* is a named collection of grading objects that enables you to perform certain important functions with multiple grading objects simultaneously. For example, you can create a surface from a grading group or calculate cut and fill values by comparing a grading group to a surface in the drawing.

Understanding Grading Objects and Sites

Like feature lines, grading objects must exist in a Civil 3D site. When two or more grading objects occupy the same site, there is potential for them to interact. There is also the potential for grading objects to interact with other feature lines in the same site. This interaction can benefit some designs, but there are cases where this interaction will cause the design to be incorrect. Therefore, it's important to proactively manage sites while you're working with grading objects and feature lines.

Creating Grading Objects

You begin creating a grading object by launching the Grading Creation Tools command. This opens the Grading Creation Tools toolbar (see Figure 17.10), which is similar to the Alignment Layout Tools and the Network Layout Tools toolbars that you used in previous chapters. Like those toolbars, the Grading Creation Tools toolbar provides the commands to configure your design, create new design objects, and edit those objects.

Certification
Objective

FIGURE 17.10 The Grading Creation Tools toolbar

Exercise 17.4: Create Grading Objects

In this exercise, you'll build a pond using grading objects.

1. Open the drawing named Creating Grading Objects.dwg located in the Chapter 17 class data folder.

   The drawing is zoomed in to the proposed location of a stormwater detention pond. You'll use grading objects to build a model of the pond, starting with the green feature line that represents the top inside edge of the pond.

If you haven't already done so, download and install the files for Chapter 17 according to the instructions in this book's Introduction.

I THOUGHT DETENTION WAS A BAD THING

The pond you design in this exercise is referred to as a *detention pond*. Its function is to slow the release of stormwater to the same rate that existed prior to development. When it rains, runoff is collected by the inlets and conveyed to the pond through underground pipes. The pond outlet is restricted to reduce the flow of water. This causes the water to back up, hence the need for a pond to *detain* it. After the storm is over, the water will stay in the pond for a bit until it empties out.

(Continues)

I THOUGHT DETENTION WAS A BAD THING *(Continued)*

What's the reason for all this? Before grass, soil, and forest were replaced with pavement, runoff water was released from this area of land at a relatively slow rate. Now, less of the water is being absorbed, and it's traveling much faster along the pavement and concrete that carries it. This increase in flow and velocity causes erosion damage and must be mitigated. A common way to accomplish this mitigation is by including a pond in your design.

2. On the Home tab of the ribbon, click Grading ≻ Grading Creation Tools.

3. On the Grading Creation Tools toolbar, click Set The Grading Group. Select Pond, and click OK. On the Site dialog, select Pond and click OK.

4. On the Create Grading Group dialog, type **Pond** in the Name field. Verify that Automatic Surface Creation is turned on, and then click OK. Click OK to dismiss the Create Surface dialog box.

5. Expand the criteria list, and choose Grade To Relative Elevation, as shown in Figure 17.11.

FIGURE 17.11   **Selecting grading criteria on the Grading Creation Tools toolbar**

6. Expand the list of creation commands, and click Create Grading, as shown in Figure 17.12.

FIGURE 17.12   **Selecting the Create Grading command**

7. When prompted to select a feature, click the green feature line. When you're prompted to select the grading side, click a point inside the feature line.

8. Press Enter to apply the grading to the entire length.

9. When prompted for the relative elevation value, type -7 (-2.13), and press Enter. When you're prompted for a format, press Enter to accept the default of Slope.

10. When you're prompted for a slope, type 3 and press Enter to apply a slope of 3:1.

   After a pause, a new grading object is created that represents the inside slope of the pond. A surface is also created, and it's displayed as red and blue contours in plan view.

11. Expand the list of creation tools, and select Create Infill. Click a point near the center of the pond.

   The 3D view now shows that the pond has a bottom. The infill created in this step is a special type of grading object that simply fills a void in a grading group. It doesn't provide additional elevation points; instead, it enables the grading-group surface to extend across an open area. An infill can be placed in any closed area created by one or more feature lines that occupy the same site.

12. Select the Grade To Distance criteria.

13. Expand the list of creation tools, and select Create Grading. When you're prompted to select a feature, click the same green feature line that you picked in step 7.

14. When prompted for the grading side, pick a point outside the pond. Press Enter to apply the grading to the entire length.

15. Press Enter to accept the default distance of 10.000' (3.000m). When you're prompted for a format, type G to invoke the Grade option, and press Enter.

16. Press Enter to accept the default grade of 2 percent.

   A new grading object is created that represents the berm of the pond.

17. On the Grading Creation Tools toolbar, click Set The Target Surface. In the Select Surface dialog box, select EG and click OK.

18. Select the Grade To Surface criteria. Expand the list of creation tools, and select Create Grading.

19. Click the outside edge of the grading object created in step 18. Press Enter at all prompts to accept the default values.

This creates a 3:1 daylight slope that intersects with the EG surface. This also completes the surface for the pond, as indicated by the red and blue contours (see Figure 17.13).

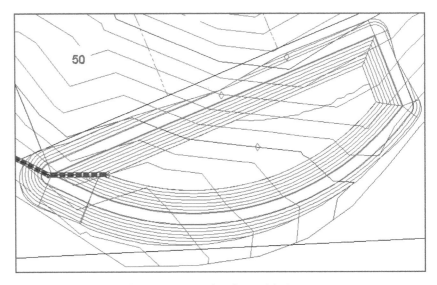

FIGURE 17.13   Contours representing the pond design

20. Save and close the drawing.

You can view the results of successfully completing this exercise by opening `Creating Grading Objects - Complete.dwg`.

Editing Grading Objects

Because of the dynamic nature of grading objects, any edits to a feature line that serves as a grading-object baseline will automatically trigger an update of the grading object. This makes most grading-object editing fairly easy. In addition, there are two tools you can use to edit the criteria that were used to create the grading object: Grading Editor and Edit Grading. The Grading Editor command opens Panorama, enabling you to edit the criteria in a table format. The Edit Grading command is a command-line interface.

Exercise 17.5: Edit Grading Objects

In this exercise, you'll edit the pond grading objects that you created in the previous exercise.

If you haven't already done so, download and install the files for Chapter 17 according to the instructions in this book's Introduction.

1. Open the drawing named Editing Grading Objects.dwg located in the Chapter 17 class data folder.

2. Click the green feature line that represents the inside edge of the pond berm. Click the grip at the northeast corner, and then use the Center object snap to select the center of the red circle to the east.

   The grading object recalculates, based on the new shape of its baseline. The grading-group surface also updates, enabling the contours to match the new shape as well.

3. With the feature line still selected, click Raise/Lower on the Edit Elevations panel of the ribbon.

   You're prompted to specify an elevation difference.

If the Edit Elevations panel isn't visible, click Edit Elevations on the ribbon.

4. Type -1 (-0.3) and press Enter to lower the feature line by 1' (0.3m).

   The entire grading group and associated surface update. Now the bottom of the pond is too low and needs to be raised.

5. Press Esc to clear the selection of the feature line. On the Modify tab of the ribbon, click Grading.

6. Click Grading Editor, and then click a point within the inside embankment of the pond.

   The edges of the grading object are highlighted to help you make your selection.

7. On the Grading Editor tab of Panorama, type -6 (-1.83) for Relative Elevation, and press Enter.

   The grading group is updated, and the pond bottom is raised by 1' (0.3m).

8. On the Grading tab of the ribbon, click Edit Grading. Click a point within the area representing the top of the berm.

9. When you're prompted to specify a distance, type 12 (3.6) and press Enter.

10. Press Enter twice to accept the previous settings. Press Enter a third time to end the command.

The grading group and surface update to accommodate the wider berm. The pond model now reflects the wider berm along with the shape and elevation changes made in earlier steps (see Figure 17.14).

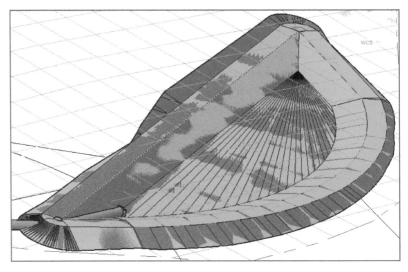

F I G U R E   1 7 . 1 4   **The pond model after several edits**

11. Save and close the drawing.

You can view the results of successfully completing this exercise by opening `Editing Grading Objects - Complete.dwg`.

Now You Know

Now that you have completed this chapter, you understand feature lines and grading objects. You're able to create feature lines from objects in the drawing or by drawing them from scratch. You can edit feature-line geometry and elevations using the appropriate tools. You also can create and modify grading objects to design specific terrain shapes.

You're ready to begin performing grading design in a production environment.

CHAPTER 18

Analyzing, Displaying, and Annotating Surfaces

In Chapter 17, "Designing New Terrain," you experienced a few examples of using the AutoCAD® Civil 3D® software to design new terrain in the form of lot grading and pond design. With more time, you would have completed the shaping of all the lots, resulting in a grading design for the entire project. Now that all the major grading design components are complete (roads, lots, and a pond in this example), it's time to combine them into one complete design. Once you have done this, you can analyze the design to ensure that it meets several additional design and construction requirements. This analysis may result in the need for an adjustment to the design, at which time you'll begin an iterative process: design, analyze, adjust, design, analyze, adjust, and so on. You'll repeat this cycle until the design is the best that time and resources permit. When the design is optimized, you can then provide annotation that provides the necessary information for the contractor to build your design for the land's new shape.

In this chapter, you'll learn to:

▶ **Combine design surfaces**

▶ **Analyze design surfaces**

▶ **Calculate earthwork volumes**

▶ **Label design surfaces**

Combining Design Surfaces

In Chapter 17, you created a pond design that resulted in a surface representing the shape of the pond. You also performed some lot grading, and if you had continued working on the lot grading for a few hours, you eventually would have finished all the lots, creating a surface that covered nearly the entire project. In Chapter 9, "Designing in 3D Using Corridors," you created a corridor surface to represent the model of the roads. This approach of designing the shape of the terrain in parts is common and recommended. For even the most talented designer, it's difficult to design all aspects of a project at once. It's easier, and often more efficient, to divide the design into "mini-designs" such as the road, lots, and pond that you experienced for yourself.

Once the parts are in place, it's then time to combine them into one master surface. To accomplish this, you use a simple but very powerful capability of surfaces in Civil 3D: *pasting*. Just as you're able to paste a paragraph of text into a document, you can paste one surface into another. The similarities between surfaces and documents end there, however. For example, when you paste one surface into another, the pasted version is a live copy of the original, meaning if the original is modified, the pasted version is also modified. To find the command to paste surfaces, right-click Edits in a surface in Prospector or choose the Surfaces ribbon tab (see Figure 18.1).

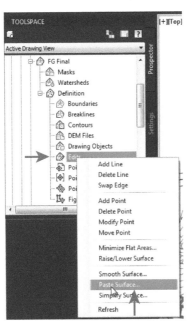
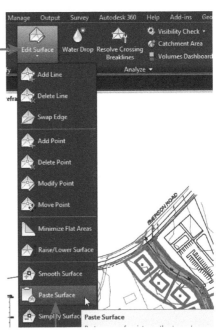

FIGURE 18.1   The Paste Surface command, located in a Prospector context menu (left) and the Surface ribbon tab (right)

When you're working with multiple pasted surfaces, you can use the order in which they are pasted to achieve a desired result. The way this works is that when two overlapping surfaces are pasted, the second one overwrites the first in the area where they overlap. You can control the order in which surfaces are pasted on the Definition tab of the Surface Properties dialog box (see Figure 18.2). Here you can rearrange the order of operations not just for pasting surfaces but for other operations as well.

FIGURE 18.2 You can change the order of operations using the arrow buttons. This can affect the result of pasting multiple surfaces together.

Exercise 18.1: Combine Surfaces

In this exercise, you'll create an FG Final surface by combining surfaces representing lot grading, road elevations, pond grading, and a small area of daylighting.

1. Open the drawing named Combining Surfaces.dwg located in the Chapter 18 class data folder.

   In this drawing, the lot grading design is complete, as shown by the blue, red, and green feature lines. There is also a small area between lots 73 and 76 where a grading group was used to calculate daylighting.

2. In Prospector, expand Surfaces, and note the surfaces that are listed. Right-click Surfaces, and select Create Surface.

3. On the Create Surface dialog, enter **FG Final** in the Name field, and select Contours 1' and 5' (Design) (Contours 0.5m and 2.5m (Design)) as the style. Click OK.

   The new FG Final surface is listed in Prospector.

4. In Prospector, expand Surfaces ➢ FG Final ➢ Definition. Right-click Edits, and select Paste Surface.

If you haven't already done so, download and install the files for Chapter 18 according to the instructions in this book's Introduction.

Make sure your background color is set to white before beginning the exercises in this chapter.

All the surfaces except EG have a style of _No Display assigned to them. That is why no design contours are shown in the drawing.

5. On the Select Surface To Paste dialog, select Lots – Exterior, and then click OK.

   Contours representing the grading for exterior lots appear in the left viewport. In the bottom-right viewport, you see a 3D model of the interior grading.

6. In the left viewport, zoom in to the interior lot area, and note the haphazard contours extending across the road and through this area.

7. Click one of the red or blue contours to select the surface, and then click Edit Surface ➤ Paste Surface on the ribbon.

8. Select Road FG, and click OK.

   In the road areas, the contours you saw in step 5 are replaced with contours that accurately represent the road elevations. In the 3D model, the roads are accurately represented, and if you zoom in, you can see the curb and the crown of the road clearly. The interior lot area is empty because this area has a hide boundary applied to it in the Road FG surface.

9. Repeat steps 7 and 8, this time selecting the Pond surface.

10. Repeat steps 7 and 8, this time selecting the Lots – Interior surface.

11. Click one of the red or blue contours, and select Surface Properties on the ribbon.

12. On the Surface Properties dialog, on the Definition tab, click Add Surface Lots – Interior and then click the up-arrow icon (see Figure 18.3).

   This moves the Lots – Interior surface above the Pond surface in the paste order.

> **Contours now appear in the area of the pond, and the surface model reflects the shape of the pond.**

> **Surface information is now shown for the interior lot grading, but the pond area has been overwritten with inaccurate information. You'll fix this in the next few steps by changing the order in which the surfaces are pasted.**

FIGURE 18.3 Clicking the up arrow changes the order of operations so that the Lots – Interior surface is pasted before the Pond surface.

13. Click OK, and then click Rebuild The Surface.

    The lot grading contours and the correct pond contours are now shown. This is an example of the importance of managing the order of pasted surfaces to achieve the desired result.

14. Repeat steps 7 and 8, this time selecting the Lot Daylight surface.

    Contours are now shown in the area between lots 73 and 76, and all design grading for the project is represented as one surface (see Figure 18.4).

FIGURE 18.4 **Grading for the entire project is represented by one surface.**

15. Save and close the drawing.

You can view the results of successfully completing this exercise by opening `Combining Surfaces - Complete.dwg`.

MODULAR DESIGN

In the preceding exercise, you saw five design surfaces listed in Prospector, each representing its own mini-design. The origin of these surfaces is as follows:

Lots – Exterior   This surface is created from the feature lines used to grade all the lots except those enclosed between Jordan Court, Madison Lane, and Logan Court. The feature lines were added to the Lots – Exterior surface as breaklines. A polyline was drawn along the back edges of the lots and added to the surface as an outer boundary. The surface was allowed to triangulate across the road and interior lot areas. The following image shows the Lots – Exterior surface in 3D.

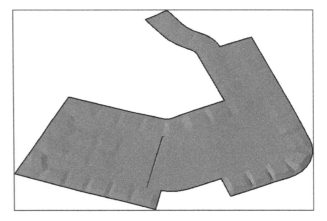

Lots – Interior   This surface is created from the feature lines used to grade all the lots enclosed between Jordan Court, Madison Lane, and Logan Court. The feature lines were added to the surface as breaklines. A polyline was drawn along the front edges of the lots and added to the surface as an outer boundary. The surface was allowed to triangulate across the pond area. The following image shows the Lots – Interior surface in 3D.

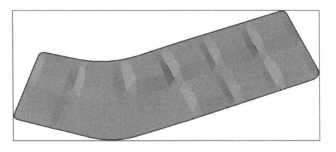

(Continues)

MODULAR DESIGN   *(Continued)*

Pond   This surface is created from the grading group used to design the pond south of lots 69 and 70. The following image shows the Pond surface in 3D.

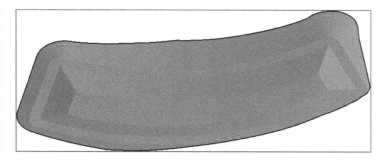

Road FG   This surface is created from the road corridor. The following image shows the Road FG surface in 3D view.

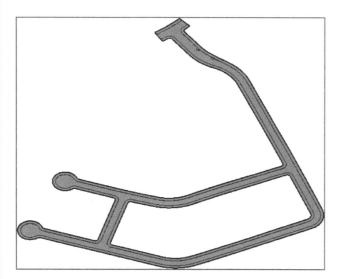

Lot Daylight   This surface is created from a grading group used to design the daylighting between lots 73 and 76. It's shown in the following graphic in red along with the Road FG surface and Lot – Exterior surface in tan.

(Continues)

MODULAR DESIGN *(Continued)*

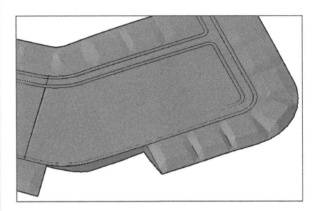

In the preceding exercise, you combined all these surfaces to create a single finished ground surface, as shown in 3D view in the following image.

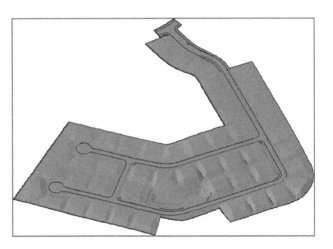

Analyzing Design Surfaces

Certification
Objective

You can do many more things with a Civil 3D surface than just display contours. Unfortunately, I can't discuss them all in a single chapter, let alone a section in a chapter, but I will cover several of the most commonly used surface-analysis features available in Civil 3D. I've grouped these features into three categories: surface analysis, hydrology tools, and quick profiles.

Using Surface Analysis

In the context of this category, *surface analysis* refers to the functions that appear on the Analysis tab of the Surface Properties dialog box. Here you can perform detailed analyses relating to elevations, slopes, contours, and watersheds (see Figure 18.5). The results of an analysis are shown graphically in the drawing and, depending on the type of analysis, can appear as shaded areas, arrows, contours lines, or even 3D areas—all color-coded for the identification of different ranges of data. In addition, you can create a legend to help convey the meaning of each color.

A *watershed* is a discrete area of land that directs the flow of runoff to a specific point or area.

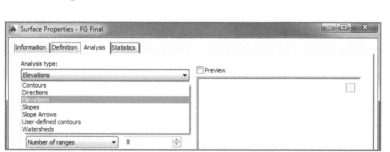

FIGURE 18.5 The Analysis Type choices available on the Analysis tab of the Surface Properties dialog box

Performing an analysis can be thought of as a two-step process. The first step is to create the analysis ranges in the Surface Properties dialog box. This step doesn't produce anything visible in the drawing, but it creates the data that will be used to generate graphical output. To create something visible in the drawing, you must perform the second step, which is to assign a style to the surface that displays the components of that analysis. For example, to display the slope arrows for a surface, you must first create the slope ranges and then apply a surface style that has slope arrow display turned on.

If you haven't already done so, download and install the files for Chapter 18 according to the instructions in this book's Introduction.

This drawing contains the FG Final surface that you created in the previous exercise.

Exercise 18.2: Analyze Surfaces

In this exercise, you'll perform a slope analysis to identify steep slope areas in the project. You'll then adjust one of the lots to demonstrate how an analysis can be used as a design tool.

1. Open the drawing named Analyzing Surfaces.dwg located in the Chapter 18 class data folder.

2. Click one of the red or blue contours in the drawing, and then click Surface Properties on the ribbon.

3. On the Surface Properties dialog, on the Analysis tab, select Slopes as the analysis type. Under Ranges, enter a value of 4 to the right of Number of Ranges.

4. Click the Run Analysis icon (downward-pointing arrow).
   Four ranges are listed in the Range Details section of the dialog box.

5. Edit the slope ranges as follows:

For ID 3, you must enter the Maximum Slope value first and then the Minimum Slope value.

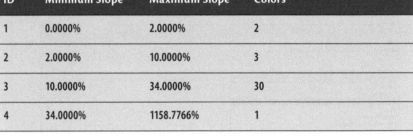

ID	Minimum Slope	Maximum Slope	Colors
1	0.0000%	2.0000%	2
2	2.0000%	10.0000%	3
3	10.0000%	34.0000%	30
4	34.0000%	1158.7766%	1

The red areas are of particular concern because they represent slopes that aren't stable with the type of soil found on this site.

This displays the feature lines and other drawing graphics on top of the colored shading rather than hidden beneath it.

6. Click the Information tab, and change the style to Slope Banding (2D). Click OK, and then press Esc to clear the selection of the surface.
   As shown in Figure 18.6, the drawing displays colored areas indicating excessively flat slopes (0%–2%) in yellow, moderate slopes (2%–10%) in green, steep slopes (10%–34%) in orange, and excessively steep slopes (>34%) in red.

7. Click one of the colored areas to select the surface, and then right-click and select Display Order ➤ Send To Back.

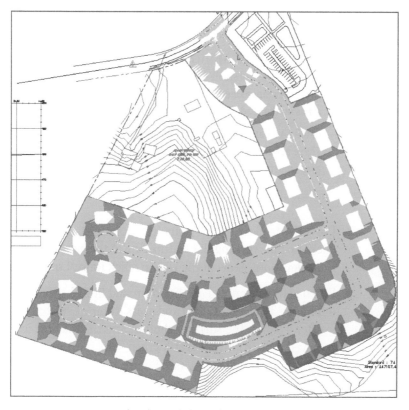

F I G U R E   1 8 . 6   Colored areas indicate different slope ranges in the FG Final
surface.

MORE ABOUT SLOPES

Slopes are a significant aspect of land development design. For every project,
certain slope ranges are targeted for specific purposes. These ranges can vary
from project to project.

For the example project, you're interested in knowing where there are excessively
flat areas (yellow, 0%–2%) because those areas could potentially have drainage
problems. Yellow areas on building pads are OK because there will be buildings
in those locations, but yellow areas on roads could represent drainage issues.

Green areas (2%–10%) represent slopes that can be traveled safely on foot or
with a vehicle. You want the entire road surface to be green, and there should
be enough area between each building pad and the street to install a driveway.

(Continues)

MORE ABOUT SLOPES *(Continued)*

Orange areas (10%–34%) represent places where travel isn't possible but where the slopes are still stable and safe from collapse. In this project, you would expect the pond embankments and the backs of some of the lots to be orange. Orange areas on the road and entire front yards that are orange aren't acceptable.

Finally, red areas represent slopes that are too steep for the soil to support. These areas would be subject to collapse and are considered dangerous. Red areas must be removed.

If the Edit Elevations panel isn't visible, click Edit Elevations.

8. Press Esc to clear the previous selection. In the upper-right viewport, click the blue rectangular feature line at the center of lot 70. On the Edit Elevations panel of the ribbon, click Raise/Lower.

9. When you're prompted on the command line to specify an elevation difference, type **-5** (**-1.524**) and press Enter.

    After a pause, the surface rebuilds, and the red area in lot 70 is removed. The front yard is still green, which means it's in the slope range to install a driveway (see Figure 18.7).

You may need to redo steps 2–6 to reestablish the ranges and colors.

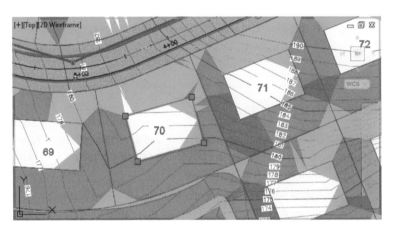

FIGURE 18.7   Lot 70 after the building pad has been adjusted downward to eliminate the steep slope

10. Save and close the drawing.

You can view the results of successfully completing this exercise by opening `Analyzing Surfaces - Complete.dwg`.

Using Hydrology Tools

Civil 3D provides two very useful tools to help you analyze the drainage performance of your surface: Water Drop and Catchments. The Water Drop tool shows you the theoretical path of a drop of rain as it flows downhill from a location you specify. By analyzing this path, you can determine the direction of flow and find low spots where water will stop flowing and begin to accumulate. A catchment shows you the area that drains to a point you specify. This is helpful for stormwater-management design, such as determining how large an inlet opening needs to be based on the size of the area contributing runoff to it.

Exercise 18.3: Analyze Hydrology

In this exercise, you'll use the Water Drop tool to analyze the flow of runoff to two inlets. Then you'll use one of the catchment tools to determine the area contributing runoff to that inlet.

1. Open the drawing named Using Hydrology Tools.dwg located in the Chapter 18 class data folder.

2. Click the Analyze tab of the ribbon, and then click Flow Paths ➤ Water Drop.

3. When prompted to select a surface, press Enter to indicate that you would like to select the surface from a list.

4. On the Select A Surface dialog, click EG-FG Composite, and then click OK.

5. On the Water Drop dialog, click OK to close the Water Drop dialog box.
   In the left viewport, click a point in lot 29 near the road. A blue water-drop path is drawn from lot 29 down the curb line to the inlet near station 2+50 (0+080). You can see the path in the lower-right 3D viewport as well.

6. With the Select point: prompt still active, click a point near the southeast corner of lot 23.

7. Press Esc to clear the current command. On the Analyze tab of the ribbon, click Catchments ➤ Create Catchment From Surface.

8. When prompted to specify a discharge point, in the left viewport, use the Center object snap to choose the center of the red circle at the end of the second water-drop path you created.

If you haven't already done so, download and install the files for Chapter 18 according to the instructions in this book's Introduction.

In this drawing, the feature-line layers have been turned off. Also, a new surface named EG-FG Composite has been provided. This surface was made by creating a new surface and pasting EG and FG Final into it. The purpose of this surface is to enable the analysis of the entire project as though it has already been built.

This water-drop path travels toward the west along the curb line of Madison Lane. It ends at the inlet near station 7+25 (0+220) on Madison Lane.

Catchments are visible only in plan view, so you don't see the catchment in the lower-right model view.

9. On the Create Catchment From Surface dialog, select EG-FG Composite for Surface, and click OK.

    A blue outline indicates the shape of the catchment area that drains to the inlet at the location you selected.

10. Save and close the drawing.

You can view the results of successfully completing this exercise by opening Using Hydrology Tools - Complete.dwg.

Using a Quick Profile

In Chapter 7, "Designing Vertically Using Profiles," you learned how to create surface profiles using alignments and surfaces. You also learned that a profile is a useful tool that enables you to slice through your design and view it from a different perspective. Well, what if you could create a profile from a whole list of entities that are readily available in your drawing? You can, and the command that does it is called Quick Profile.

The Quick Profile command creates a temporary profile along the path of a line, an arc, a polyline, a parcel line, a feature line, a survey figure, or a selected series of points. Once you have selected the object to represent the path, you're presented with a dialog box that enables you to select any surface in the drawing that you would like to display in the temporary profile view. If you have selected a 3D object such as a 3D polyline or feature line, you're also given the option to represent that object as a profile.

If you modify the object you used to define the path of the profile, the quick profile view updates automatically. This is a great tool for viewing slices of your design at many different locations very efficiently. Quick profiles are intended to be temporary, and they disappear whenever you save the drawing.

Exercise 18.4: Analyze Using a Quick Profile

If you haven't already done so, download and install the files for Chapter 18 according to the instructions in this book's Introduction.

In this exercise, you'll use quick profiles to study the interaction between existing ground and proposed ground in the pond area and in the area between the interior lots.

1. Open the drawing named Using a Quick Profile.dwg located in the Chapter 18 class data folder.

    In this drawing, a heavy red polyline in the left viewport crosses through the entire project at the location of the pond.

2. Click the Analyze tab of the ribbon, and then click Quick Profile.

3. When you're prompted to select an object, click the heavy red polyline that crosses through the pond.

4. On the Create Quick Profiles dialog, verify that the box next to Select All Surfaces is unchecked; then check the boxes next to EG and FG Final. Select Design Profile as the profile style for FG Final.

5. Click OK, and then click a point in the lower-left corner of the upper-right viewport.

    A new profile view shows existing ground in red and proposed ground in black. As you study the profile, you should be able to identify the shape of the road in two locations and the shape of the pond in between (see Figure 18.8).

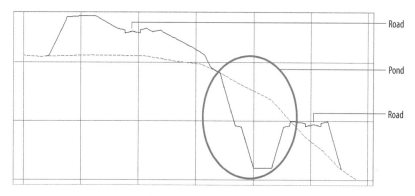

Road

Pond

Road

FIGURE 18.8 Several prominent design features can be noted in the quick profile.

Notice the change to the quick profile. Use the red polyline and the quick profile to study the design of the project at several different locations.

6. Click the red polyline to show its grips, and then click one of the grips and move it to a new location.

7. Press Esc to clear the selection of the red polyline. Zoom in to the interior lots, and identify the green feature line that forms the back sides of lots 68–70.

The 3D Entity options weren't available the first time you used the Quick Profile command because the red polyline you selected was a 2D object.

8. Click Quick Profile on the ribbon. When you're prompted to select an object, click the green feature line described in the previous step.

9. On the Create Quick Profiles dialog, check the box next to EG. Make sure the Draw 3D Entity Profile option is checked, and then select Design Profile as the 3D Entity Profile Style value.

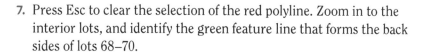

10. Click OK, and then click a point to the right of the first profile view. A new profile view is created that shows existing ground in red and a profile of the feature line in black. Notice how the feature line matches existing ground except for a certain length at either end where it ties into the finished ground elevations (see Figure 18.9).

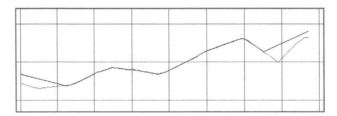

F I G U R E   1 8 . 9   **A quick profile view showing a feature line and a surface profile**

11. Save and close the drawing.

You can view the results of successfully completing this exercise by opening `Using a Quick Profile - Complete.dwg`. Note that the "Complete" version of the file isn't much different from the original because quick profiles are removed when the drawing is saved.

Calculating Earthwork Volumes

Moving earth is one of the most expensive construction activities in a land development project. For this reason, there are two important questions you'll need to answer about nearly every grading design you do:

▶ How much earth must be moved?

▶ How much earth must be brought to or transported away from the project site?

As a designer or an engineer, one of your most important tasks is to answer these questions with the smallest values possible. The less soil that is required to be moved for a project, the more money you save the client and/or owner. Transporting soil to or from the site is also a very costly construction activity, so it's also one you should minimize.

Understanding Earthwork Volumes

When talking about earthmoving, you'll often use the terms *cut* and *fill*. Cut is soil material that is removed from the ground, and fill is soil material that is added to it. When an excavator takes a scoop of soil out of the ground, that soil is called *cut*. When that scoop is carried to another location on the site and dumped, the soil becomes *fill*. Grading the site is nothing more than a complex series of scoops and dumps—that is, cuts and fills. At the end of the project, all the scoops added together represent the cut value, and all the dumps added together represent the fill value. If these values are equal, then no soil needs to be transported to or from the site, thus reducing the cost of construction (not to mention the environmental impact). When cut and fill are equal, the condition is referred to as a *balanced site*. As a designer, you should strive to balance the earthwork of your designs whenever possible.

Using the Volumes Dashboard

Although you can use several methods to calculate earthwork volumes in Civil 3D, I'll cover only one of them in this book in detail: the *Volumes Dashboard*. The Volumes Dashboard command is found on the Analyze tab of the ribbon. Clicking this opens Panorama, which displays the Volumes Dashboard tab. Here, you can add or create one or more TIN volume surfaces and the cut and fill results are shown. You can also create *bounded volumes*, which are smaller areas within a volume surface that might represent individual lots or project phases. You can even generate detailed reports that are displayed in a browser or in Civil 3D, as shown in Figure 18.10.

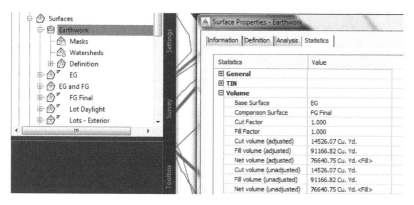

FIGURE 18.10 A TIN volume surface named Earthwork shown in Prospector, and its volume results shown in the Surface Properties dialog box

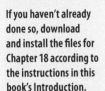

If you haven't already done so, download and install the files for Chapter 18 according to the instructions in this book's Introduction.

Exercise 18.5: Analyze Earthwork

In this exercise, you'll use the Volumes Dashboard to analyze the cut and fill for the entire project as well as three individual lots.

1. Open the drawing named `Calculating Volumes.dwg` located in the `Chapter 18` class data folder.

2. Click the Analyze tab of the ribbon, and then click Volumes Dashboard.

3. On the Volumes Dashboard tab of Panorama, click Create New Volume Surface. In the Create Volume Surface dialog box, do the following:

   a. For Name, enter **Earthwork**.

   b. For Style, select _No Display.

   c. For Base Surface, select EG.

   d. For Comparison Surface, select FG Final.

   e. Click OK.

WHAT'S A TIN VOLUME SURFACE?

As you may recall from Chapter 4, "Modeling the Existing Terrain Using Surfaces," the acronym TIN stands for *Triangular Irregular Network,* which is a method of creating surfaces by drawing lines between 3D points to form triangles. A TIN surface is any surface that is created using this method. When you create a TIN *volume* surface, Civil 3D superimposes one TIN surface over another and creates a point at each location where the triangle edges cross. New triangles are then created by connecting the calculated points. The resulting surface has the same distinctive triangular shapes, but instead of elevations, the values it represents are differences in elevation between the two surfaces. These differences in elevation are referred to as *cut* when they are negative and *fill* when they are positive.

The cut and fill results are shown in Panorama. Here, you see that the Cut Volume value is much smaller than the Fill Volume value. The project isn't balanced, and the requirement for extra fill means soil will have to be delivered to the project site. The design should be adjusted to bring it closer to balance. This can be accomplished by lowering the profiles and building pad feature lines to create more cut while eliminating the need for fill.

4. Click Earthwork, and then click Add Bounded Volume. When you're prompted to select a bounding object, click the parcel area label of lot 1.

5. Repeat the previous step for lots 2 and 3. Click the plus sign next to Earthwork to expand the information below it.

Note the individual cut and fill results that are shown for lots 1, 2, and 3.

OTHER VOLUME METHODS

Civil 3D provides three additional methods for calculating cut and fill:

TIN Volume Surface You can create a TIN volume surface without using the Volumes Dashboard by simply using the Create Surface command and choosing TIN Volume Surface as the type. You can view the volume results for the surface by opening Surface Properties and clicking the Statistics tab.

Grading Volume Tools You use the Grading Volume Tools with grading groups that have been assigned a volume base surface. Not only can the Grading Volume Tools report cut and fill, but they can also be used to adjust the design and even balance the design automatically.

Quantity Takeoff Criteria You use Quantity Takeoff Criteria to generate section-by-section volume calculations based on a sample line group. This method is nearly always associated with a corridor model for a transportation design project.

6. Change the name of Earthwork.1 to Lot 1, Earthwork.2 to Lot 2, and Earthwork.3 to Lot 3. Check the boxes next to Lot 1, Lot 2, and Lot 3, and then click Generate Cut/Fill Report.
   Your browser should open, displaying a detailed cut-and-fill report for the overall earthwork as well as the three individual lots.

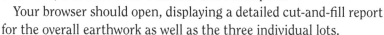
Checking the boxes tells the Volume Dashboard to include information for these items in the report.

7. Save and close the drawing.

You can view the results of successfully completing this exercise by opening Calculating Volumes - Complete.dwg. Although there is no change to the drawing itself, you can open the Volumes Dashboard and view the volume calculations.

Labeling Design Surfaces

Certification
Objective

As you have done with every other type of design in this book, you need to annotate your surface design. As with all annotation, the information you convey here is almost as important as the design itself, particularly with regard to grading.

From a strictly documentation standpoint, the primary final product of a grading design is a set of design contours. By themselves, the contours aren't very useful for construction. Once they are labeled, however, they begin to show the contractor exactly how to shape the land to meet its desired function. In some areas, contours alone don't provide enough detail and must be supplemented with labels that call out specific elevations and slopes. Labels that refer to the elevation of a single point on a drawing are often referred to as *spot elevations* or *spot grades*.

Although it was some time ago, you learned how to create contour, spot, and slope labels in Chapter 4. You'll apply those skills once again, but this time you'll label proposed elevations rather than existing elevations.

If you haven't already done so, download and install the files for Chapter 18 according to the instructions in the Introduction.

Exercise 18.6: Label a Design Surface

In this exercise, you'll create contour, spot elevation, and slope labels for lot 2. You'll use these labels to adjust the design of lot 2.

The upper-right viewport is zoomed in to the first few lots at the beginning of Jordan Court. You'll add labels in this area to provide information about contour elevations, slopes, and spot elevations.

1. Open the drawing named Labeling Design Surfaces.dwg located in the Chapter 18 class data folder.

2. Click the Annotate tab of the ribbon, and then click Add Labels.

3. In the Add Labels dialog box, do the following:

   a. For Feature, select Surface.

   b. For Label Type, select Contour – Multiple.

   c. Click Add.

4. When you're prompted to select a surface, click one of the red or blue contours in the drawing.

5. When prompted to specify the first point, pick two points that draw a line through the contours in the front yard of lot 2 (see Figure 18.11).

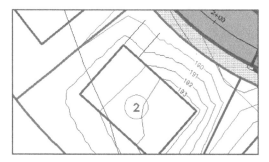

FIGURE 18.11   Contour labels in the front yard of lot 2

6. In the Add Labels dialog box, change Label Type to Contour – Single. Click Add.

7. When you're prompted to select a surface, click one of the red or blue contours in the drawing.

8. Click several contours on the Jordan Court road surface.

9. In the Add Labels dialog box, change the label type to Slope. Click Add.

10. When prompted to select a surface, click one of the red or blue contours in the drawing to select the surface.

11. When prompted to choose between the One-Point and Two-Point labeling options, press Enter to select the One-Point option. Pick a point near the center of the front yard of lot 2.

  The slope label indicates that the grade here is greater than the allowable 10%. This is something you'll address at the end of this exercise.

12. In the Add Labels dialog box, change the label type to Spot Elevation.

13. Click Add, and select a red or blue contour when you're prompted to select a surface.

14. Using an Endpoint object snap, select the four corners of the lot 2 building pad. This places a spot-elevation label at each corner.

15. Press Esc to clear the previous command. Click the blue building pad feature line for lot 2. On the Edit Elevations panel of the ribbon, click Raise/Lower.

If the Edit Elevations panel isn't visible, click Edit Elevations.

16. When you're prompted to specify the elevation difference, type -2 (-0.691) and press Enter.

    After a pause while the software rebuilds the surface, the contour labels, slope label, and spot-elevation labels all update to reflect the change (see Figure 18.12). The slope in the front yard of lot 2 is now less than the maximum of 10%.

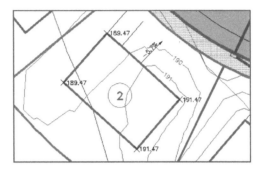

FIGURE 18.12 The labels update, indicating that the maximum slope requirement is now met for lot 2.

17. Save and close the drawing.

You can view the results of successfully completing this exercise by opening `Labeling Design Surfaces - Complete.dwg`.

THE NEW WAY TO BUILD

Although contours are the most common final product of a design surface, there are other ways your grading design can be used. One in particular is becoming more popular every day: a *machine model*. Contractors are now able to use GPS-guided excavation machines that can synchronize their operation with a computer-generated model representing the design of a project. Where does this model come from? You guessed it: Civil 3D and other programs like it. Although the contractor will often have your model checked and reworked before uploading it to a machine in the field, it all starts with your grading design in Civil 3D. A well-defined, accurate, finished ground surface translates directly to a well-built, well-functioning project.

Now You Know

Now that you have completed this chapter, you understand the concept of building your grading design in parts, and you know how to combine those parts by pasting surfaces. You're able to analyze surfaces and use the results to make changes to your design. You have practiced the application of slope, hydrology, and earthwork analyses and can apply those on projects of your own. Finally, you can label your design surface, not only to provide information to people viewing the drawings, but also as a tool to identify design issues and correct them.

You're ready to begin compiling, analyzing, and labeling design surfaces in a production environment.

AutoCAD Civil 3D 2016 Certification

Autodesk® certifications are industry-recognized credentials that can help you succeed in your career, providing benefits to both you and your employer. Getting certified is a reliable validation of skills and knowledge, and it can lead to accelerated professional development, improved productivity, and enhanced credibility.

This Autodesk Official Press guide can be an effective component of your exam preparation. Autodesk highly recommends (and we agree!) that you schedule regular time to prepare, review the most current exam preparation roadmap available at www.autodesk.com/certification, use Autodesk Official Press guides, take a class at an Authorized Training Center (see www.autodesk.com/atc to find ATCs near you), and use a variety of resources to prepare for your certification—including plenty of actual hands-on experience.

Certification Objective

Table A.1 is for the AutoCAD® Civil 3D® 2016 Certified Professional exam and lists the topics, exam objectives, and (where possible) chapter where the information for each objective is found. Certification icons like the one in the margin here appear in each chapter next to the corresponding information. This book will give you a foundation for the certification, but you will need further study and hands-on practice to complete and pass the exam.

These Autodesk exam objectives were accurate at publication time. Please refer to www.autodesk.com/certification for the most current exam roadmap and objectives.

Good luck preparing for your certification!

TABLE A.1   AutoCAD Civil 3D 2016 Certification exam sections and objectives

Topic	Learning Objective	Chapter
User Interface	Navigate the user interface	1
	Use the functions on Prospector	1
	Use functions on the Settings tab	1
Styles	Create and use object styles	2, 4, 6, 8, 11, 13, 16, 18
	Create and use label styles	2, 4, 6, 8, 11, 13, 16, 18
Lines & Curves	Use the line and curve commands	1
	Use the Transparent Commands toolbar	1
Points	Create points using the Point Creation command	3
	Create points by importing point data	3
	Use point groups to control the display of points	3
Surfaces	Create and edit surfaces	4, 17
	Use styles and settings to display surface information	4, 17
	Create a surface by assembling fundamental data	4, 17
	Use styles to analyze surface display results	4, 17 / 18
Parcels	Create parcels using parcel layout tools	12
	Design a parcel layout	12
	Select parcel styles to change the display of parcels	13
	Select styles to annotate parcels	13
Alignments	Create alignments	5
	Design a geometric layout	5

(Continues)

TABLE A.1 (Continued)

Topic	Learning Objective	Chapter
Profiles & Profile Views	Create a surface profile	7
	Design a profile	7
	Create a layout profile	7
	Create a profile view style	8
	Create a profile view	8
Corridors	Design and create a corridor	9
	Derive information and data from a corridor	9
	Design and create an intersection	9
Sections & Section Views	Create and analyze sections and section views	10
Pipe Networks	Design and create a pipe network	14, 15
Grading	Design and create a grading model	17
	Create a grading model feature line	17
Managing and Sharing Data	Use data shortcuts to share/manage data	2
	Create a data-sharing setup	2
Survey	Use description keys to control the display of points created from survey data	3
	Use figure prefixes to control the display of linework generated from survey data	3
		3
	Create a topographic/boundary drawing from field data	3

INDEX

Note to the Reader: Throughout this index **boldfaced** page numbers indicate primary discussions of a topic. *Italicized* page numbers indicate illustrations.